Medicine as a Human Experience

D1576239

There are those who will tell you that being a physician is a curse, a life of endless and ambiguous work, where at best we are consumed in a holding action—and all that, without experiencing appropriate appreciation of our sacrifice.

I do not feel that way. Being a physician I consider the highest privilege I can imagine. Along with the joys from my family, my life as a physician has provided me with moments of epiphany, transcendental moments of lucidity . . . To be a physician—to be permitted, to be invited by another human being into his life in the circumstances of that crucible which is illness—to be a trusted participant in the highest of dramas—for these privileges I am grateful beyond my ability to express . . .

Lorin L. Stephens, M.D.

Medicine as a Human Experience

David E. Reiser, M.D.

David H. Rosen, M.D.

Foreword by Norman Cousins
Consulting Editor, George L. Engel, M.D.

With contribution by John Rosenberg, M.D.

University Park Press · Baltimore

University Park Press
International Publishers in Medicine and Allied Health
300 North Charles Street
Baltimore, Maryland 21201

Sponsoring Editor: Marjorie Nelson
Production Manager: Berta Steiner
Cover and text design by: Caliber Design Planning, Inc.

Typeset by: Bi-Comp, Inc.
Manufactured in the United States of America by: Halliday Lithograph

Library of Congress Cataloging in Publication Data

Reiser, David E., 1946–
    Medicine as a human experience.

    Includes index.
    1. Sick—Psychology. 2. Physician and patient. 3. Medicine and psychology.
I. Rosen, David H., 1945–   . II. Title. [DNLM: 1. Patients—psychology.
2. Philosophy, Medical. 3. Physician-Patient Relations. W 62 R375m]
R726.5.R4   1984   616'.001'9   84-7375
ISBN 0-8391-2037-0

This book is dedicated to our families:

Kathleen and Mark

Deborah, Sarah, Laura, and Rachel

We owe special thanks to the following organizations and publishers: the American Medical Association for permission to reproduce in the Foreword adapted excerpts from "The Physician as Communicator" by Norman Cousins, *Journal of the American Medical Association* 248:587–589, 1982; Belknap Press of Harvard University for poem number 1129 from *Poems of Emily Dickinson,* edited by Thomas H. Johnson, Cambridge, Mass., 1981; Holt, Rinehart and Winston for "The Silken Tent" from *The Poetry of Robert Frost,* edited by Edward Connery Lathem, New York, 1967; the American Psychiatric Association for "The Clinical Application of the Biopsychosocial Model" by George Engel, *American Journal of Psychiatry* 137:535–544, 1980; The Johns Hopkins University Press for "The Care of the Patient: Art or Science?" by George Engel, *Johns Hopkins Medical Journal* 140:222–232, 1977; The Williams & Wilkins Company for an excerpt from *Patient Interviewing: The Human Dimension* by David Reiser and Andrea Schroder, Baltimore, 1980; Simon and Schuster for excerpts from *Heartsounds* by Martha Weinman Lear, New York, 1981; the American College of Physicians for excerpts from "A Life Setting Conducive to Illness: The Giving-up/Given-up Complex" by George Engel, *Annals of Internal Medicine* 679:293–300, 1968 and "Culture, Illness and Care: Clinical Lessons from Anthropologic and Cross Cultural Research" by A. Kleinman, L. Eisenberg, and B. Good, *Annals of Internal Medicine* 88:251–258, 1975; Viking Penguin for an excerpt from *The Youngest Science* by Lewis Thomas, New York, 1983; David McKay for "A Noiseless Patient Spider" from *Leaves of Grass* by Walt Whitman, Philadelphia, 1900; and St. Martin's Press for excerpts from *A Parting Gift* by Frances Sharkey, New York, 1982.

Contents

Foreword

Physician as Humanist

Norman Cousins

Drs. Reiser and Rosen have written a book filled with compassion and insight not only for patients but also for the singular and often complex young men and women who take upon themselves the healing role. I have been trying in recent years to find out as much as I could about the direction medicine seems to be taking. The authors provide some encouraging answers and point a path toward the resurrection of the principles of integration that are essential. By "integration" I am thinking not of a murky principle but of the need to affirm the importance of the human spirit, dignity, fullness, and hope in the philosophy of medicine.

Few things are more encouraging about modern medicine than the recognition that the psychological and the physiological are part of a totality; psychological and psychiatric problems are not merely aspects of medicine but are central to all medical practice. It is difficult to think of *any* relationship between a doctor and a patient that does not involve psychological and psychiatric competence by the physician. This is a fundamental issue.

Medical training tends to divide most subjects between "soft" and "hard." The hard subjects are defined as, or equated with, science: pathology, pharmacology, biochemistry, biophysics—everything that utilizes facts and numbers in one way or another. The soft subjects involve psychology, patient-doctor relationships, the philosophy of medicine, and the history of medicine.

When some subjects are defined as soft and others as hard, one makes value assignments. The hard is "good" and "dependable." The soft is "weak" and therefore to be disparaged. Yet 15 to 20 years after medical school, what happens? One discovers that the so-called, the supposed "hard" base of medicine breaks up—that the fact base of medicine is vulnerable. All one has to do is to look back over the past 25 years and certainly the past 50 years to see how much of medicine that was considered to be hard and indisputable has been refuted or replaced.

In many respects, the "soft" subjects have greater longevity. The way a doctor listens to a patient, his ability to inspire the patient's confidence, to communicate that which must be communicated in a way that does not destroy hope are the things referred to as the "art of medicine." This is what medicine is all about, and this is what endures. As for science, certainly the scientific aspects of medicine are the foundation, but the "hard" facts keep changing because of the nature of both pure and applied research.

These matters Reiser and Rosen clearly grasp, and their book is an attempt to integrate "soft" and "hard," "science" and "art"—in short, to be truly scientific in the best sense of the term. Many textbooks have already been written that aspire to present students with a unifying view of patients and the practice of medicine. In this regard, *Medicine as a Human Experience* is not unique. What makes it unique, in my view, is the spirit its words embody, the attitude its pages communicate. The authors understand, and repeatedly demonstrate in this book, that the patient-physician relationship is a powerful, sometimes mysterious, frequently healing interaction *between human beings*. At the core of this interaction is communication.

Five years ago, I accepted an invitation to teach literature and philosophy to medical students at the University of California, Los Angeles, and to study problems in patient-physician relationships from the standpoint of patients. I also wanted to pursue research in a field of deep interest to me, the biochemistry of the emotions.

I thought I would have to brace myself for all the shocks that go with a new career, but I quickly discovered that physicians and writers have at least one thing in common: Communication is an important part of their trade. In journalism you live or die by your ability to use words. In health care the words a physician uses have a profound effect on the well-being of the patient. A doctor's words can be gate-openers or gate-slammers: They can open the way to recovery, or they can make a patient dependent, tremulous, fearful, resistant. The right words can potentiate a patient, mobilize the will to live, and set the stage for heroic response. The wrong words can produce despair and defeat or impair the usefulness of whatever treatment is prescribed. The wrong words can complicate the healing environment, which is no less central in the care of the patients than the factual knowledge that forms the basis of treatment.

Being able to diagnose correctly is one good test of medical competence. Being able to tell the patient what he or she has to know is another (and, as the authors later explain, both are essential skills of a "competent" physician). Now, I recognize the problems involved for the physician in proper communication. There is not only the problem of language itself—how to use words that do not confuse or mislead. There are also the professional problems—the obligation of the physician to inform the patient, the difficulties caused by the fact that patients vary in their ability to deal with the truth, the ease with which poor communication with the patient can spill over into tangled relationships and even malpractice suits.

Let me hover over some of these problems.

First of all, proper communication is one of the most difficult undertakings on earth. The older I get, the more I am forced to recognize that many or even most failures and breakdowns have their origin in faulty communication. Whether we are talking about the predicaments of human beings or the confrontations of nations, the inability of people to convey intention and meaning has been one of the prime causes of confusion and violence over the centuries. On a small but accessible level, you need go no further than the administration of hospital affairs to see how many errors, some of them serious, proceed out of faulty communications. Consider the wrong medications in the intravenous bottle, or the wrong pills, or the wrong quantities, or the hospital attendant who misinterprets instructions intended for one patient and applies them to another. Not infrequently, that attendant can fault ambiguous communications: the orders just were not clear enough.

Imprecision in communications, it goes without saying, is not confined to the medical profession. It is in the air. In the business world, blurred or faulty use of language represents the biggest single problem and single largest expense confronting any organization.

In my own contacts with patients, I have been made aware of the frequency with which they seem frightened or confused or immobilized as the result of their medical encounters. I allow for the possibility that their reactions may be the result of their own failures in understanding, but I am nevertheless struck with the fact that the relationship between patient and physician is often impaired because of sloppy communications.

Now we come to an entirely different problem. Even when the physician's message *is* clearly delivered and clearly understood, its effect may run counter to the well-being of the patient. Patients are not equally adept in their ability to handle the truth. Some may even be exposed to iatrogenic hazards if they are confronted at point-blank range with the fact of extreme illness.

One of the residents at UCLA spoke to me about a conference with a patient and the family, during which they were all expecting the attending doctor's verdict after a biopsy. The oncologist came into the room; the family was seated. He sat down, spread his hands, and said, "Well, I've got to let you have it." He said, "Your kidneys have crapped out." He said, "Your liver is crapped out. As a matter of fact," he said, "everything is crapped out. That's the way it is." And he left.

Truth is the fashion these days. No one wants to stand against the truth. We all want the truth. But there are some problems here. The issue, it seems to me, is not do you tell the truth, but first do you really know the truth? Does any doctor really know enough to make a pronouncement of doom? Yes, he knows the basis of the evidence and on the basis of the averages that this patient may live just 3 or 4 months, but he is diagnosing an average—he is not really diagnosing a patient. No one knows enough about a human being to make a precise pronouncement of doom, and yet such pronouncements are made all the time. A good habit to get into is to ask yourself: Do you really know the truth in the first place?

Second, how do you deliver the truth? Do you deliver it as though you have a truckload of bricks to unload on a patient, or is a certain sensitivity called for? Do you deliver it in a way that crushes the patient's hope? Or could you find some way of allowing that patient to stay alive psychologically?

It may be said that the physician has no choice but to convey the facts flat out, that the danger of malpractice suits is such that the physician is forced to tell the patient the worst in unmistakable terms. At least, if the worst should happen, the physician cannot be accused of failing to prepare the patient—a failure for which he could be held legally accountable.

The essential question, perhaps, is whether the hard facts and nothing but the hard facts are always necessary or useful. Now, if the reason for the hard facts is the doctor's fear of legal reprisal, then we have to ask ourselves if there is a conflict of interests between the patient's need for treatment and the physician's need for legal protection. Consider the case of the San Francisco patient who had a biopsy of a lump in her breast and who telephoned the oncologist 3 days later asking about the result. She was told that such serious matters were never discussed over the telephone but that she would be informed in due course. She was. She was informed by *certified* letter. The letter was completely unambiguous. It said in the tersest language that she had a malignancy. There was certainly no failure here in communication, but there was certainly little regard for the effect that communication in this form would produce. With a registered receipt in his possession, the physician could protect himself against any possible accusation later that he had failed to make an accurate diagnosis. The woman was not so much told as notified, not so much instructed as sentenced.

Is it reasonable to ask if insensitive reference to the worst helps to bring on the worst? To what extent does the *unvarnished* recital of a negative prognosis have the effect of a hex? Physicians are obligated to use all the science at their command—chemotherapy, radiation, surgery—in an attempt to reverse or slow down a malignancy. For the same reason, the wise physician calls up his humanity to potentiate and motivate the patient. The mood and attitude of the physician as well as that of the patient are potent factors affecting treatment. For that reason alone, the physician should try to avoid a situation in which either one leaves an encounter in sheer terror and defeat.

In my current position, I have a chance to see patients at the request of doctors: patients who have given up and who need emotional support. The most difficult thing in dealing with these patients is not the illness but the psychology it engenders. Nothing is more inevitable in serious illness than the panic that accompanies it. Panic is the intense fire of disease. Panic is a disease by itself. Panic makes biochemical changes in the body. What happens when the doctor communicates with a patient in a way that intensifies that panic? Perhaps it might have been better in some instances not to have gone to the doctor at all.

The authors of this book draw for you a clear picture of the way panic and stress can throw the entire endocrine system into disarray. It is no accident that disease frequently and suddenly becomes intensified as the diagnosis is pronounced. The way a patient receives a diagnosis can have a profound effect on the course of the disease. This does not mean that the truth must be deferred or denied. It is a matter of attaching as much importance to the manner and style of communication as to any other aspect of medical care.

We are accustomed to thinking of iatrogenic problems in terms of the wrong medication, or mistaken surgery, or harm done in diagnostic procedures. But there are also psychological iatrogenic situations—what happens after a patient is sent into an emotional tailspin with physiological consequences as the result of the exchange with a physician?

Everything we have said so far points to this question: Is it possible to communicate negative information in a way that is received by the patient as a challenge rather than as a death sentence?

I believe it is. As the authors of this book repeatedly demonstrate, understanding how patients are affected by serious illness, as well as what illness they happen to have, paves the way for communicating without crippling.

Throughout the book, an attitude is evidenced that is conducive to treatment and recovery. The authors do not minimize the seriousness of a patient's condition. What they do, instead, is to put their emphasis on healing as a partnership. They describe what it is that modern medical science has to offer, what it is that the patient has to offer, and finally what the physician as a human being has to offer. They talk about the patient's resources and, equally important, about the resources of the healer.

We make a great mistake if we think that in a serious or terminal illness victory is represented only by some miracle that reverses the illness—some beautiful remission—and that defeat is represented only by death. An illness is similar to existence inside the concentration camps. There are many victories short of escape, many victories short of cure, and many defeats that are not marked by death. Even though we cannot expect ultimate victory, our existence is enriched or impoverished by the interim victories or failures within our reach.

A young boy says, "It was wonderful when mother opened her eyes and recognized me." Another patient is able to turn over in bed by himself, and yet another patient is able to hold out her hand. These are the moments that are made possible by the physician as humanist, the physician who does not equate healing with some rigid and narrow definition of biomedical cure, the physician who appreciates the importance in medicine of such imponderables as hope, dignity, courage, and, yes, love.

I am reminded of one of the doctors at Encino Hospital, who had a judge as a patient. The judge was willing himself to die. The family was bereaved not just because of his impending death but because his character had changed so drastically under circumstances of extreme adversity.

The judge had always been a fighter, strong and resolute. Now he was giving up, and all he wanted to do was to die. His family hardly recognized him, but the doctor was wise enough to ponder, "You know, if we can just give this family one week—one week—with the judge as he used to be, not in terms of health, but in terms of the spirit as they have recognized it, it would make a very big difference to them for the rest of their lives.

The next day I was leaving for China, so at the doctor's request I went to the Encino Hospital that night. The judge—a tall man, six feet three inches—was wasting away. He was down to about 90 pounds. He could barely speak. He had been a reader of the *Saturday Review*,* so there was some way for me to reach out to him and have him reach back.

He whispered. He spoke about the magazine and how he had read it all those years, and I said "Dr. Bluming asked me to come and see you because of the family."

He said, "What about the family?" in a high whisper; and I said, "Well, you know, cancer is the most contagious of diseases."

He said, "No, it's not."

* N. Cousins was editor of this magazine for many years.

I said, "Well, it is contagious in the sense that grief is the virus, and sometimes the way we die helps to determine what happens to others; and when you look at the records, you find that wives follow husbands within a few months and husbands follow wives—and the inability to handle grief is really a virus.

"You know, your family has always seen you as a great fighter, and now you're going out of character."

He said, "I gotcha."

The next day, when I arrived in Hong Kong, I telephoned the Encino Hospital and talked with Dr. Bluming. He said, "Gosh! Something very strange and wonderful has happened. When they tried to hook the judge up to his intravenous this morning, he said, 'Turn the damn thing off and give me my breakfast the regular way.' I don't know how he got it down—but he did."

The doctor reported, "Two hours later, he asked his wife to come over to play a game of bridge. How they played that game of bridge, I'll never know." The next day, the judge even walked around the room.

When I got back 3 weeks later, I discovered that he had died just 2 days before my return. He not only lived out 1 week, he lived out three—and he did so with spirit. He found his victory, and the family found its victory, in an altered context that was real.

There are victories that are possible, and a physician is responsible for helping us to get the most out of whatever may be possible. In the final analysis, medicine is the science and the art of the possible.

As this volume makes clear, the doctor's job is not just to deal with the ultimates. The doctor's concern is with the intermediates that make up our day-to-day lives. Nothing is more wondrous than the ability of the human spirit to produce profound biochemical, physiological, attitudinal, and behavioral change, even though a cure is not possible. I have been mystified by this and at times ennobled. This, it seems to me, is the great experience within the reach of physicians. The present text offers a path toward that full realization.

Patients need and look for qualities in their doctors that go beyond technical competence. They want reassurance. They want to be looked *after*, not just looked *over*. They want to be listened to. They want to feel that it makes a difference to the physician, a very big difference, whether they live or die. They want to feel that they are in the doctor's thoughts. In short, patients are a vast collection of emotional needs. Yes, psychological counselors are very helpful in this connection, and so are the family and clergy; but the patient turns most of all and first of all to the physician. It is the physician's station that has most to offer in terms of those emotional needs. It is the person of the doctor and the presence of the doctor, just as much as—and frequently more than—what the doctor does that creates an environment for healing. The physician represents restoration. The physician holds the lifeline. The physician's words and not just his prescriptions are entwined in that lifeline.

This aspect of medicine has not changed in thousands of years. Not all the king's horses and all the king's men—not all the tomography and thallium scanners and two-D echograms and medicinal mood modifiers—can preempt the physician's primary role as the keeper of the keys to the body's own healing system. To the students who read, and more important *understand*, the spirit and the essence of this book, I would say, without hesitation or fear of hyperbole, you are medicine's future. You are also its only hope.

I pray that you will never allow your knowledge to get in the way of your relationship with your patients. I pray that all the technological marvels at your command will not prevent you from practicing medicine out of a little black bag if you have to. I pray that when you go into a patient's room you will recognize that the main distance is not from the door to the bed, but from the patient's eyes to your own—and that this distance is best traveled when the physician bends low to the patient's fear of loneliness and pain and the overwhelming sense of mortality that comes flooding up out of the unknown, and when the physician's hand on the patient's shoulder or arm is a shelter against darkness.

I pray that, even as you attach the highest value to your science, you will never forget that it works best when it serves your humanity. For, ultimately, it is our respect for the human soul that determines the worth of our science.

Preface

This book has been written for medical students out of our appreciation for their creative ideas, compassion, empathy, social concern, and humanism. We hope it will help future physicians to sustain and expand these attributes throughout their careers, so that they may truly say their experience of medicine has been a joyous and human one. Beyond this, we hope that this book will be useful to all professionals involved in the healing role—nurses, psychologists, social workers, clergy, and so many others—everyone, in short, who cares for patients; everyone who truly *cares*. This is something that goes way beyond technical degrees.

The book evolved out of our teaching experiences at three medical schools. Dr. Reiser was in charge of the Introduction to Clinical Medicine Interviewing course at the University of Colorado and then participated in the Psychiatric Aspects of Medical Practice course at the University of California, San Francisco, which Dr. Rosen directed. When we worked together in San Francisco, we discovered that we had several things in common: a love of teaching medical students; a desire to help them maintain their self-awareness and humanism; and a belief in the soundness of a new scientific paradigm in clinical medicine based on George Engel's biopsychosocial model. In the context of hosting a National Conference on Teaching the Psychiatric Aspects of Medical Practice and Psychosocial Factors in Healing, we met Dr. Engel. Now we are at the University of Rochester where Dr. Engel has taught for nearly 40 years and continues to inspire. Need we say more?

Here at the University of Rochester, Dr. Reiser is in charge of the first year course, Psychosocial Medicine I, which introduces the student to the biopsychosocial model, becoming a physician, the doctor-patient relationship, and beginning interviewing—in sum, the human dimension of medicine. Dr. Rosen directs the Psychosocial Medicine II course, which was established and directed by Dr. Engel from 1946 to 1983. In this course students learn psychosocial skills, patient-centered interviewing, clinical reasoning, and knowledge essential for clinical work. The course involves a lot of contact with patients and aims to provide a bridge between the students' evolving knowledge of basic sciences and application of this knowledge to their work with patients and patients' families during the clinical years. The course covers adaptation to loss and life change, pregnancy and human sexuality, child and adolescent care, long-term care, psychopathology, and clinical reasoning utilizing the biopsychosocial model.

We are both involved in teaching in the General Clerkship, which is a unique University of Rochester transitional clerkship focusing on the student's ability to conduct a patient-centered interview, obtain a complete history, and carry out a complete physical examination utilizing a biopsychosocial approach. It is a very faculty-intensive, apprentice-type, clinical educational experience. In addition, we are both involved in the development of a comprehensive Psychosocial and Psychiatric Aspects of Medical Practice course modeled after the one in which we both taught at the University of California in San Francisco.

We wrote this book because we believe students need a text that can help make the transition from the classroom to working with patients easier and more meaningful. It provides *general precepts and principles*, illustrated clinically, that are designed to elucidate and enhance the practice of humane, empathic, patient-centered care in the clinical settings where students learn.

Medicine as a Human Experience emphasizes the student-physician's special role in caring for patients as unique individuals, focusing on their psychological and social realities as well as their biological needs. Many physicians have expressed increasing concern over the trend toward fragmented and dehumanized medical care. We share this concern, and the present book is an attempt to address it. Throughout, we attempt to convey the message that being knowledgeable about, and sensitive to, the human being we care for is an essential feature of effective, successful medicine.

The book concerns itself with caring for the whole patient and outlines basic precepts involved in an empathic, biopsychosocial approach to medical practice. The Prologue by John Rosenberg is a medical student's moving summation of his own experiences during the clinical years in medical school—a piece that takes a candid look at the traumas as well as the triumphs of those years. The first chapter outlines the basic principles of medicine as a human experience and provides a template for the book. The next two chapters by George Engel concern the clinical application of the biopsychosocial model and the care of the patient. Chapter 4, "The Doctor-Patient Relationship," underscores the key nature of the human bond between patient and physician as a partnership that is essential to the healing process. Chapter 5 concerns itself with the patient-centered interview, a basic tool utilizing the biopsychosocial approach in patient-centered medicine. Chapter 6 focuses on the experience of illness and utilizes a developmental schema which highlights a patient's potential for growth during illness. The last chapter, "The Nature of the Healing Process," emphasizes that the known tangibles of scientific medicine (in the broadest sense) must be coupled with the intangibles of compassion, empathy, hope, and meaning if healing is to occur. In the Epilogue, "Desiderata," guideposts are offered to help medical students find their way through the difficult maze we call medical education.

Didactic principles are always drawn from clinical experience, keeping the focus of the book throughout where it should be—on the patient, a suffering fellow human being. Throughout the text, we insist that patients be seen as people struggling with life and its often traumatic disruptions and never as "interesting cases" or "examples of pathology."

We sense a change in medical education toward a more holistic paradigm, and the challenge and responsibility for changing the medical profession rests with all of us. Recently our own medical school reviewed its educational goals and one of its five objectives is *to foster an understanding of medicine as a profession and as a personal human experience.*

It is our hope that this book will contribute in a small but meaningful way to making the practice of medicine more comprehensive, more meaningful, and more human. We intend this book of precepts and general principles to be a guide, a comfort, and an inspiration to young doctors as they pursue their own healing and the healing of their patients.

David E. Reiser
David H. Rosen
Rochester, New York

Acknowledgments

This book has been long in the making, and numerous people helped it at various points along the way. We wish to thank the following individuals for the energy and effort that went into the process of developing the book and its concepts: Eugene Shatkin, Richard Crayne, Carol Wolman, Herbert Ochitill, Carl Jonas, Harrison Sadler, Morton Weinstein (deceased), Katherine Unger, Barbara Blackwell, Jeffrey Mandel, Paul Moscovich, Loma Flowers, David Schwartz, William Prescott, Robert Hoffman, Christie Kiefer, Yonkel Goldstein, Martin Glasser, Carl Viesti, Nancy Adler, Al Jonsen, Evelyn Gendel, Carlos Sluzki, and Jerome Motto. We also wish to thank the following individuals who supported us while this work was being written: Robert Wallenstein, I. C. Kaufman, Julius Krevans, Howard Goldman, Robert Glaser, Haroutun Babigian, Robert Ader, Jules Cohen, Roger Sider, and Frank Young.

We are grateful to Dennis Kraus, Christine Borghi,

David Nagel, Thomas Davis, Robert Mick, Stephen Ray, Jean Strachan, Michael Schwartz, Dorothy Wood, and Jean Vincent for reviewing portions of the manuscript.

A special thanks is owed to Martin Lipp, who suggested the idea for such a work in the first place. We owe gratitude to the patience and assistance of the editorial staff at University Park Press, especially our editor Marge Nelson.

We are indebted to Vickie Gordon, Nina Colgrove, Gail Connor, Cindy O'Keefe for typing sections of text. Additional secretarial support was provided by Kate Deegan, Diane Knechtges, and Laurel Ley. Above all, we are indebted to Mary Ellen Capezzuto who did the lion's share of bringing this book to the light of day. Her patience, intelligence, exacting standards, and skill made the birth process of this book *almost* painless!

Our special appreciation goes to Salli Kernaghan, our personal editor in Chicago. Her ability to see the forest for the trees, to truly *understand* the project, is what makes her editing so sensitive and special.

We are above all else grateful to George Engel for his contributions, which obviously go way beyond his two chapters—the innumerable hours of editing, the countless discussions, the generous proferring of encouragement and support throughout the ups and downs of the whole process of bringing this book into the world. He is not only one of the most brilliant people we have known, he is also one of the most magnanimous. It's been a joy to work with him.

Finally, we owe a special debt to our families (Kathy Gresh and Mark Reiser, Deborah Voorhees-Rosen, Sarah, Laura, and Rachel Rosen) for all they endured while this book was in the making.

Medicine
as a Human
Experience

Prologue

Life on the Wards: One Student's View

John Rosenberg*

When I was asked to add a medical student's perspective to the ideas presented in this book, I was slightly bewildered. I wondered what I could find to contribute to these pages which would add something substantive to the principles already elaborated here. Clearly, the authors are more experienced as physicians, more knowledgeable than I. I have had just a brief glimpse of medicine; I have no great familiarity with any particular field, no brilliant thoughts to add to George Engel's discussion of the biopsychosocial model of illness. As I pondered my assigned task, images of *me* kept crossing my mind: images of a naive me before medical school and images of an exhausted me coping with the tremendous workload of my preclinical years. I saw images of myself in conflict, at times totally alienated from my previously

* John Rosenberg is currently a resident at the University of California in San Francisco. This prologue was written when he was a senior medical student at U.C.S.F.

held beliefs about my role as a practitioner and at times horrified at the cold realities of medical education and practice.

One image in particular kept recurring, unwanted but unforgettable. It was in my fourth week of medical school, during the one afternoon each week we were let out of the lecture hall in small groups to see patients and physicians interact, sort of a role-modeling session for freshmen, anticipating responsibilities yet to come. Al and I were the two students assigned to the pulmonary specialist at a San Francisco hospital, and on this particular day we were watching Dr. Thompson perform a bronchoscopy. The patient, Mr. Benelli, a 55-year-old seaman with a recently intensified cough, was sitting bolt upright in a dentist's chair, wringing his hands. Dr. Thompson sprayed his throat with Xylocaine; I held his chin up while Dr. Thompson dropped the bronchoscope down his throat, discussing the miracle of fiberoptic instruments. Mr. Benelli gagged and choked; Al comforted him while Dr. Thompson kept advancing the tube down his trachea. The coughing and gagging echoed off the tiled walls of the procedure room. Dr. Thompson stopped his prattle, spying something worthy of biopsy. Three or four bits of tissue from Mr. Benelli's bronchi dropped into the formalin jar. As he withdrew the scope, Dr. Thompson proclaimed his satisfaction with the procedure. The tube out, Mr. Benelli continued to gag and cough, looking up at us with eyes tearing from the pharyngeal irritation. Dr. Thompson seemed so pleased to have found an answer that he could not wait for the gagging and coughing to stop before pronouncing judgment, "Well, it looks like you have cancer." That said, he left the room with brisk stride, waving Al and me out before him. We could hear the gagging cease as Mr. Benelli was left stunned, sitting motionless and alone.

This memory tells me what I have to say; I know what I can offer. I am a medical student—that is my area of expertise. I may not have extensive experience in medicine, but I have spent 4 years watching medical care, and I know that there is madness in this system. The irony is profound—we are here in medical school learning to take care of patients, and yet far too often we graduate having learned nothing of caring. This is not what I expected from the medical profession; and as the authors of this book make clear, the loss of humanity that so many young physicians experience should not, and need not, persist. Yet I must also say that far too often persist it does. Medical education has its dark side, one that is painful and sometimes tragically deforming to young spirits. I know this and so does every medical student who is really honest. This dark side is not all of medicine, but it is too much of medicine for those of us going through the educational process as it is currently constructed. I think it is time that we all admit it.

I entered medical school with idealized notions of the healing role I would play as a physician. I brought with me certain interpersonal skills and what might be described as naive compassion for the ill and ailing. I had understanding of and certainly an appreciation for the complexity and the importance of biological, psychological, and social elements of health.

Four years later, I now know that we are taught a brand of medicine that is often cold, inhumane, and incomplete: Cold, in that we do not learn how to be comfortable with our patients, relating as fellow human beings, so we distance ourselves, adapting airs of professional detachment and indifference. Inhumane, in that this professional detachment can keep us from considering the patient's experience of his illness as we contemplate only the organic aspects of his disease. Incomplete, in that our ignoring the social, behavioral, and psychological components of the patient's experience of his illness thwarts our attempts to help him.

I have been changed by my educational experiences; I am not the person I was when I began medical school. Though I would not want to be unchanged by medical school, I am not sure that my professionalization has always fostered changes for the better. I have felt myself pushed to adopt technological and pseudoscientific attitudes toward patients and their diseases *in place of* the more humane compassion and empathy that was all I had to offer 4 years ago. I have lost some appreciation for the empathic skills and strengths that can help me to establish meaningful and beneficial relationships with my patients. I believe this to be a direct result of the way in which I was trained. Yet there are too few individuals in academic medicine who understand this problem or attempt to correct it.

This book has been written by physicians who *do* understand the problem. The authors' objective is to teach students to understand how the patient experiences illness. They believe that by learning a rational approach to patients that encompasses commonly overlooked aspects of patients' lives students will be able to establish more effective and therapeutic relationships with their patients. I have involved myself in this project because I have seen enough to know that their perspective is vital if the profession of medicine is to reverse the trend of alienation from the people whom the profession claims to serve.

Being a Medical Student

What the other contributors to this book may not discuss, but I must, is the experience of being a medical student. Though it is valuable to understand what is going on in the patient's mind, and the way such perceptions influence his health and medical care, often we medical students cannot give adequate attention to these concerns because we are overwhelmed by the challenges of our role as students. Ironically, perhaps, the structure of our education at times prevents us from learning about integrated patient care when the needs of the people entrusted to us most demand it.

This irony is evident even before we become clinical practitioners. The preclinical years are structured in a way that emphasizes and reinforces the biases of the biomedical model of disease. The mammoth workload and the pressures to perform encourage us to focus our energies on that which is most stressful—the basic sciences—to the exclusion of courses that teach us about the behavioral, psychological, and social aspects of patients, their families, and their health problems. Compounding the problem is the fact that we are given scant opportunity or encouragement to integrate what the experience of becoming a physician is doing to *us*. How can a system that treats its students unempathically possibly hope to turn out doctors who treat their patients with exquisite concern? This skewed orientation leads us to complete our classroom training with a reasonable background in pathology, biochemistry, and physiology but with an inadequate knowledge of, and often diminished appreciation for, the psychological and social skills that are essential aspects of comprehensive and humane patient care. Moreover, and just as serious, the result is too often a student who is cold, joyless, and out of touch with himself.

What of the clinical years, the meat and potatoes of our preparation for a medical career? Is this unbalanced perspective of disease corrected when we begin the actual laying on of hands? Unfortunately not. In fact, when we begin our clinical training, there are myriad ways in which the ward experiences continue to interfere with our learning how to care for patients.

The First Clerkship—A Nontransition

My introduction to clinical rotations was nonexistent. One day I was a student in a classroom for 8 hours a day, and during that same time the next day I was taking care of patients on a medical ward. There was no transition, no time for me to prepare for the quantum leap in my responsibilities.

My first rotation was tremendously difficult. I appeared on my assigned ward on the first morning sporting a freshly pressed white coat. I looked around the ward nervously, wondering when and if I should begin to take notes. I was in luck that morning—some beneficent soul showed me the layout of the ward, explaining all too rapidly where to find the 5 cc syringes, where the EKG machine was kept, how to call a "code" ("What's a code?"), and where I could or could not leave my lunch. As I toured the ward I peeked into the patients' rooms, wondering how I could possibly help these people and praying that I did not have to start helping them until tomorrow. The chief resident of the service came over for introductions and assured me that the interns and residents on the service were extremely capable and good teachers to boot. The chief resident then gathered all the students together and divided us up, assigning us to particular teams. My team was on call that night ("They don't really expect me to stay late today, do they?"), and my intern was mumbling something about wanting all of his "hits" before midnight. We all ran down the hospital stairs, 10 flights, to exchange a little light banter for a few minutes over coffee in the cafeteria. Those scant 10 minutes were no doubt allocated so that all of us, the interns, residents, and students, could get to know one another thoroughly before we began our assigned tasks. When we got back to the ward, my resident said, "Okay, it's time to get to work"—and I wished that somebody would just tell me just what work he meant. After all the introductions, tours, and banter, it suddenly became apparent that my orientation had one glaring deficiency—nobody had told me what I was expected to do and on what basis I was to be judged.

This paucity of guidance and explanation has continued beyond the first day. We have come to the wards nervous and naive, not understanding the practical realities of patient care and ward life. Quite often no one is there to help us understand and clarify the very nature of our presence on the medical team or to define expectations for our performance.

This contributes to tremendous confusion about our role for the first few months of clinical training. We cannot possibly make good use of our time to learn medicine when we are coping, often poorly, with such an abrupt change of role. Who is available to help us out? Interns and residents, perhaps, but they are in a similar bind. They have just begun their year. They too are feeling insecure in their new roles. As their energies are directed toward coping with their own monumental self-doubts and presentiments of inadequacy, they often lack the strength or desire to help us adjust to our new surroundings, and we are left to fend for ourselves in the difficult task of role clarification.

Halfway through my first clinical clerkship I was still in a daze. I was struggling to understand what I was supposed to be doing on my team. I sometimes felt as if I were walking circles around the hospital floor, counting laps as I passed the nursing desk, wondering what in the world I was supposed to be doing next.

During an afternoon's didactic session with our resident, with all students and interns attending, I mentioned that my time on the floor was half over and that I would like to have some idea as to how the team perceived my work and how I might improve. I mentioned that I did not want to wait until the end of the clerkship to find out what I had done right or wrong by reading my evaluation—that I would prefer to have some feedback at that midpoint so that I might use that information to reassess my role. After I had asked from some response, there was absolute silence in the room for about 20 seconds. Then the resident said, "I think that you're all doing just fine." End of lecture.

If the medical staff withhold their comments and criticism, as they are sometimes known to do, we are left with little means to evaluate our performance on the ward. This can and does increase the stress that we feel as we struggle to clarify our role on the medical team. Without assistance from those who might guide us toward the realization of our potential as physicians, we are left to other means.

Trial and Error

One of these means is trial and error: We often learn to define our roles as students and later as physicians by cataloging those behaviors that have either brought us praise or scorn. This trial and error process is taxing, for our behavior is shaped to conform to prevailing notions of patient care. On my second week of clinical rotations, I embarrassed myself in front of my team by not understanding exactly what my position was on the ward. For 1 week I had been following Mr. A., a friendly, talkative man who was continuously in great pain from a lumbar disc problem. Every morning I came into his room to greet him and to test his foot dorsiflexion strength. On this particular day, when I saw him before our team's formal morning rounds, Mr. A. informed me that it was his 50th birthday. Later, as our team stood outside Mr. A.'s room, I mentioned that it was his birthday and suggested we sing happy birthday to him. The interns and residents turned to me, staring incredulously, as one of them expressed their collective view—"We're not a bunch of singing waiters." Throughout the rest of the day, I was subjected to ridicule for my naive suggestion.

This experience left me very hurt and confused—obviously my suggestion was ridiculous, at least to the medical staff, and I learned from this episode never again to suggest such ideas. However, I did not quite understand the reaons for their mockery. Considering how little I knew about medical care at that point, I was much more a friend than a doctor to Mr. A., and thus my suggestion seemed appropriate to me. Though this experience left me confused about my role with patients, I learned what I thought to be an important lesson: I vowed that never again would I suggest anything that might not jibe with the prevailing view of patient care in front of those who sat in critical judgment of my behavior on the ward. It was only a year later that I realized that I had overreacted to this rebuke—that in this situation my expression of interest in joining or initiating the celebration of this patient's 50th birthday was a fitting expression of care and concern. Although the appropriateness of group singing might have been questionable, the medical team, instead of squelching my interest, could have discussed ways in which my concern for this patient could have been appropriately, even creatively, expressed. As is commonly the case, however, the medical staff made no attempt to directly address their expectations for my performance; it was through the not-so-subtle technique of ridicule and scorn that the medical team guided me toward what they considered to be proper behavior.

Whom to Please—Conflicting Demands

This process of discovering my place through trial and error was difficult enough, but I also found myself perpetually beset by the dilemma of not knowing whom to please. It has always been difficult to decide if I ought to aim to please myself, my patient, my medical team, or the attending staff. On my Medicine rotation, for example, it soon became evident that my intern and resident had vastly different notions regarding what I was supposed to be doing on the ward. My intern, a somewhat scattered, frantic young man, liked to encourage my enthusiasm and involvement, but only in certain aspects of patient care. He wanted me to draw all blood samples, perform all procedures, and run to the laboratory at every opportunity to deliver specimens. He stated that when *he* was a medical student his primary role had been to do all the scut work; learning medicine had been a tangential concern, and he enthusiastically assumed that I should now follow suit.

The resident, on the other hand, kept telling me that he expected me to be off the ward, reading and digesting every little fact about my patients' conditions. I saw very quickly that I was in a bind: If I disappeared from the floor to study and read, the intern would later angrily pull me aside, telling me that I had missed this or that piece of work to be done, intimating that I was shirking my duties. If I stayed on the ward doing the various time-consuming chores and ended up having to ask questions during morning rounds the following day, the resident would turn to me impatiently and tell me that I was not reading enough and indignantly refuse to answer my questions. On this rotation I never *did* decide whom I was supposed to please—but both intern and resident were responsible for evaluating my performance. Talk about binds!

Being Influenced by Medical Staff

As I recall my interaction with different patients with whom I have worked over the past few years, I am impressed with how the character of my memories varies from individual to individual. As I think back to a few of my patients, all I can remember are the technical details of their work-up and their treatment. With others I find that I remember a multidimensional view of the patient and the patient's life style and background. I attribute this variation to the fact that on some rotations I have been urged in subtle ways to attend only to technical details, whereas on others I have been encouraged to broaden my involvement with patients.

I have been strongly influenced by certain residents and attending physicians to adopt their patient-care priorities. Indeed, their views color my memories still. Unfortunately, too many of my superiors have had rather narrow biomedical views of their patient care roles. I remember a typical but dramatic experience from one of my third-year clerkships in which I realized that I was being groomed to be a certain type of medical student, yet I was not sure that I approved of the direction in which I was being pushed.

I had been on one team on a medical ward for 3½ weeks, doing the requisite "work-ups" and presentations to my attending physicians. One morning, my resident announced that our team was to be blessed by the presence of the hospital's Chief of Medicine 3 days hence, and he wanted us to decide which patients would be presented. After our team "rounded" on our patients, the resident came up to me and offered me the opportunity to present one of my more interesting "cases" to the Chief of Medicine. He told me that this was quite an opportunity for me, that I should consider it seriously, and that I should decide to present "a case" only if I intended to study intensely every relevant aspect of the case before the Chief's visit. My resident as much as told me that if I were going to do less than a superior job he did not want me to do it at all. After considering this "opportunity," I declined and chose to let the intern present a different case—but I was quite irritated.

It seemed to me that this resident was much more concerned about his own reputation than he was about my education. An opportunity of sorts had indeed been offered to me—but only if I could assure my resident that I was not going to embarrass him or perform in some way that might jeopardize his position in the good graces of the Chief of Medicine. What sort of priorities were operating here, anyway?

Another aspect of this "golden" opportunity that offended me was the sense that my role there was not to be authentic, but to perform—to make my presentation a superior, faultless, all-inclusive show. My resident was implying that this was of the utmost importance, both to him and to the Chief of Medicine. I thought it odd that so much importance should be placed on one "case presentation," especially since nobody seemed particularly concerned about how the "case" being presented was actually cared for.

Ultimately, I decided to reject others' notions of what my priorities ought to be on the ward. I declined my moment in the spotlight and asked not to present. This was not easy, however, and I wondered for days if I had made a mistake in opting not to take advantage of this "opportunity."

Looking back at this incident with 2 years' distance, I realize how vulnerable I was to criticism from my residents. It was not easy for me to appreciate the extent to which this sort of attitude was detrimental to my patients' best interests and to me. At times, however, I was able to see this quite clearly as a crass attitude toward patient care which paled by comparison with the views of the few physicians who were true masters at caring for their patients.

One experience stands out in my memory of these more positive learning experiences. On my Medicine clerkship, I worked with a middle-aged American Indian man with cholecystitis. As part of the work-up, this patient underwent the myriad tests that our tertiary care, high-technology center had to offer. I spent a great deal of time learning about the various tests—what they could or could not show—and I worked hard to piece together a tight diagnostic picture for the presentation to my attending physician.

I presented my patient in the style I had been taught—hurried, dispassionate, and thorough—but I was stopped about halfway through my remarks by a question from the attending. "What tribe is this gentleman from?" I was not sure, but I thought he was Sioux. "Yes, but what particular branch of Sioux tribe is he from?" my attending asked. I could not answer. The attending then proceeded to give a brief discourse on Indian history and Indian lore, and he told me that I should know this about my patient. He instructed me to research the Sioux history and to report back to my team on the next day. He emphasized that we should all know something about our patients' backgrounds—that their personal history is a key to compassionate understanding and that it also enriches our experience as physicians involved in patient care.

This particular physician was quite a fixture at our school. He had attended the school as a medical student, had served as a chief resident, and then had been on the faculty for 30 years or so, involving himself wholeheartedly in patient care and clinical teaching. His influence molded my dealings with patients because I knew he himself appreciated his patients as unique individuals with meaningful personal histories, and he wanted his medical students to do the same. By routinely inquiring about the life histories of his patients, this attending physician inculcated in us a sense of the importance of the psychosocial aspects of care, the uniquely individual, the interpersonal. He worked hard to teach us that there was more to medicine than the rapid recall of yesterday's SMA-12 results. We also learned from him that we could appreciate the personal aspect of our relationships with patients purely for the enrichment of our own human experience, not just for the sake of elegant presentations to our attending physicians.

This is how medicine should be taught, and this physician made it look easy and effortless. My contact with him proved to me that we should be learning more about how to know our patients as human beings as well as we know their organ-system problems.

I'm Still Here

The positive experiences that this physician and a few other special teachers have shown me over the years have helped to modify the rather dismal overall picture I have formed of medicine and medical education. However, the positive experiences have been far too few. The authors of this book tell me that my perspective may be too one-sided, that medical education need not be so narrowly technological and dehumanizing—

that the system which educates us *can* improve in the future, is not (for all its grave problems) mortally flawed. I believe they are right or I would not be putting pen to paper here. At the same time, I stick to my assertion that the education of many, perhaps most, medical students *is* seriously flawed, that too often we wind up as narrow and dehumanized as the system which has trained us. I believe the authors may be worried about the impact of my bitterness on you, the readers. Anger, I think, they can brook and even encourage as constructive. However, I think they fear that bitterness might infect and discourage, when what medical education needs so desperately now is an infusion of hope, inspiration, and optimism. I understand their point. This book exemplifies hope. It reduces my bitterness—but I *am* bitter! Fortunately, I do not feel hopeless, but the rage and frustration I feel will not go away. My education has done this to me. This book, and others like it, will *not* undo this. I hope the authors understand that it could not be otherwise.

Yet I am still here—and I fervently hope the reader can believe this—I still love medicine! In many ways, I love it more and more. This fact alone gives me great hope and solace. Even without the benefit of progressive educational reform, I have wound up loving my work. It seems to me that medicine, at its core, offers such immense rewards, such beauty, drama, and richness, that even our teachers cannot ruin it for us. I *have* been outraged by many of my educational experiences. They *have* been immensely destructive. Yet I remain deeply affirmed in my decision to be a doctor. I continue to feel privileged to participate so fully in life. I have experienced the full range of significant human events, from the first cries of birth to the final rasps of impending death. What a privilege! There must be few other life opportunities in which someone can expect to absorb such wisdom or to be so enriched.

Death and Dying

There is little in our day-to-day nonmedical experience to prepare us for the first time we sit at a patient's bedside as the intangible spark of life is extinguished and we watch a warm body turn cold. The mysterious processes of death are frightening to us all.

On most wards there seems to be unspoken communications regarding those whose life-spark is dimming. Nursing staff may find that they spend less time in the dying patient's room; medical staff may find that they focus on particular aspects of the patient's care to defend against the hopelessness of the patient's medical status. The medical team may compulsively follow the trends in electrolytes, as if keeping track of the sodium level obviates the need to understand or contemplate the incomprehensible surge of death.

I have seen ward staff treat the dying differently from other patients; they begin to detach the personal bonds between caretaker and the cared-for, as if it is too painful to acknowledge the humanness of those who are dying. I have been surprised to find myself viewing dying patients as excessively demanding, irritable, problem patients, somehow trying to protect myself from feeling responsible for the unavoidable truth that the patient's ultimate demand, continued life, cannot be met.

In these upsetting situations, we can choose various levels of involvement with the patient and family. The tendency is to avoid difficult, close interaction with the family and to concentrate on the cognitive aspects of the "case" by studying the diagnostic, pathological, therapeutic, and prognostic aspects. Though this is often the type of involvement promoted and reinforced by the house staff, it is incomplete as well as inhumane.

One of my closest friends immersed herself in the life of a family she worked with on a Pediatrics rotation. Here is her story, in her own words (at her request I am not disclosing her identity):

> One of my saddest, most profound experiences was my involvement in the world of a dying 6-year-old during my first clerkship.
>
> A young divorced couple had brought their 6-year-old son in from Northern California for evaluation and treatment of jaundice and ascites. The father had contracted hepatitis in the recent past, and several months later the son began to show signs of impaired liver function. The family was accustomed to holistic/nutritional alternatives to medical care and had for years consumed megavitamins, vegetable juices, raw milk, and medical herbs. The child had been given enormous amounts of vitamin A supplements (as had the entire family) before the onset of liver dysfunction. The parents, hoping to "help his liver along," began to augment the already near-toxic levels of vitamin A and to feed him large quantities of raw carrot juice. By the time he was referred from an outlying hospital, he was bright yellow, and his little belly had tense ascites. The diagnosis was not clear, but the most likely was vitamin A induced cirrhosis. There was a small chance that he had chronic active hepatitis, a form of liver disease with more potential for reversal. Only a liver biopsy would tell for sure, and David was admitted to our hospital to undergo this procedure.
>
> My resident said, "Never felt a liver edge before? Go feel David's—it's down to his belly button." As I gingerly approached him and asked if I could take a quick look, the solemn child said nothing but raised his T-shirt and surrendered to yet one more stranger. His parents watched protectively. After a few seconds, I felt too uncomfortable examining him; he pulled his T-shirt back down and without a word went back to watching TV from his position in bed. The parents asked where the local natural foods stores and restaurants were, and I made them a list and a map.
>
> I felt helpless, but I wanted to be around this child. My intern needed to draw serial platelet and clotting studies several times a day, and I tried to help her hold David still. It was agony to watch him close his

eyes and brace himself for the needle. It had happened to him so many times that he could no longer be distracted or fooled into thinking about something else. He simply gave in and felt the pain, asking only that his mom or dad hold his hand.

Every day I felt myself becoming closer to this family. I baked them whole wheat banana bread, brought them things to read, tried to explain the significance of each test we did. We spoke to the parents in our Psychiatric Aspects of Pediatrics seminar, and even I was astonished to learn how they really felt about their son's illness and about each other. The psychiatrist instructor, with gentle skill, allowed them to begin to work out their fears and hopes for their child.

The liver biopsy was to be done as soon as David's clotting functions were in the safe range to protect him from uncontrolled bleeding secondary to the biopsy itself. There were delays during which he was transfused with platelets and plasma, but finally he was ready. We were all praying that the biopsy would show him to have a treatable disease. The GI attending physician did the biopsy and took it down to pathology himself. I went with him and felt the pain in his voice as he reviewed the slides with the pathologist: severe cirrhosis with no reversible inflammatory component; consistent with, but not diagnostic of, vitamin A toxicity.

The prognosis was clear: This child was going to die—soon—by bleeding to death from portal hypertension. I started to cry as we went to tell the parents. I decided not to go into the conference room, but the attending took my elbow and said, "This is something that you should be here for." Solemnly and with obvious personal sadness he told them the diagnosis. The mother started to cry, and he held her a moment. Then we all tried to accept his description of how things would be for this special child: that they would live with the uncertainty that he might at any time have a major bleed. As many times as that might happen, and as terrifying and awful as each episode might be, the worst part was that there was no cure. He did not tell them how long he thought David had to live, and they did not ask.

David recovered uneventfully from the biopsy, and we discharged him. By then he felt relatively well and was horsing around with the other kids on the ward. He wheeled up to me on his bicycle, kissed me good-bye, and told me how glad he would be to see his little kitten when he got back home.

Several weeks later, I got letters from both the father and the mother. I think they tell the rest of the story better than I could hope to.

[From Al, David's father]:

Thank you very much for sending David the card and the note you sent me. David was really pleased with your care. He does love his cats; the card was beautiful. He is staying with Barbara now, so yesterday he took it with him to her house. He remembers you well. I told David I was going to write to you and he said to say hello for him. Please tell Q,

K, and B hello for us too [the medical student, intern, and resident on my team].

I had my liver biopsy last Thursday. I am glad the process has begun for me, too. It will be good to know what may be going on inside my body.

It has been a hard 2 years for David and myself, and I pray that we both, but especially David, are beginning the seemingly slow process of healing. If we can make it through this winter without a relapse, I will be so glad.

David has been under the weather this past week, but he is pulling out of it now it seems. Michael [David's brother], David, and I went back to King's Canyon Park a week ago to camp and swim in the river. (Beautiful!) In spite of how careful I was in making sure he was not getting sunburned, he did anyway. But it was not noticeable due to his jaundice. He developed a huge blister on each shoulder. The pediatrician put him on penicillin just in case it might not be sunburn but staph. The culture was negative. But the penicillin, which he took for 2 days I think disturbed the equilibrium of his intestinal flora. Some bad bacteria took hold and he has had diarrhea and fever on and off all week.

I wish I could take all his ills upon myself; he does not deserve what has happened to him. Caring friends like you are really nice to have around. You are a special lady. Write when you can.

Love,
Al and David

[From Barbara, the mother]:

Since I have so much free time on my hands at the moment, I thought I'd take the opportunity to thank you for the card you sent David. We're all looking forward to seeing you if you're able to come visit with Dr. O. He may have told you that David is in the local Children's Hospital now. He'd had an up and down fever for a week and a half, and a sore foot. Over the weekend, he became edematous and his fever stayed high so we brought him into the hospital. He was put in intensive care for the night, put on a cooling pad, given oxygen and a blood transfusion (his hemoglobin count had dropped to 10). He had three IVs, two of which pulled out, and got a fourth one last night for his foot infection. His urine remains dark, but his skin color is less yellow. He still feels very tired, but at least he's not delirious now (on Monday his mind was rambling and he had difficulty recognizing me).

All this is very frightening, to say the least. I don't think I want to dwell on it much more, as it makes me very shaky. I need to remain positive for his sake. I did want to let you know what was going on, but I'm glad you weren't here to see him as he was, since I know how much you care about him. On the other hand, it's good to share the hurt with someone.

Al has worsened, too. He became feverish after spending that first day here with David, and he's been home sick ever since.

What a difference in hospitals! Some of the rules here are more stringent—parents aren't allowed to eat in the rooms, for instance, and only two visitors are allowed at a time during the day. They do have a good dietitian, though, who will go along with many of our ideas in regard to diet—goat's milk, whole grain bread, tofu, alfalfa sprouts, raw vegetable juices.

I think I'm rambling now . . . not enough sleep in the last 3 days. The one really bright spot was last night when a group of 15 clowns from a clowning class came through the ward, and one spent time with David and made him balloon animals. In fact, David got his picture in the papers this morning. David was still very solemn, but his eyes brightened quite a bit.

P.S. later . . .

David has been out of the hospital for a week now. He's recovered enough to start back to kindergarten Monday, but he's still irritable. Al is likewise better, though always tired. I'm looking forward to hearing from you. And thanks again for that card to David of the kittens. I brought it to the hospital and put it on his bed to look at while he was sick. It helped to bring up his spirits.

[And then a final letter]:

I wanted to write a note of appreciation for your letter concerning David's death. Al, Michael, and I passed through San Francisco on Tuesday but apparently the wrong time of the day to locate anyone from the hospital. It was strange to return to the hospital. When we were there in July, the experience was unreal, especially after the doctors pronounced such a doom on David—It was then that I first became truly frightened for him. When we returned to University Hospital [not its real name] I realized that it was a real place and David had really been there . . . and he's really gone now.

I feel your compassion for us. It was very difficult, that last week of David's life. We both wondered if he'd still be alive if we'd insisted he be moved up to University Hospital—but probably not. I don't know. Right now I can't handle any more discussion of why he died, could it have been prevented. It was simply horrible, that's all. David grew weaker, wouldn't eat or wasn't allowed to. He had diarrhea constantly—his fever went up and down, and his belly filled with fluid, causing him trouble with his breathing. In the end, his little heart couldn't handle it, and he stopped breathing. Both Al and I were there. David had been unconscious for 3–4 hours by then, so he wasn't suffering anymore. The doctor on call and the nurse tried to revive him but . . . no good. I don't know how I can calmly relate all this. Inside I feel chilled. Maybe by repeating it often enough, I won't have to cry as much when the full reality hits.

What hurts worst is that I feel as if I'm still looking for him. Everything I see or do reminds me of him. I miss him always. Sometimes when I'm laughing with Michael, I feel David is sitting right there with us, laughing right along. But I can never cuddle him again, never hold his hand again, never help him get dressed or kiss him or sing to him or even get angry and then forgive each other. I grieve always.

At the same time I feel a purpose for David's short but blessed life. He touched everyone he came into contact with and even people he never knew. In our county, 60 people gave blood for him. A memorial fund has been started for him, and a musical benefit will be given in his memory in our town.

We handled the funeral arrangements ourselves. Al made David's coffin, and I provided the padding inside, the shroud, and a pillow. We picked up David's body from the morgue; I was incredibly frightened of seeing his body—we weren't prepared for death in our society—but David's body was so beautiful, so peaceful—and his parting gift to us was a little smile on his face. He was so beautiful, in death as in life. We took him to the crematorium and left the coffin open for half an hour or so. Three friends were there with us. Then we left his precious body for the last time.

After we were given back his ashes, we held a wake. I estimate that over 100 persons came to my house that night, all friends of David's. They brought food, candles, flowers, and musical instruments. It was great—I felt David was there enjoying with all of us, especially later when we formed a circle and sang.

On Thursday morning about 30 of us caravanned up into the mountains to the home of a friend of ours. There we scattered half of David's ashes in a little sunlit glade. There were about eight children, and they gathered around Al and me after we had cast the first handfuls and asked for help. Afterwards, they left flowers on the ground. A friend played two or three songs on his fiddle and another played and danced briefly. We spent the rest of the day walking about the mountains, sharing food, singing, and just being.

I'm rambling on and on, but I thought you'd be interested in knowing how we said good-bye to our beloved son. You know, he really enjoyed these cards you sent him, and he felt you to be his friend. I wish he were still with us—how I miss him. I hope that someday medical science can find help or a cure for liver diseases. At the least, I hope hospitals can become even more individually oriented and not so tuned in to procedure. Al and I regret most that we couldn't hold David in our laps during that last week—the nurses discouraged it because it made his temperature go up. We can't hold him anymore.

I also wonder if the doctors knew David's life span would be so short. I wouldn't want to ask them right now, and I don't know if I would have wanted to know back in July. Still, if I'd known, I would have given David much more time in his last months. There would have been that many more good memories to treasure. How hard to be a parent, but how hard also to be a doctor and to have to make decisions: How much should be told to the patient or his survivors? But I think I always knew, underneath, once they said there was nothing they could do for David. I didn't want to accept it and every time the thought surfaced that David might die, I shoved it down and forced a positive thought in its place and prayed for a miracle of healing. That miracle was not to be for David. I believe his life had a purpose, that he left this place when he knew his time had come to return to whatever living force it is that fills us all. I'm glad he's not tired anymore, or hurting. But I miss him; God, how I miss his little arms around my neck.

I'll stop now . . . . This is all very painful to write, but I know it's equally painful to read. Hoping to hear from you . . .

Barbara

Two weeks later, I received a phone call from Barbara telling me that Al had bled to death from a repeat liver biopsy.

It took me a long time to digest this whole epic—so much had happened to these people over such a short period of time. I was glad that I had gone through this experience with them—though there were days when I was emotionally overwhelmed. I think I'm less afraid of my own patients' illnesses, and I'm not so afraid of having them show me how much they hurt.

My friend chose to involve herself with David's family rather than to distance herself, as others might have done. As is evident from these letters, she remained in contact with the family over many months, feeling the pain of David's and Al's illness and Barbara's excruciating grief; and she, as much as anyone, endured the agony of David's eventual death. . . . It all hurt terribly; yet my friend's love was *so* beautiful! And to be invited in so trustingly by David and his parents, was so incredibly meaningful! It is hard to describe how one can be so saddened and yet ennobled at one and the same time.

There is no easy way to learn to accept death. Our learning progresses out of our willingness to make ourselves vulnerable to our patients' pain and suffering and our ability to grow as we confront the incredible and wonderous mysteries of life itself. Being a doctor demands, and offers, nothing less.

Toward Change and Fulfillment

Unlike the medical student who befriended David and his family, many of us often lose sight of the original ideals and conceptions of medical care that attracted us to the medical profession. Medical education tends to teach a philosophically narrow approach to patients, following the biomedical model. Many facets of the patient's experiences—home life, social situation, life style, personality traits, coping mechanisms, and feelings about being ill and what that means—receive inadequate attention. For us to ignore them limits our potential effectiveness as physicians and healers.

Many aspects of the educational experience, clinical and preclinical, promote this narrow perspective. Preclinical teaching stresses a disease-oriented perspective of patient care, often inadequately supporting concepts of psychological or social importance. During the clinical years the role models to which we are exposed all too effectively reinforce this. Threatening and anxiety-provoking experiences contribute further to our disequilibrium, which in turn leads us to adopt the accepted narrow approach to patients without challenge. Time constraints and pressures to conform to "high academic standards" also urge us to limit our perspective of patient care to disease-specific concerns.

We do not need to accept the limitations of the predominant concept of patient care. In fact, we must not. We can be powerful instruments of change within medicine, but first we must recognize the ways in which our ideals of proper interactions with patients are reshaped by our clinical experiences. The principles and concepts outlined in this book can help us to ensure that our ideals can prevail. We do not need to passively adopt the views and attitudes of those around us.

Our medical education offers us the opportunity to mature and grow adept at handling new dimensions of responsibility. Our status as students does not limit the deeply engrossing and satisfying relationships we can develop with our patients. We can use our personal strengths and develop skills to help patients through times of illness, even though we might not have mastered the fine points of medical diagnosis and treatment.

Only one who has been on the receiving end of medical care can adequately express the paramount importance of the caring relationship with one's patients, as is demonstrated in the following letter to a third-year medical student from one of his former patients, a 60-year-old woman with metastatic cancer.

Dear Robert:

I found my 3 weeks in University Hospital to be interesting and stimulating as well as frightening and uncomfortable. I had had little experience with illness and hospitals for 60 years; and here are some thoughts which I would like to share with you and your fellow students.

The patient must assume that her physicians have absolute knowledge of technology, surgical procedures, medications. She finds herself helpless in a world of battalions of people asking questions; she rides down long corridors and is introduced to strange machines. Nothing she has ever known before seems to be of any use to her.

Then there is human contact, which for me made all the difference.
What follows is a kind of subjective code of ethics, which I hope that
physicians of the future will attend to. I am aware that it was the senior
physicians who made the ultimate decisions and performed the surgical
procedures, but it was the young nurses, the medical students, the
residents who taught me many of the things I am about to say and who
were my salvation. May their numbers increase!

There is the all-important first encounter with the patient—the
immediate establishment of confidence, rapport, dependence, and
friendship with a perplexing variety of patients. For a patient, especially
one of my generation, indoctrinated early to worship the medical
profession—turned away from that worship even as she was turned
away from the inadequacies of her religious instruction—it was a
miracle to meet young physicians and medical students who seemed
immediately to *know* me, to *care* about me, young people whose feelings
are close to the surface, who could move from a kind of
tongue-in-cheek jocular bedside manner, to tenderness, to the
birth of confidence in a matter of minutes.

There comes the answering of questions. A physician must be a teacher,
able to translate the most intricate aspects of modern medicine to the
most basic facts, understandable by the most uninformed patients. Since
I am professor of literature and have been prescribing poems, novels,
and drama to the multitudes for 40 years, here I go again. A physician,
in my opinion, can only be a good teacher in this most difficult area of
instruction if he is first a poet, because it is only by the use of metaphor
that the abstractions of one kind of learning can be transformed into
the concrete facts of another. He should therefore steep himself in
literature so that he can comprehend the defiance of Ahab, the
gentleness of Christ, the patience of Job, the rapture of Keats dying of
tuberculosis. Then, if he has also been reading quantities of lyric verse,
the metaphors will come.

He must also be a teacher who holds out no false promises but does so
not without hope, as Emily Dickinson said:

Tell all the truth but tell it slant—
Success in Circuit lies
Too bright for our infirm Delight
The Truth's superb surprise

As Lightning to the Children ease
With explanation kind
The Truth must dazzle gradually
Or every man be blind—

He must know that to let his feeling show is not a sign of weakness. In
his black bag should be a vial of tears to be used unhesitatingly but with
discretion. Of far more importance, in my opinion, is his ability to
inspire laughter, be it ironic, corny, slapstick, sophisticated. He should
know that behind Falstaff's most dreadful jokes lay much love and

tragedy, that in the ironic laughter of Mark Twain and Jonathan Swift there was anger and frustration. I laughed more while in the hospital than I had in a long time; there is where I learned how close laughter and tears are to each other and how necessary they both are.

For his own salvation, the physician needs to learn to retreat deep within himself for renewal; he should spend time climbing mountains, sailing, running wild rivers, living alone in the wilderness. He should spend much time with small children so as not to forget their direct simplicity; he should not forget that the very old are frequently very wise.

He must always be capable of wonder—at the variety of human experience, at the magic of healing, at what was surely meant to be the awesome and exciting experience of death. I grew up in Appalachia where physicians and hospitals were few and far between and where, I am sure, many people died before their time and in unnecessary pain. Nevertheless, they died at home, surrounded by their kin, and the manner of their deaths was an important part of the folklore of their lives; their last words and embraces were important conclusions to the other stories about them that were told to us as children. And so finally a physician must attempt the difficult task of being a guide for the patient and the patient's family through the lonely valley of death. For this most difficult of all his duties, I prescribe large doses of Emily Dickinson.

All of this takes time and energy. And so, in order not to destroy himself or to turn away from his feelings in order to save himself, a physician must, no matter how much his services are in demand, limit himself. He must never allow himself to be persuaded to deal with too many patients at any one time. If he does not remain whole, how can he heal?

Robert, this did not come out the way I feel it in my heart. It's didactic and sentimental. But you know how I feel about you and the other students who helped me; you turned me around in ways that will make all the difference for as long as I live.

>   With much thanks and love,
>   Elaine

This letter encompasses, in a briefer form, everything that this book is attempting to convey: our patients are unique human beings with histories, with meaningful stories to tell, with emotional reactions to their illnesses, with thoughts and criticism to share regarding their medical treatment. We must not let the extraneous complications and difficulties of our education overshadow our realization that we have a great deal to offer to our patients, and that they in turn have a great deal to give back to us.

1 Medicine as a Human Experience

The inspiration for this chapter—indeed for much of this book—comes from a challenge posed to us by one of our students. We had just finished bedside rounds during which we had interviewed a dying man. The interview had been sensitive. Subsequent discussion was lively but thoughtful. We asked why this suffering man felt compelled to deny how sick he was. The group felt animated and engrossed. Soon the students began linking events from the man's childhood to his coping style in the present. The connections seemed to make sense and helped us all to understand the patient better.

Then Jeff, a bright but skeptical student, pursed his lips.

"Okay," he said. "I buy it. Losing his father as a kid *does* relate to the way he is coping now. And I feel I understand him better as a person, which is good. . . . But so what?"

Silence.

"Really," Jeff persisted. "I'm not putting this stuff down. I *agree* it's nice to understand our patients and that often doctors don't. But I still say—so what? What can I do *practically*? Now that I know all this, how do I *help* him?"

Slowly, several students in the group began to nod in tentative agreement.

As instructors, we had heard this concern from medical students many times. We both fought an initial urge to counter Jeff with some remark like, "There *are* no cookbooks, Jeff! You have to get used to that!"

But we bit our tongues and tried to understand what lay behind his question.

What finally dawned on us was this: Jeff was not being simple-minded, prejudiced, or oppositional. He really did not understand what we ourselves had come to take so unquestioningly for granted—that empathy, understanding, and insight do help our patients, often help them a lot. At that moment, we also realized something else. The failure to comprehend lay less with Jeff than with ourselves. Despite the best intentions, we had still failed to make it clear to Jeff why understanding patients is not simply "nice" and "interesting" but absolutely essential to good medical care. Moreover, we must finally confess, the explanation that Jeff needed and deserved turned out not to be so simple to deliver.

On the other hand, the answer to Jeff's question—but put in reverse—is no more simple. The question is: Why is the importance of understanding the whole person, and not just fragments of him, so widely ignored and denigrated in modern medicine? How could this *not* be clear? How could it happen that Jeff's medical education would leave him bewildered about such fundamental truths instead of enlightened and reassured?

It is not our intent, however, to answer these questions, though they do cry out for answering. Rather, we will attempt to respond to the question Jeff asked, for it is a pivotally important one. Is the concept of medicine as a human experience really practical? Does it, in fact, make a difference with patients in the office and at the bedside? In short, is it merely "nice"—or does it help?

A historical perspective is revealing. Clearly, the plea for empathic physicians is not in itself new. It is at least as old as medicine and as new as this text. The idea has had impassioned and articulate proponents all along. From this we must infer that the champions of empathy down through the decades also encountered resistance and perplexity, from colleagues and students who were just as incredulous as Jeff. Conceptually, this is important, for it means that contemporary medical education is not wholly to blame for the problem. Certainly, medicine is currently fraught with serious shortcomings. However, too many of its critics assume, naively and incorrectly, that dehumanization and lack of true holism in medicine are somehow new and therefore exclusively the fault of science and high technology.

The problem is not new. If it were, Osler would not have been pleading the same case with his colleagues 80 years ago and Hippocrates long before that. All along, at least some physicians seem to have been saying rather skeptically, as Jeff did, "Okay, but so what?"

Our purpose in this chapter and throughout the rest of this book is not to diagnose the problem's origins so much as it is to take yet another crack at correcting the age-old misconceptions that still abound. We address the essence of Jeff's question—the "so what?" part—by delineating what we believe to be four essential principles that underlie all of medicine as a human experience. They are: *acceptance, empathy, conceptualization,* and *competence.* We believe that these four elements comprise the foundation of what might be termed *patient-centered medicine.* And as we hope to make clear, this is where the most effective, most human kind of medicine should always be centered. In elaborating on each of these principles, we especially try to make a case for their practical importance—why they are therapeutic, indeed essential, to our patients' welfare. Essential, not just "nice."

The Four Principles of Medicine as a Human Experience

Acceptance

At a conference on healing, Dr. Stephen Ray, an unusually sensitive, open physician who practices plastic surgery at the University of Rochester, expressed his feelings about working with the severely deformed:

> Before I enter the room to see such a person, I clear my mind of prejudices and preconceptions. I remind myself that all of nature is part of some universal order and is therefore harmonious and beautiful. Then, if I walk into the room and see a man or woman whose face has been scarred beyond recognition, I do not see the grotesqueness but find myself thinking of spiritual things—ancient craggy rock faces, gnarled old trees. It's odd—but with this attitude, where others find ugliness, I can discern beauty.

What Dr. Ray is displaying is acceptance, a trait that we believe is fundamental to all truly effective patient care. It is important to be clear about what we mean by this simple word. Certainly "acceptance" has many commonplace meanings—acceptance of responsibility, acceptance of obligation, acceptance of assignments, tasks, and deadlines. Of course, we mean all of these, but we also mean something much more specific, more basic to the warp and weft of medicine itself. In its most fundamental sense, acceptance means that the doctor takes the patient—the person as he is—into his mind, his heart, and his conscience. It is not an action but an encompassing attitude. Furthermore, this attitude is not "mystical." Rather, it is embedded in what is most phylogenetically and ontogenetically basic to the human being. The doctor who fails to perceive this will never understand the essence of patient care and healing.

To develop this line of reasoning, permit us two excursions from what one normally thinks of as being a part of medicine. The first excursion is into etymology, the origins of our symbols and the conceptions of ourselves that are embedded in our language. *Accept* comes from the Latin verb *accipere*. It means literally "to take or receive." The word in turn is derived from a preposition, *ad* (meaning "toward") and *capere* (meaning "to take"). Note how similar *capere* is to two closely related Latin words: *caput* and *cephalicus*. Both of these words mean, literally, "the head". The origins of our language most likely reflect an innate appreciation that acceptance, on its deepest level, is mental, not physical. We embrace people most intimately not with our arms, but with our minds, and with that universal metaphor for mind, our hearts. Thus the fourth listed definition of "accept" in *Webster's Third International Dictionary* is just this—"to receive into the mind."

Why is this concept important? What does it have to do with modern medicine? The answer, we believe, lies in its intrinsic emphasis on receptivity rather than on action. Progressively, medicine (and indeed technological society itself) has grown more action-oriented. Yet acceptance reminds us that at the deepest level humans need to be received, embraced, taken in, incorporated—all far more quiet and receptive modes of relatedness than we are usually accustomed to.

A key line of evidence for the importance of acceptance in medicine as a human experience is found in the phenomenon of human bonding. As many studies now make abundantly clear, maternal acceptance is no mere nicety. Along with food and warmth, maternal acceptance is essential for normal human development. Observe a mother with her young infant, a 3-month-old for example. She holds the infant to her breast, almost always with its head on the left, over her heart. She gazes into its eyes, and the child gazes back. Vocalizations are minimal, and those present consist of sighs, soft whispers, and coos. There is little motor activity. The mother's expression is serene. The baby's body tone is relaxed. If the baby is breastfeeding, its hand may reach out and gently stroke the mother's breast, or perhaps explore the contours of her mouth or hair. The mother, in turn, strokes the baby gently and coos. It is a moving and beautiful sight. It is also the biology of survival.

Now observe the child when it is not being held or, equally distressing for the infant, being held *improperly, unempathically* by a tense, distracted, or indifferent mother. It may begin to cry and scream. Its body tonus becomes tense, its back and neck arch. When such distress occurs in a well-nurtured baby, the mother who is sensitive to her child responds quickly, knowing "instinctively" what her child needs—more milk, a dry diaper, a good burping, to be warm.

We are all moved by such a sight. It *is* lovely. However, such a response, unamplified by a scientific understanding of what is actually transpiring in the dyad, misses the fundamental point: We are witnessing here a basic biological process, one essential to the survival of the species. This early trust contains the origins of later forms of human acceptance—embracing, receiving, taking into the mind. Note especially what is *not* present. The baby's motor activity is greatly reduced. His vocalization and the mother's are minimal and muted in tone. Silence, touch, and eye contact predominate. In fact, an increase in vocalization and motor activity usually signals increased infantile tension and distress. Note, finally, how the mother handles this. She holds the child, presses it to her, thus reducing the internal and external stimuli that are causing tension and distress. The entire sequence occurs with a minimum of action, conscious thought, or words. We see the absence of this process at times when the mother is having difficulty with her child or is emotionally unavailable. Such mothers typically talk a lot and move a lot, alternating between detachment and activity. Their voices are loud. They may tickle the baby, say "There, there!" loudly, and shift the baby from shoulder to shoulder. As the mother's frustrated activity increases, the infant in turn becomes progressively more distressed, vocal, and hyperactive. What does this have to do with understanding patients? The answer is—a great deal!

Let us go back to the healthy, secure baby. Time passes and, with trust and acceptance as building blocks, the infant grows. Cognition increases, and his world expands. He gains motor control and explores his environment. Soon he develops language and, with language, the capacity for abstraction, symbol formation, and reason. By the time our baby has grown into adulthood, he is a bundle of symbolic possibilities and abstractions—words, actions, ideas, and purposes. During adulthood only the most intimate and special of circumstances, such as sexual intimacy, permit the typical grown-up to let go and revert to that earlier state of tension release and nonverbal bliss. It is this capacity to surrender willingly to the care of another, to let go of one's customary and excessive self-control, that many adults find so exceedingly difficult. Commonly, we say, "I just can't relax." Often we really mean, "I can't entrust myself totally to another."

Consider now the plight of our patients. When a person is very sick, in pain, in a hospital, nature has potentially played a cruel trick on him indeed. Though he is not a baby, he is at risk of becoming or being as helpless as a baby. He is dependent, passive, and frightened, sometimes terribly afraid to move. Once again he is dependent on caretakers. For the first time since he was a tiny baby, feeding and bowel care are again in the hands of others. The nature of severe illness itself triggers a regression to such a state of dependency (so similar to infancy). Patients fight it in different ways, but the regression itself is usually inevitable. We see the most extreme example of it in the total passivity and helplessness of the patient who has given up, but lesser degrees abound. Many patients fight the dependency very hard. Cassem and Hackett suggest, however, that patients who can accept this inevitable regression and allow themselves to become dependent and place total, even idealized faith in their doctors may sometimes be better off. The patients who fight this dependency, on the other hand, may tend to encounter more problems. Perhaps this is why doctors are such notoriously poor patients. As a rule, physicians are reluctant to relinquish control, even when it would be entirely appropriate to do so.

Here we have it then: a patient who is disorganized, suffering, and regressed, but usually hating the regression itself and actively fighting it. Enter the doctor—a person who, for many reasons, may be especially afraid of such disorganization and helplessness in himself. Typically, we doctors tend to talk a lot. From the outset, our questions are very focused, content-oriented, and paced in rapid, staccato succession. We issue instructions. We move constantly, fidgeting and probing, fingering our reflex hammers and stethoscopes. Too often the result is a patient who does not feel accepted. Akin to the agitated baby in an anxious mother's arms, the jostling and shaking that characterizes too many physicians' styles increases the patient's fearfulness and tension. This is why doctors need to learn attentiveness, receptivity, openness, increased tolerance of feelings, and silence—so the patient can begin to relax, feel protected, and begin to trust. Such acceptance is an ingredient of healing, one that goes far beyond any mere polishing of bedside manner. It is an essential response to yearnings locked deep in all human beings. The effective doctor must learn to resonate with this basic longing and give over and submit to trust in his patients.

Consider again how this basic, evolutionary need is expressed in our language. Listen to how we speak of a "good doctor." We say he is a compassionate person who is *warm, feeling,* possessing a big *heart.* When a patient feels understood by such a doctor, he frequently states that "the doctor accepted me," and the patient is *touched* by such acceptance—"I can trust him." As you listen to these phrases, consider their physicality, think back to that baby once again held in its mother's arms, warm and safe, head against the breast, listening to the rhythmic pounding of the heart. The doctor-patient relationship is rooted in biology and evolution, not in mysticism or mere sentiment.

To accept the patient, we must learn to listen better. We must learn to permit feelings to emerge more. We must become more receptive. We need to master the difficult act of being quiet. Although this aspect of healing has been woefully neglected, scientific exploration in this area is both important and possible, just as it has proven to be in the study of the infant-mother dyad, another subject originally relegated to sentiment and mystery. The clue to many illnesses may lie in the physiological response of a distressed organism when it needs soothing, comfort, and quiet nurturance. Just as was true for the infant, the *lack* of these responses (internally or from the environment) could conceivably lead to altered physiological states predisposing to disease. Identifying such phenomena would obviously be important in understanding illness onset. Similarly, learning how to soothe may be a neglected yet critical aspect of healing that is required even after the disease has been cured.

Whether through ignorance or for other reasons, modern medicine too often seems to have lost sight of these human requirements. Instead of listening, we talk. Instead of accepting the patient, we subject him to tests and procedures. In place of a gentle touch, we offer Valium. We have lost sight of too much that is essential to healing, including the importance of acceptance, and we cannot afford to be so unscientific about these matters.

Empathy

Empathy is the second principle of patient-centered medicine. Its importance has been widely stressed and its dimensions described by many writers concerned with the doctor-patient relationship. It has been defined variously, most of the definitions attempting to connote an emotional stance that avoids extremes of overidentification on the one hand and excessive emotional detachment on the other. A useful definition describes empathy as the ability to fully understand and share in another's feelings, coupled with the ability to know that those feelings are not identical to one's own. Defining empathy may be difficult, but achieving it is even harder. Most students find that they tend to oscillate between periods of overidentification with patients and periods of excessive detachment. The notion of striking a balance is obviously appealing but not simple to effect. In truth, accurate and consistent empathy with patients is an exacting skill, one that requires years of experience and effort to develop fully.

For the student who is first approaching the task, it is important to understand empathy's dynamic quality. It is a fluid process, not some ideal fixed point between "too close" and "too far." It is useful to think of the empathic process as analogous to multiple frames in a motion picture. Even though the movie one sees on the screen seems smooth and consistent, slowing the frames down reveals rapid and remarkable shifts. Imagine that observing empathy is a bit like observing a film of a hummingbird, apparently poised in one spot. If we could slow down the action and study each frame, we would see thousands of small corrections, constant shifts and changes in the yaw and pitch of the bird's beating wings. Analogously, a doctor does not really stay poised at some ideal distance from a patient in order to empathize, though it might appear so. Actually, with a speed and fluidity that does indeed resemble the beating of a hummingbird's wings, an empathic physician moves about constantly—extremely close to a patient one minute, more detached the next, somewhere in between these extremes most of the time. To illustrate this process more clearly, we will turn our focus to two hypothetical cases. For didactic purposes, let us indulge in the luxury of modern cinematography: stop-action, slow-motion, and instant replay.

The first case is a relatively simple one. We need only to observe it in slow motion. Imagine that a doctor is interviewing a young woman in her twenties hospitalized for a flare-up of diabetes that worsened after her mother died the month before. The patient's lips begin to quiver, and tears well up in her eyes. The doctor, in turn, feels himself growing teary-eyed and momentarily fears that he too will burst into tears. He draws back and regards his patient for a moment from a safer distance. Quickly regaining his composure, he almost instantaneously draws closer again and says softly, "You still miss her terribly, don't you?" The patient now sobs openly. The net effect of the interaction could be described as "empathic," but the actual process was far more fluid and dynamic.

The physician who has achieved empathy possesses a very potent tool. First, he can articulate for his patients what they are actually experiencing. This can be highly therapeutic in its own right. Perhaps more important, accurate empathy enables a physician to avoid many of the communication breakdowns, frustrations, and hostilities that so often arise in clinical work. In our experience, the vast majority of these disruptions begin with a breakdown in empathy.

The usefulness of accurate empathy goes further. As everyone knows, doctors do not treat patients in a vacuum. Patient care occurs in a complex social system—typically during the student's clinical years in a hospital ward. The tensions, hostilities, counter-hostilities, flirtations, and minor irritants that so frequently spring up in these settings can bewilder physicians and hurt patient care. Such occurrences are common, perhaps, but we believe they warrant a closer look. Again, let us turn our magic camera on and view another hypothetical case. This one turns out to be more complex and unsettling.

Michael Smith is a youthful-looking junior student doing his first rotation on Internal Medicine. The setting is a crowded, hectic ward in a city hospital. Michael's patient is a 47-year-old unemployed "waitress" named Johnnie. In fact, Johnnie is a prostitute. She is also an alcoholic and, intermittently, a heroin addict. She has been in prison several times. Currently, she is in the hospital for severe abdominal pain, possibly alcohol-induced pancreatitis.

A hard-edged, boisterous woman, she seems to get along well enough with the resident and intern who are taking care of her. Their interactions at the bedside seem amiable enough, filled with gruff joking and double entendres. However, this apparent ease of rapport is not destined to be for Michael. We pan in on the action as he approaches her bedside, just after the intern and resident have left. Michael has been assigned to do her admission history and physical and draw all her blood samples. The resident has told him earlier, snidely and barely out of the patient's earshot, "Have we got a good one for you."

From the outset, Michael senses that she absolutely hates him. In order to illustrate what soon transpires, we will stop the action at several points and see what is going on in the individual frames.

Initially, Michael fidgets nervously, the back of his neck heating up, as Johnnie beholds him with a silent but scornful scowl. He fumbles as he tries to get his ophthalmoscope set up.

Suddenly Johnnie crows out, "How old are you anyway, twerp?"

"Twenty-three," Michael mumbles uncomfortably.

"What the hell are they sending *you* in here for anyway?" she retorts. "Am I suppose to be your guinea pig?"

Michael squirms and mumbles something.

"I don't think I like your attitude, Sonny," she says snidely. "I may be a city hospital patient, but I ain't nobody's fool. You go get one of the *real* doctors to examine me!"

Mike withers inside, his palms now perspiring profusely. He trembles with humiliation and rage.

Stop action! Let us observe what is happening.

Clearly Johnnie has seen right through Michael's insecurities, attacking him precisely where he is most vulnerable—his concerns about his youth, inexperience, and ineptitude.

Let the camera roll again. Initially Michael tries to handle the problem by being polite and conciliatory, but it does not work.

"I ain't going to be your guinea pig, Sonny boy!" Johnnie snaps. "You ain't examining me!"

At this point, Michael decides to sound more "authoritative," as he imagines his resident would in this situation.

"Listen, Ms. Johnson!" he says in his gruffest voice. "I am here to examine you. This isn't a private hospital, you know. This is important! Now, come on and stop giving everyone a rough time!"

Stop action!

Michael has now puffed up his chest and tried to seem as stern and "physicianly" as he can. He hopes this will force his rambunctious patient to comply, but it is not to be.

Roll the camera. Johnnie now squints at Michael with sardonic amusement. A wry smile then breaks through the leathery dissipation of her worn face. With slow and deliberate measure, she says, "Back off, Sonny boy. Come back when you grow up!" She grabs her IV pole, which beings to totter dangerously. "Now I ain't kidding, Sonny boy! If you don't beat it, I'm going to smash this thing over your stupid little head!"

Cut!

What has happened? For very understandable reasons, Michael has not been able to empathize. This is hardly surprising, and Johnnie is no gem; but such an explanation does not suffice. To begin with, Michael is already self-conscious about his inadequacies. Confronted with this difficult, belligerent patient, his composure quickly evaporates. He then tries to act tough, but to no avail. Moreover, from the looks of the IV bottle tottering menacingly on its pole, he is in some danger of getting clobbered.

What went wrong? Essentially both parties were too wrapped up in themselves to have empathy for the other. It is hard to know precisely what was on Johnnie's mind; she probably was angry about being treated as an object by the house officers, enraged yet intimidated. So she took her fury out on the inexperienced, vulnerable medical student, Michael. Michael too had entered the interaction already distracted, preoccupied with his own feelings of inadequacy. As soon as she shot off her "zinger," Michael reacted as though the attack were all too real. We repeat: *as though it were real.* Michael, as is so typical of doctors, then responded to Johnnie in suit. Assuming that her accusation had legitimacy, he felt he had no option except to refute her logic. As doctors often do, he initially tried to be conciliatory and play nice. When that failed, he tried to pull rank. Essentially, however, he responded to her accusation at face value and attempted to restore his position by proving her wrong.

Because this is a hypothetical situation, we can indulge in the luxury of an instant replay. Let us imagine that Michael seeks the counsel of an attending physician whom he respects and trusts. Let us be a little frivolous and imagine the attending right there in the hospital, though it is 11:00 o'clock on a Saturday night.

The attending listens to Michael nonjudgmentally and then says, "Try to detach yourself from the immediacy of the situation. [Note how empathy involves distance as well as closeness.] Pretend you are invisible and looking down at the interaction between the two of you from a spot on the ceiling. Forget about yourself—watch that guy named Michael down there. Ask yourself: Why is it that Johnnie might be reacting with such hostility to Michael? Give her the benefit of the doubt. At least *try* to see it from her point of view. What do you come up with?"

"Well," Michael muses, "she seems determined to prove that she's the one in control down there! She seems angry."

"True. What else?" the attending prods.

"Well," Michael continues, "there's no doubt that she's putting me down. She's trying to make me feel like two cents."

"And succeeding. But why would she need to do a thing like that?" the attending persists.

"I remember something now," Michael says suddenly. "Just before I was going to examine her, before the intern and resident left, one of them made a pretty crude joke. Something about how many men she must have slept with. She laughed it off; but I could tell she was hurt. I think she even blushed a little, but they were already leaving the room. They didn't see it."

"Then you came in," the attending notes.

"Right. Maybe they hurt her pride?"

"Sure! Maybe she was making *you* feel as humiliated and inadequate as they had just made *her* feel!"

"I can understand now why she reacted that way toward me."

"So what are you going to say to her now?" the attending asks.

"That's harder. *You* tell me what to say."

"Okay," the attending obliges. "Agree with her!"

Michael looked puzzled.

"Agree with her!" the attending repeats. "Empathize with her plight. Not only is she insulted and degraded, but on top of that they send a junior medical student in to do her history and physical."

"Well," Michael says somewhat skeptically, "I'll give it a try."

Cameras! Action! Scene one, take two!

Michael approaches the bed again. Johnnie still sits there, a contemptuous scowl on her face. This time, however, Michael notices something else—something sadder, a weariness and vulnerability that this tough woman tries hard to hide.

"I'm Michael Smith, a junior medical student. Has Dr. Jones explained that I need to get a history and physical from you?"

"How old are you, twerp?!" Johnnie starts in, "I ain't going to have no student experiment on me!"

Michael bites his lips this time and gives the new approach a try.

"You're not having much luck around this place, are you?" he begins. "It's bad enough to be sick and have to go to City; but on *top* of that, they send in 'the bargain basement special' to examine you—a junior medical student! Me? I'd be upset too!"

Johnnie looks momentarily nonplussed. Then her expression softens. "Well, I guess you kids have it hard, too. You've got to learn."

"I think it's important for you to know," Michael says, "I'll be the one taking care of you. The other doctors are also going to be following you. I'm very concerned about this pain you've been having."

"Ah, what the hell," Johnnie says. "It don't matter that much anyway. Where do you want me to begin, Doc?"

Clearly, we could have bypassed this lengthy dissection of the empathic process by simply saying, "Put yourself in the patient's shoes," or "Empathize but don't identify." Yet such admonitions, nice as they sound, seldom help a great deal. To make sense of it, one needs to look at the process in more detail. Several themes emerge when we do:

1. Breakdowns in empathy usually begin when a patient pulls the doctor's chain. The specifics can vary, but patients are good at it. In Michael's case the patient misdirected her anger and lashed out at

Michael, who was vulnerable to attacks on his youth and inexperience. Other patients can, and do, throw other kinds of brickbats—seductiveness, hostility, passivity, demandingness, etc.

2. The empathic bond ruptures further when the doctor assumes that the attack on him is based on objective reality. This prevents him from asking, "Why does the patient feel compelled to see me like this?" Instead, the doctor becomes defensive and feels compelled to disprove the validity of the patient's attack. This approach rarely succeeds. Typically, a doctor first redoubles his efforts to be kind, smart, wise—whatever the patient is accusing him of being deficient in. When this fails, as it almost always does, the doctor then typically responds with increased authoritarianism and hostility.

3. This completes a self-fulfilling prophecy in which the doctor becomes the very person the patient fears.

4. As the cases above show, empathy requires that the doctor almost literally be in several places at once. If the doctor is insensitive to the painful messages the patient is sending out in the first place, he will never be able to understand the patient's real anguish. He *must* feel the pain that the patient intends him to feel. At the same time, he must be able to detach himself from the immediate situation and realize that what is being directed toward him comes more from the fact that he is a symbol than from any reality that has to do with him.

5. While achieving this kind of equanimity can be difficult, it permits the physician to speak sincerely "over his patient's shoulder," so to speak, so that the cliche, "Being in the patient's shoes," takes on real meaning.

Empathy is one of the hardest skills to perfect. It is also one of our most effective tools. Nothing is foolproof, of course, but most situations that go awry do so from lack of empathy. Even enormously explosive situations can often be defused with accurate empathy. Obviously, the uses of empathy are not limited to understanding patients. One can also use empathy better to understand the complex and sometimes painful interactions that occur among various hospital personnel, including ourselves.

One final point: Note that oversimplified prescriptions for actions and interventions are down-played throughout this text. Students do, understandably, find the absence of such prescriptions frustrating. However, despite students' understandable wishes for specific courses of action, remedies, or antidotes, we have chosen to refrain. It is our contention that the student who truly accepts the patient and empathizes with the patient's plight *will* know what action to take and when to take it. Plenty of books offer easy "tricks of the trade," guaranteed recipes for sure-fire success. Though these cookbooks reduce anxiety momentarily, they ultimately ring hollow. Patient-centered medicine is simply too complex! The proper intervention must come from true understanding and empathy. When these are achieved, what to do usually becomes extremely obvious. Without understanding and empathy, no lexicon of tricks or list of techniques will ever succeed.

Conceptualization

The conceptual basis for patient-centered medicine that we advocate is derived from George Engel's biopsychosocial model described in Chapters 2 and 3. Essentially, Engel's thesis is based on principles of systems theory and holds that no change can occur within one component of a system without eventually making an impact on other components of that system. Further, each system (e.g., a molecule, a human being, or a family) holds a lower or higher place in relation to other systems in a hierarchy of systems. Approaching patient care from this perspective requires a shift in thinking away from a simplistic disease orientation toward the more complex and more effective stance that we describe here as patient-centered medicine. The following two chapters, which describe the theoretical basis of this approach in greater detail, underscore how difficult a challenge it is to make this shift in perspective. To be a good doctor, a truly complete one, a physician must understand molecules and cells, organelles and organs, but he must also understand the complex, ineffable miracle we call "the person." Even this will not suffice, however; for as Engel's diagrams make clear, people relate primarily in dyads but live in still larger systems—families, communities, and the biosphere itself.

Once upon a time, being a doctor must have seemed easier. Now it is more difficult than ever. The onslaught of new information at all levels of the systems hierarchy has accelerated at an astonishing rate. These are not trivial advances but major new trends, fundamental and far-reaching discoveries that the doctor must integrate and understand.

A man who loses his business has a heart attack. Six months later he drops dead. Once we would have attributed it to coincidence. Now new information tells us otherwise. Farmers in Montana spray insecticide over a wheat field. A month later poisoned waterfowl in 30 states endanger the entire food chain. Important information! The doctor must know it! Take one final example, a tiny glitch on the screen of knowledge, this one occurring at the molecular level. A scientist discovers a practical method for splicing new DNA into the genetic structure of *E. coli.* Important new information! Only now are its far-reaching effects beginning to resonate through the entire system of humankind all the way to the most fundamental ethical and spiritual tenets of civilization.

What is a conscientious doctor to do? Students are already overwhelmed with the amount of new knowledge to be mastered. The mind reels with emotional and intellectual vertigo at the prospect of encompassing so much more.

Certainly no one can master all of this information. One of medical education's greatest failures, in fact, has been its failure to help students accept this. Doctors who try to master everything ultimately become haunted by a driving perfectionism—and they are doomed to fail, try as they may.

What most doctors do to solve this dilemma is to draw a box around an area of relative "expertise" into which they then withdraw. They put a perimeter around some section of the huge and momentous total picture. Where the doctor draws his box depends on many factors. Some draw it around molecules. Others draw it around an organ system. As one very sincere and successful academic physician expressed it, "I'm a liver man." A few brave souls try to draw larger boxes and speak of themselves as generalists or family practitioners. Clearly, the fear—an eminently understandable one—is that the larger one draws the box, the greater the risk that one's knowledge base will be vitiated and ultimately prove faulty. No one wants to be a dilettante, and life has simply grown too complicated in the twentieth century for there to be any more "Renaissance" men and women. So, understandably, doctors try to specialize. Quite reasonably, they attempt to draw an appropriate box.

Here the game gets tricky, however. The biases, misconceptions, and prejudices that accompany all territoriality emerge (once you have drawn your box, you have defined what is, and is not, in your territory). Thus the gastroenterologist sneers at the family practitioner who does not know how to interpret a technetium scan. The family practitioner scoffs right back, noting the gastroenterologist's inability to treat the same patient's tennis elbow. The neurochemist laughs at the psychoanalyst. The psychoanalyst in turn condescends to the biochemist.

On a practical, day-to-day basis the typical junior and senior medical student learns that his box is being drawn at the organ system level. Anything beyond this level is likely to be disparaged or ignored. It is easy to see why. It is difficult enough to endure the rigors of a typical admitting night. The nuances of acid-base balance, chemotherapy, and electrocardiology seem staggering. Who has time for even these critical matters, let alone subjects more encompassing of the entire human condition?

Reluctantly, somewhat uneasily, somewhere during the clinical years the typical student is tempted to turn his back on the larger problems of his patients. He says, implicitly if not explicitly, "I do not hear. It's not that I don't want to hear. It's just that I can't afford to hear. Not right now, anyway, not for the next few years."

Obviously, we have no simple solutions, but we can offer a general principle: Do not expect the impossible of yourself. If students and doctors can learn to accept ambiguity, learn to live with the lack of mastery that is inevitable during any period of knowledge explosion, it may still be possible to embrace a broader view of patient care—one that modern medicine clearly demands.

By all means, draw your boxes. We all must. Specialization is both desirable and necessary at this point in history. However, draw your boxes with less acrimony and paranoia. Be very suspicious of those around you who seem to mock everything outside their own particular box. This attitude signals insecurity more often than it does conviction.

It is *not* necessary to be an expert at every level of the total ecosystem to be a good doctor. It would be presumptuous to try and impossible to succeed. What we do need to begin to appreciate more is the way things fit together as well as the infinite manners in which they fall apart. We have gotten a better education in dissecting sick people than we have in appreciating how healthy people stay harmonious and whole.

In "The Silken Tent," Robert Frost wrote:

She is as in a field a silken tent
At midday when a sunny summer breeze
Has dried the dew and all its ropes relent,
So that in guys it gently sways at ease,
And its supporting central cedar pole,
That is its pinnacle to heavenward
And signifies the sureness of the soul,
Seems to owe naught to any single cord,
But strictly held by none, is loosely bound
By countless silken ties of love and thought

To everything on earth the compass round,
And only by one's going slightly taut
In the capriciousness of summer air
Is of the slightest bondage made aware.

Frost was talking about the interdependency of all humankind. Yet the metaphor also extends to medicine. Instead of quarreling with each other from the safety of our theoretical boxes, we must begin to appreciate that medicine as a human experience involves all of us at all levels of the systems hierarchy, embracing "everything on earth the compass round." Each of us, with our own legitimate expertise, must begin to realize that we are all strands linked by a silken tent, a tent woven from the fabric of our shared humanness.

This is a very simple notion, yet one that is heeded too rarely. To medical students, we would say: As you dig your way through the mountains of facts, beware of those who burrow their own little holes in those mountains and then growl at approaching strangers. We are all miners.

Patient-oriented medicine most definitely is not easy. The real challenge of the biopsychosocial model comes from its demand that doctors view patients both so broadly and in such depth. It demands, above all, a perspective whereby the doctor tries to understand both himself and his patients, and how things fit together, instead of all the artificial and pathological ways they can be induced to fall apart—from self-destructiveness and despair to the ravages of the disease process itself. Good patient care requires this integrating perspective.

The observant student will note that Engel's diagrams in Chapter 2 consider "the biosphere" as the most encompassing unit in the systems hierarchy. We believe there is still another dimension. Whether one calls it spirit, religion, the existential nature of life—questions about the meaning of life—some order seems to prevail in the universe. In saying this, we do not wish to foist our view on anyone. Yet we feel compelled to state our own beliefs candidly. We are troubled by contemporary medicine's lack of appreciation for the human spirit. Where is our awe when we contemplate the mystery and miracle of life itself? For ourselves, this sense of awe has brought us our greatest moments of transcendence, peace, and lucidity in settings that would otherwise depress, frighten, and elicit unremitting despair. Somehow, there have been precious moments that justify all our strivings, when the endless knowledge that we have had to absorb, the unrelenting ambiguity of our work, the impossibility of ever knowing all that we want and need to know have truly been worth it. At special moments a remarkable clarity has emerged; and at these moments we have felt fulfilled and serene.

We appreciate that many will not relate to our own views, and this is fine. Yet even if students do not see the relevance of such a perspective for themselves, they should realize how important spiritual concerns are for many of their patients, and how abysmally neglected they have been in the prevailing ethos of contemporary medicine.

Competence

In concluding the four basic principles of patient-centered medicine, it seems appropriate to end with competence. Ultimately, knowledge and intellect alone are not sufficient to make one a good doctor, but neither are compassion and empathy alone. We are dealing with live patients, real people who place themselves in our hands. What we do or do not do can make the difference between life and death, recovery and degeneration, health and illness. Even if we do not kill a patient through gross incompetence (something that students dread, though it is rarer than they fear), ultimately it is our competence that determines the quality of our patients' lives on countless levels.

Allow us to return once more to Johnnie, our suffering alcoholic prostitute. If Michael had not been able to empathize with her, Johnnie would not have died as a result. However, his insensitivity would have left another small wound, one more tiny cut in a lifetime of slashes and piercing misfortunes. One could, we suppose, sigh and say, "So what?"

Yet we believe that in a subtle but not trivial way Michael would have been incompetent. At the same time, Michael's empathy alone would not have been enough to ensure competence. He also must understand how to work up an acute abdomen. He must know how to formulate a good differential diagnosis. Johnnie could have had alcoholic pancreatitis, as everyone suspected, but she could also have had a stone in her common duct, pancreatic carcinoma, even myocardial disease. The list is long, and Michael must learn it to be competent. He must also know how to manage and treat the disease he ultimately diagnoses. He must, finally, know how to avoid the countless iatrogenic complications that treatment itself causes.

Beyond this, let us assume it was pancreatitis, and Michael's choice of treatment brought the amylase level down. Still, how competent would he and the other doctors have been if they simply send Johnnie back into the streets, back into the social cauldron that fomented her self-destructiveness in the first place? It is worth thinking about, though the vision is frightening and dreadful.

We cannot possibly be all things for all patients. We cannot even be all things for one patient. Yet competence does demand that we do many things. Above all, competence requires one to see the big picture. For Johnnie, this might include an attempt to get her into an alcohol treatment unit. (Yes, we *know* it has been tried before!) We must at the very least consider the destructive social context that contributes so heavily to her disease. Obviously, this is far from easy, but competence demands no less. Doctors who stubbornly pretend that their responsibility is limited to a narrow box drawn around Johnnie's pancreas are woefully and willfully wrong. They are incompetent. Finally, when a doctor reaches a patient, as Michael did Johnnie, he does something special. Perhaps it is just a touch or a look of understanding. One less tiny cut in the patient's life. A small wound that heals instead of festering. That is competence.

The real meaning of competence was brought home to us recently and all too personally.

Dr. Philip Johnsen* is a San Francisco psychiatrist who has co-taught with one of the authors (Dr. Reiser) and is also a very dear friend. Commencing in the summer of 1981, Phil had complained for several weeks of general malaise with no specific localizing symptoms. He attributed this to "depression" (a typical box that psychiatrists draw, ignoring how often depression is an early sign of somatic disease). On Thursday night, he called the author and said, "I think I have melena—my stools are dark." What ensued was the spectacle of two doctors trying to rationalize serious illness away, a spectacle as common as it is dumb. We speculated about whether he was ingesting larger amounts of iron in a

* This is a pseudonym. The doctor is real.

new vitamin. Together we hemmed and hawed. Finally, because he had no symptoms of shock or overt bleeding, and because it had been only one stool, we decided on a wait-and-see attitude.

The next day, however, Phil did not go to work. That morning, he began to bleed from his rectum, steadily and briskly. Bright red blood. Like most doctors, Phil had no doctor of his own. Neither did I, but I gave him the name of one who had once treated my wife. Phil, however, was worried that the man I suggested might be "too young." He called another colleague and got the name of an older internist who immediately told him to go to the emergency room. At this point, Phil did not take a cab or an ambulance, nor did he ask one of his many friends for a lift. Instead, he struggled down four flights of stairs in his Victorian flat, drove himself across town to the hospital, and circled the block several times until he found a choice parking space. He then walked—unaided and alone—to the emergency room.

There he met his internist and proceeded to have another bloody stool. He was admitted to the medical floor. A number of things happened in rapid succession. First, he was typed and cross-matched for blood. When his hemoglobin fell from 16 to 12, his physicians began to transfuse him. Second, a small army of experts began arriving on the scene. The internist called a general surgeon, the general surgeon called in a proctologist, and of course I could not stay away either. Finally, Phil's father, a prominent general surgeon in another city, immediately drove to San Francisco. Soon the small army of experts surrounded the bed, haggling among themselves about the diagnosis and treatment indicated. I sided with Phil's father—it was a duodenal ulcer, bleeding briskly from a nicked arteriole. The proctologist insisted it was "definitely lower GI." The surgeon and internist thought it was "too soon to tell." That night, as I sat by Phil's bed, I felt overwhelmingly helpless and frightened.

At some point during my vigil, a nurse came in to hang a new mixture of saline and whole blood. His uniform was dirty. He kept looking at his watch because the shift was ready to end. As he fiddled with the IV lines, he kept saying under his breath, "Shit!" He glanced constantly at the TV set that Phil had turned to a ball game but then abandoned. Every time the nurse said "Shit," Phil grimaced and turned paler. His eyes became riveted to his IV line. Every time it slowed, he fretted. Every time it sped up, he worried. He worried about the pain he was feeling in his vein. He focused on countless little details. He implored his nurse for guidance and advice—why was the blood running too slow? Too fast? Etcetera. Now mind you, this is difficult to explain rationally on the basis of Phil's training and experience. In addition to being a psychiatrist, he had worked in emergency rooms for a number of years and knew how to insert IVs blindfolded. He also knew how to work-up a GI bleed.

Now he was a patient, however, and it was clear, despite his tendency to talk in jargon, that he was scared, helpless, and dependent. When the nurse cursed because the IV line was giving him trouble, Phil felt immediate panic and fear that some impending disaster was about to occur. Rational? Perhaps not. But my doctor friend was a patient now.

And he was being treated incompetently.

The following day, he was too sick to see visitors. Phil and I did, however, speak at length on the phone. Over and over, he emphasized his confidence in one of his doctors, his surgeon.

"This guy really knows what he's doing." Phil kept repeating. "He's really *competent*. You can tell."

He went on to cite the data for this surmise, ranging from what he heard through the grapevine to the fact that his doctor's hair was liberally sprinkled with gray. He came across to Phil as calm and confident. Phil was especially impressed with his knowledge of the latest procedures. In addition to the usual upper and lower GI series, Phil told me they would do a technetium scan to rule out a Meckel's diverticulum. If that did not work, they would try a new more sophisticated technetium scan in which they would label red blood cells and see where they collected, thus localizing the probable site of bleeding. Phil was impressed, as was I, with this surgeon's command of the latest facts and technological procedures pertinent to the diagnosis and management of Phil's frightening condition.

"This guy is really good!" Phil repeated again.

After the call, I found myself thinking. Here was my friend and my co-teacher in a course on patient-centered medicine, a course that emphasized empathy, compassion, and understanding of the whole human being. Yet, over and over, Phil kept emphasizing the reassurance he felt from his surgeon's *competence*. By this he clearly meant his surgeon's knowledge and technical expertise, not his "bedside manner."

To say I had a crisis of faith that night would be putting it too strongly, but I could not fail to heed Phil's own emphasis on technical competence. This was clearly much higher on his own list of priorities than warmth and "bedside manner." My thoughts drifted back to a senior psychoanalyst whom I had known during my residency training. He had once talked to me, years before, about his own open heart surgery. This very empathic, gentle man had said, with much feeling, "I don't give a *damn* if the surgeon has any empathy in the way he relates to me or not. I want someone who's good! In fact, *I don't* want somebody who's too compassionate and involved with me. It might mar his judgment at a critical point in the operation."

So here were two doctors, both big on empathy, both now insisting that *when it came to them* technical expertise was what really counted. They sounded no different from the numerous house officers I have dealt with over the years who have said to me, "Sure, it's good to be nice to your patients, but knowing what to do is what gets them better!" The haunting question of my medical student—"So what?"—echoed that night in my mind.

Were my own priorities all askew? Was all the stuff I *talked* about and believed in just the "soft" side of a hard-edged, technological field after all?

On Sunday I spoke to Phil again. This morning he was in a panic. He had continued to bleed. His doctors had continued to tranfuse him and elected a conservative course. Meanwhile, the etiology of his bleeding remained a mystery. The usual common conditions that could be diagnosed on endoscopy and barium studies were all negative. There was no consensus about whether his bleed was in the upper or lower GI tract, much less about its precise cause. However, this Sunday morning Phil was in a panic about something else. His proctologist had entered the room, flipped quickly through the chart, and said, "Yep. This is definitely a lower GI bleed all right."

"What does that mean?" Phil had asked. "I mean, for me?"

"We'll do an angiogram. STAT!" the proctologist said. "It's time to stop pissing around. We'll localize it and then we'll cut."

"Will the angiogram hurt?" Phil asked. "What are its side effects? What about allergies?"

But the proctologist was already at the door.

Technically, the proctologist was thinking clearly enough. I, too, was worried about the general hesitancy, but his behavior had reduced my friend to a state of abject panic.

For the first time, Phil now requested Valium.

Three hours later he called me back, much calmer, more reassured. He was still bleeding. Objectively, nothing had changed; 2.5 mg of Valium could not explain this change. I learned that his trusted surgeon had meanwhile come in and talked with him.

"Boy, that guy knows what he's doing!" Phil said again.

This time, as I listened to Phil, I realized he was describing competence of a very different sort. The surgeon had sat with him for a long time. He had empathized with his apprehension. He had reassured him, not by contradicting the proctologist but by underscoring his own quiet confidence in himself and his own sense of when to act.

"Not yet," the surgeon had said

Again, technically, he may have been right; he may have been wrong. It was not the deferring of an immediate angiogram that reassured Phil, it was this surgeon's capacity to accept Phil, to empathize, and to pay attention to all of Phil's concerns. And Phil immediately felt better.

It began to dawn on me that this surgeon was indeed special and truly very competent! His competence came from his ability to see my friend on many different levels. On the cellular level, this surgeon understood what red cell tagging was and had informed views regarding the latest indications for angiography. Had he not understood this, he would have been incompetent, and Phil would have known this instantly. Yet he also understood Phil's apprehension and dread. He knew when to listen, when to reach out and reassure. By contrast, the proctologist, technically adequate as he was, proved to be incompetent when my friend got scared. It was nakedly apparent to me at that moment that technical competence alone was not enough; nor was ill-informed compassion in the absence of technical expertise. Both were essential—a vital balance.

Note finally that the surgeon—our hero in this drama—did not know everything. He was not an expert on all levels of the biopsychosocial system. That is one reason why he consulted other specialists, as had Phil's internist—but the surgeon *grasped* the system. He also accepted and related to his patient, no small achievement! Somehow, he understood "the silken tent."

More than 3 years now have passed since Phil was hospitalized, and there has been no recurrence of his bleeding. He was discharged without a definite diagnosis and is now back at work. The suspected diagnosis is a rare one—an AV malformation in the small bowel. There is a plan for how to proceed if bleeding should recur. Technically, the plan is elegant and wise, but Phil's bleeding may never be diagnosed. Indeed, it may never recur.

Summary

In this initial chapter we have outlined four guiding principles of medicine as a human experience: acceptance, empathy, conceptualization, and competence. Acceptance and empathy are essential to developing a healing partnership with one's patients. Both stem from self-awareness, for it is difficult to accept another human being if you have not first accepted yourself. Conceptualization, utilizing the biopsychosocial model and even expanding it to include issues of existential meaning and the human spirit, is directly related to comprehensive medical care; it also relates integrally to our fourth principle, competence. It is our belief that if students develop and adhere to these precepts during medical school, they will not only become better physicians for it, they also will be more inwardly fulfilled in their choice of a career. These principles emphasize that we are all part of the human family. Osler implied as much more than 75 years ago when he stated that M.D. degree entitled physicians to a life-long education in two spheres—the inner and the special. He spoke of the necessity of aspiring to both: (1) inner education, a knowledge of one's self; and (2) special education, a knowledge of medicine. Osler also understood the importance of the human spirit, for he admonished physicians always to "mix the waters of science with the oil of faith." Shifting metaphors somewhat, we add: Into the bedrock of your hard-won technical knowledge let the tendrils of hope and compassion at long last take root; let the seeds of your humanity and love finally germinate and grow.

Suggested Reading

Cassell, E. J. 1982. The nature of suffering and the goals of medicine. New Engl. J. Med. 306:639–645.

Cassem, N. H., and Hackett, T. P. (eds.) 1978. The setting of intensive care. In: Massachusetts General Hospital Handbook of General Hospital Psychiatry. Mosby, St. Louis.

Cassem, N. H., and Hackett, T. P. 1971. Psychiatric consultation in a coronary care unit. Ann. Intern. Med. 75:9–14.

Cope, O. 1968. Man, Mind and Medicine. Lippincott, Philadelphia.

Cousins, N. 1979. Anatomy of an Illness as Perceived by the Patient: Reflections on Healing and Regeneration. Norton, New York.

Frankl, V. E. 1973. The Doctor and the Soul. Vintage Books, New York.

Lipp, M. R. 1977. Respectful Treatment: The Human Side of Medical Care. Harper & Row, Hagerstown, Maryland.

Osler, Sir W. 1906. Aequanimitas. Lewis, London.

Reiser, D. E. 1973. Struggling to stay human: One student's reflections on becoming a doctor. New Physician 22:295–299.

Rosen, D. H. 1973. Physician, heal thyself. Clin. Med. 80:25–27.

George L. Engel

Clinical Application of the Biopsychosocial Model

2

How physicians approach patients is very much influenced by the scientific model on which their knowledge and experience are organized. Commonly, however, physicians are largely unaware of the power that this model exerts on their thinking and behavior. This is because the model is not necessarily made explicit. Rather, it becomes that part of the fabric of education that is taken for granted, the cultural background against which they learn to become physicians. Their teachers, their mentors, the texts they use, the practices they are encouraged to follow, and even the medical institutions and administrative organizations in which they work reflect the prevailing conceptual model of the era.

For many years the dominant scientific model in medicine has been what is now called the biomedical model. Its origins have been traced back to the successes of Newton's mechanistic physics in the 17th century and to the decision of established Christian orthodoxy to lift the prohibition against dissection of the human body so long as physicians agreed to limit their attention to the body and leave man's soul, morals, mind, and behavior to the Church. This compact helped determine that the scientific model of Western medicine be based on reductionism and mind-body dualism. Reductionism assumes that the understanding of a complex entity can be best achieved by identifying and analyzing its component parts, from which the whole can be reconstructed. It fosters a view that nature is composed of discrete entities interacting in a linear, causal fashion and encourages the tendency to invoke simple cause-and-effect relationships. Its influence is evident in the habit of speaking of diseases not as dynamic processes but as discrete entities. Dualism predicates separation of mind from body, of the psychological from the somatic, and provides no conceptual framework, other than reductionism, whereby the two can be related.

Limits of the Biomedical Model

As a scientific framework within which to elaborate the disordered bodily mechanisms involved in disease, the biomedical model has been extraordinarily fruitful. However, its underlying reductionism and dualism have served to deflect scientific attention from the more personal, human, psychological, and social aspects of health and disease. These, biomedicine considers neither accessible to rigorous scientific evaluation nor essential for the formal education of the physician. Rather, they remain part of the "art" of medicine and of the Samaritan role of the physician, skills to be emulated but not ones possible to study or teach.

The inability of the biomedical model to include the patient and his attributes as a person, as a human being, is a crippling flaw, for in the daily work of the physician the prime object of study is a person. Much of the data the physician utilizes are gathered within the framework of an ongoing human relationship and appear in behavioral and psychological forms, i.e., how the patient behaves and what he reports about himself and his life. This fact is not acknowledged by the biomedical model which is disease- rather than patient-oriented. It encourages a view of the patient as a machine to be repaired and the physician as the repairman. Such a perspective, as frequently caricatured in cartoons, is one source of dissatisfaction of patients.

To counter such tendencies, a model is required that permits scientific attention to the psychosocial dimensions of medicine. By "psychosocial" we refer to the whole range of psychological and social issues that are germane to health and illness and that are involved in the physician's everyday understanding and care of the patient as an individual and as a social being. They include all that heretofore has been referred to crudely as the "art" of medicine, the "bedside manner," the Samaritan and healer role of the physician, and the doctor-patient relationship. They encompass the gamut of social, cultural, and psychological processes that make for the individuality of each patient and influence susceptibility to disease and requirements for individual care. For the physician, "psychosocial" refers to a body of knowledge and a set of skills that are basic for clinical competence.

An instructive way of getting a glimpse of what is encompassed by the term "psychosocial" is to consider the complaints and expectations of the public about doctors and medical care, for it is patients and families who are the most painfully aware of what their physicians lack. Patients are the ones who tell us that doctors do not communicate well, that they do not listen, that they seem ignorant of or insensitive to personal needs and individual differences, that they often neglect the person in their zeal to pursue diagnostic and treatment procedures. They stress their physician's inaccessibility—often more indicative of the psychological remoteness of the doctor than any economic barriers or problems of geographical distance.

Attention to the criteria that patients use for illness and wellness also helps to clarify what comprises the psychosocial. Patients' criteria have to do with how one feels and how one functions: with the ability to relate, to work, to play, to love, to struggle, to have opinions, and to make choices. For the patient, "healthy" means to be able to get on with the tasks and gratifications and to meet the challenges of life without pain, discomfort, or disability. Patients look to their physicians to know and understand them as individuals, to appreciate the significance for their health and well-being, of the conditions of their lives and living. Furthermore, they expect their physicians to have the scientific knowledge and professional competence to do so. "Psychosocial" as a frame of reference includes far more than what is ordinarily designated as "psychiatric."

The biomedical model has ill-served these requirements for physicians to meet the psychosocial needs of patients. Long overdue is a scientific model capable of encompassing these missing dimensions. The development of a general systems theory at long last provides the basis for such a new model. First applied by Weiss and von Bertalanffy to cope with the same problems in biology, the systems approach is equally appropriate for medicine. The new model is called the *biopsychosocial model.* Medicine based on the new model might be called "systems medicine."

Biopsychosocial Model

The advantage of the systems approach is that it provides a conceptual framework within which both organized wholes and component parts can be studied. Systems theory is best approached through the common-sense observation that nature is ordered as a hierarchically arranged continuum, with its more complex, larger units superordinate to the less complex, smaller units. This may be represented schematically by a vertical stacking to emphasize the hierarchy (Figure 1) and by a nest of squares to emphasize the continuum (Figure 2). Each level in the hierarchy represents an organized dynamic whole, a system of sufficient persistence and identity to justify being named. Cell, organ, person, family—each indicates a level of complex, integrated organization about

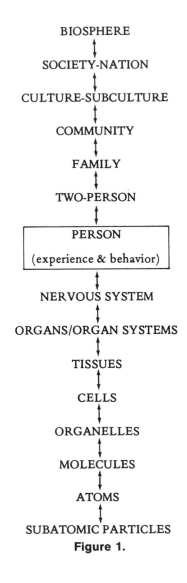

SYSTEMS HIERARCHY
(LEVELS OF ORGANIZATION)

BIOSPHERE
↕
SOCIETY-NATION
↕
CULTURE-SUBCULTURE
↕
COMMUNITY
↕
FAMILY
↕
TWO-PERSON
↕

PERSON
(experience & behavior)

↕
NERVOUS SYSTEM
↕
ORGANS/ORGAN SYSTEMS
↕
TISSUES
↕
CELLS
↕
ORGANELLES
↕
MOLECULES
↕
ATOMS
↕
SUBATOMIC PARTICLES

Figure 1.

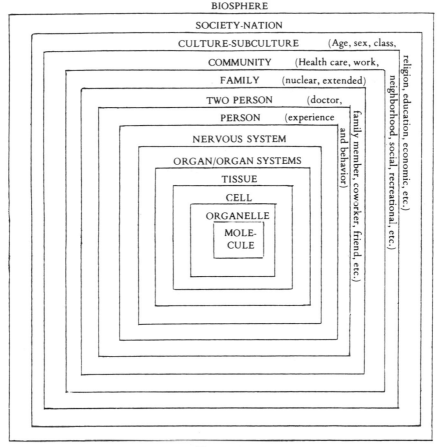

Figure 2.

the existence of which a high degree of consensus holds. Each system implies qualities and relationships distinctive for that level of organization, and each requires criteria for study and explanation unique for that level.

Consideration of the hierarchy as a continuum reveals another obvious fact. Each system is at the same time a component of higher systems (Figure 2). System *cell* is a component of systems *tissue* and *organ* and *person*. *Person* and *two-person* are components of *family* and *community*. *In the continuity of natural systems, every unit is at the same time both a whole and a part.* Person (or individual) represents at the same time the highest level of an organismic hierarchy and the lowest level of a social hierarchy. As a whole, each system has its unique characteristics and dynamics; as a part, it is a component of a higher level system. The designation "system" refers to the existence of a stable configuration in time and space, a configuration that is maintained not only by the coordination of component parts in some kind of internal dynamic network but also by the characteristics of the larger system of which it is a part and which in turn constitutes its immediate environment. "Stable configuration" also implies the existence of boundaries between organized systems across which material and information flow. Each system is interconnected with every other system by information flow through feedback arrangements. Hence disturbances at any system level may be communicated to and affect any other system level, especially those in the closest functional relationship.

Such a systems-oriented model overcomes the limitations of dualism and reductionism and replaces the simple cause-and-effect explanations of linear causality with reciprocal causal models. Health, disease, illness, and disability can be conceptualized in terms of the relative intactness and functioning of each component system on each hierarchical level. Overall health reflects a high level of intra- and intersystemic harmony. Disruption of such harmony may be initiated at any level, be it cell, organ, person, or community. Whether the resulting disturbance is contained at the level at which it was initiated, or other levels become implicated, reflects the capacity of the initially affected system to adjust to the change, i.e., to cope. Thus a modification in an individual's social environment (an imposed job change, for example) impacts first on psychological functions, e.g., perceptions and appraisal. If the change is successfully accommodated at the psychological level, there will be no perceptible reverberations in other systems. For example, the individual may have no difficulty successfully handling the situation by thinking it through and resolving on a course of action—"no sweat," so to speak. Similarly, a molecular substance introduced into the body might be broken down, excreted, neutralized, or inactivated without implicating any but the particular molecular, cellular, tissue, or organ system required for its disposal. In both examples, the systems initially involved have the capacity to handle the imposed change without disruption. Under different circumstances, or in another individual with a different past history, the very same social change or the very same molecular substance may induce profound disruptions that involve many systems in the hierarchy. Such contrasts between smooth functioning and disruption provide the basis on which health, disease, illness, and disability may be differentiated.

Central to this perspective are not only the dynamic interrelations that determine relative degrees of intra- and intersystemic harmony or disruption but also the fact that every change becomes part of the history of each system, rendering it different at each successive point in time. In the biopsychosocial model, there can be no return to the *status quo ante*. Health restored is not the same as the former state of health; it is a different intersystemic harmony than that which existed before the illness episode. Moreover, an illness not only changes the patient as an individual, it may also impact others, in the family as well as the community.

Biopsychosocial Model Applied

Let us now examine with a clinical example the application of the biopsychosocial model in everyday practice. As we said at the outset, how the physician approaches the patient is very much influenced by the scientific model he uses to organize knowledge and experience. The biopsychosocial model orients the approach in terms of the hierarchy and continuum of the natural systems that the physician must keep in mind as he undertakes the study and care of a patient.

To exemplify the systems approach, let us consider the case of Mr. Glover (a pseudonym), a 55-year-old married real estate salesman with two adult sons who was brought to the emergency department on March 1 with symptoms similar to those he had experienced 6 months earlier when he had had a myocardial infarction.

We begin consideration of the model by reminding ourselves that clinical study begins at the person level—the patient—and much of it takes place within a two-person system—the doctor-patient relationship. The data consist of reported inner experience (e.g., feelings, sensations, thoughts, opinions, memories) and reported, observable behavior. From the outset, even such minimal screening data as Mr. Glover's age, gender, marital and family status, occupation, and employment already indicate system characteristics useful for future judgments and decisions. Adding to this, the information that the patient had resisted acknowledging illness (noteworthy in the face of a documented heart attack 6 months earlier) and that he had to be persuaded to seek medical attention quickly directs attention to this man's psychological style and conflicts. This alerts a systems-oriented physician to the possibility, if not the probability, that the course of the illness and the care of this patient may be importantly influenced by the processes at the psychological and interpersonal levels of organization. At the same time, the similarity of Mr. Glover's current symptoms to those of his earlier myocardial infarction directs attention to systems derangements at the cardiovascular level, not to mention the symbolic level of "another heart attack."

Such an inclusive approach, which considers all the levels of organization that might possibly be important for immediate and long-term care, may be contrasted with the parsimonious approach of the biomedical model. In the latter model, the ideal is to find as quickly as possible the simplest explanation, preferably a single diagnosis, and to regard all else as complications or as "overlay," or as just plain irrelevant to the doctor's task. For the reductionist physician, a diagnosis of "acute myocardial infarction" would suffice to characterize Mr. Glover's problem and to define the doctor's job. Thereafter, Mr. Glover would likely be referred to as "an MI," and that would be that.

By contrast, let us now reconstruct *in systems terms* the sequence of events comprising the first 90 minutes of Mr. Glover's latest episode of illness. The critical events and their consequences for intra- and intersystemic harmony are schematized in a series of diagrams (Figures 3 through 8) Each diagram indicates the systems level on which the event in question impacted, along with its reverberations up and down the systems hierarchy. Appreciating the unity of the hierarchy—that each system is at the same time also a component of higher systems—highlights the significance of the disruption of any one system for the intactness of all other systems, especially those most proximate. These interrelationships are indicated in Figures 3 through 8 by using double arrows to connect the system levels.

Figure 3 depicts the critical event of progressive impairment of coronary artery blood flow interrupting the oxygen supply and disrupting the organization of a segment of myocardium. Note that although changes are taking place at the levels of molecule, cell, tissue, organ, organ system, and nervous system, illness and patienthood do not become issues until the *person* level is implicated, i.e., not until the person experiences something that he interprets as possibly indicating illness.

For Mr. Glover, such changes began around 10:00 in the morning. While alone at his desk he began to experience general unease and discomfort and, then, during the next few minutes, growing "pressure" over his midanterior chest and an aching sensation down the left arm to the elbow. The similarity of these symptoms to those of his previous heart attack quickly came to his mind. Thus began the threat of disruption at the *person* level and with it another wave of reverberations up and down the systems hierarchy.

The role played by the central nervous system now became critical, first in the integration and regulation of his inner experiences and his behavioral responses and second in the physiological adjustments that were occurring in response to the processes in the oxygen-deprived myocardium. For Mr. Glover these nervous-system-mediated processes were not in harmony. Whereas the infarcting of the myocardium called for reducing the demand for myocardial work and minimizing such arrhythmogenic factors as excessive catecholamine secretion, his psychological response was to oscillate between alarm and increased sympathetic nervous system activity on the one hand and denial and inappropriate physical activity on the other (Figure 3). Almost from the start, the possibility of a second heart attack came to mind, but he dismissed this in favor of "fatigue," "gas," "muscle strain," and finally "emotional tension." However, the negation itself, "*not* another heart attack," leaves no doubt that the idea of a "heart attack" was very much in his mind. Behaviorally he alternated between sitting quietly to "let it pass," pacing about the office to "work it off," and taking Alka-Seltzer.

When he could no longer deny the probability, if not the certainty, of another heart attack, a different set of concerns emerged. His new formula became, "If this really is a heart attack (but maybe it will still prove not to be), I must first get my affairs in order so that no one will be left in the lurch." In this way, he tried to sustain his self-image of competence and master and counter his fear of being helpless. But this was at

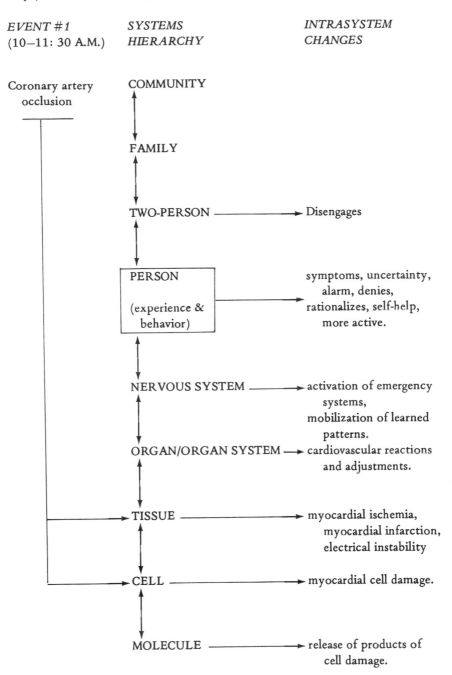

EVENT #1
(10–11: 30 A.M.)

*SYSTEMS
HIERARCHY*

*INTRASYSTEM
CHANGES*

Coronary artery
occlusion

COMMUNITY

FAMILY

TWO-PERSON ——————→ Disengages

PERSON

(experience &
behavior)

symptoms, uncertainty,
alarm, denies,
rationalizes, self-help,
more active.

NERVOUS SYSTEM ——————→ activation of emergency
systems,
mobilization of learned
patterns.

ORGAN/ORGAN SYSTEM —→ cardiovascular reactions
and adjustments.

TISSUE ——————→ myocardial ischemia,
myocardial infarction,
electrical instability

CELL ——————→ myocardial cell damage.

MOLECULE ——————→ release of products of
cell damage.

Figure 3.

the cost of imposing an even greater burden on his already overburdened heart and cardiovascular system. In systems terms, feedback was becoming increasingly positive, and a dangerous cycle was in the making. Disruptive processes at many system levels were gaining ascendancy over regulatory processes. The patient persisted in this determined, almost frenetic behavior for more than an hour, until the intervention of his employer brought it to an end and enabled him to accept hospitalization and patient status.

Figure 4 diagrams the psychological stabilization that took place as a result and how this led to stabilization of other systems. The intervention by the employer involved the *two-person* system, immediately affecting *person*. This terminated the vicious cycle, thereby lessening the impact on the damaged heart of potentially deleterious extracardiac influences.

How had the employer brought about such a felicitous result? We later learned from Mr. Glover that the employer's approach was to commend his diligence and sense of responsibility, even in the face of being so obviously ill, and to reassure him that he had left his work in suitable condition for others to take over. But she also challenged him to consider whether a higher responsibility to his family and his job did not require him to take care of himself and go to the hospital. Intuitively she had appreciated this man's need to see himself as responsible and in control, and she had sensed his deep fear of being weak and helpless. As a result, by the time Mr. Glover was admitted to the emergency department shortly before noon, he was no longer having any discomfort. The staff promptly instituted a coronary care routine. This was reassuring to the patient who had by now accepted the reality of a second heart attack. Thirty minutes later, in the midst of the continuing work-up, he abruptly lost consciousness. The monitor documented ventricular fibrillation. Defibrillation was successfully carried out, and the patient made an uneventful recovery.

Interviewed a few days later, Mr. Glover was able to reconstruct the events in the emergency department leading up to the cardiac arrest. His account raised doubts that the onset of ventricular fibrillation could be ascribed solely to processes originating in the injured myocardium, as the staff assumed. Rather it suggested a major role for extracardiac (neurogenic) influences originating in disturbances at the *two-person* and *person* levels. According to Mr. Glover, everything had been proceeding smoothly until the house officers ran into difficulty doing an arterial puncture. They persisted in their fruitless efforts for some 10 minutes and then left, explaining only that they were going for help. For Mr. Glover, the procedure was not only painful and disagreeable but, more importantly, he felt his confidence in the competence of the medical staff being undermined and with that his sense of personal mastery and control over his situation. Rather than being helped by powerful but concerned and competent professionals, he began to feel himself victim-

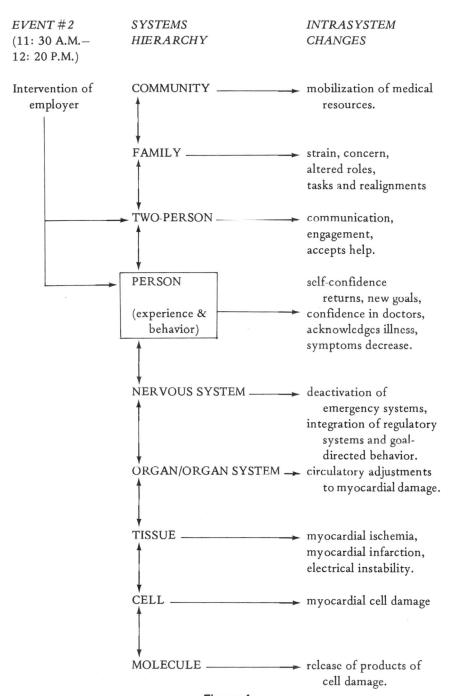

EVENT #2
(11: 30 A.M.—
12: 20 P.M.)

*SYSTEMS
HIERARCHY*

*INTRASYSTEM
CHANGES*

Intervention of
    employer

COMMUNITY ⟶ mobilization of medical
                            resources.

FAMILY ⟶ strain, concern,
                    altered roles,
                    tasks and realignments

TWO-PERSON ⟶ communication,
                        engagement,
                        accepts help.

PERSON

(experience &
behavior)

⟶ self-confidence
        returns, new goals,
        confidence in doctors,
        acknowledges illness,
        symptoms decrease.

NERVOUS SYSTEM ⟶ deactivation of
                                emergency systems,
                                integration of regulatory
                                systems and goal-
                                directed behavior.

ORGAN/ORGAN SYSTEM ⟶ circulatory adjustments
                                        to myocardial damage.

TISSUE ⟶ myocardial ischemia,
                myocardial infarction,
                electrical instability.

CELL ⟶ myocardial cell damage

MOLECULE ⟶ release of products of
                    cell damage.

Figure 4.

ized by beginners who themselves needed help. Yet he could not bring himself to protest. His tape recorded comment was:

> I didn't wanna tell 'em that I didn't think, ah, that I knew, he wasn't doing it right . . . they tried here and they tried there . . . the poor fellow was having such a tough time, he just couldn't get it.

Within a short time, the patient found himself getting hot and flushed. Chest pain recurred and quickly became as severe as it had been earlier that morning. When the staff left to get help, he first felt relieved. However, anticipating more of the same, he began to feel outrage and then to blame himself for having permitted himself to be trapped in such a predicament. A growing sense of impotence to do anything about his situation culminated in his passing out as ventricular fibrillation supervened.

The Two Models Compared

Figure 5 diagrams the unsuccessful attempt at arterial puncture. It provides an opportunity to draw a contrast between how the model that organizes a physician's thinking also influences the physician's approach. In the case of Mr. Glover, the judgment to institute an acute coronary regimen without delay is beyond dispute. Where differences emerge are in the priorities set and the behavior displayed by adherents of each model as they go about their study and care of the patient. The emergency room approach was conventionally and narrowly biomedical. It was predicated on the reductionist premise that the cause of Mr. Glover's problem, and therefore the requirements for this care, could be localized to the myocardial injury. Because of that assumption, plus the high risk attendant on such injury, they felt justified proceeding with the technical diagnostic and treatment procedures and gave only passing attention to how Mr. Glover was feeling and reacting. When the arrest occurred, the staff congratulated each other and the patient on his good fortune, pointing out that had his arrival in the hospital been delayed another 30 minutes, he might well not have survived. They assumed that the onset of ventricular fibrillation at 12:30 p.m. could be ascribed solely to the natural progression of the myocardial injury.

A systems approach to Mr. Glover would have differed in notable respects. From the outset, the decision for the implementation of coronary care would have included consideration of factors other than cardiac status, notably those manifest at the *person* level. The initial interview of Mr. Glover would have been conducted so as to elicit simultaneously information needed to characterize him as a person as well as to evaluate the status of his cardiovascular system. Particularly in the case of a possible myocardial infarction, the systems-oriented physi-

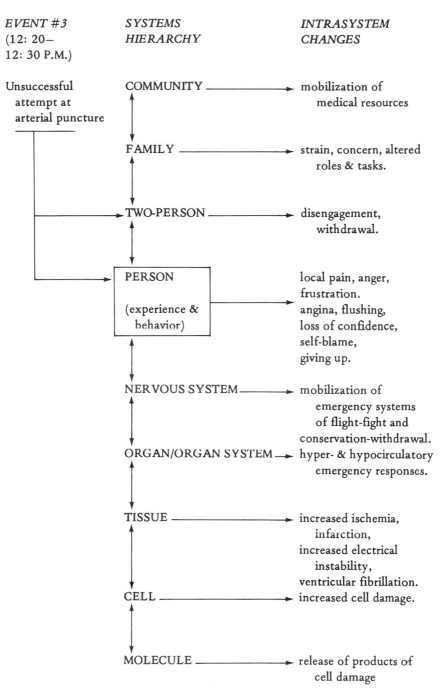

Figure 5.

cian would be alert to information about *person*-level factors that might alter the stability of the cardiovascular system. For example, to learn how the employer had helped him accept the reality of his heart attack and the need for prompt medical attention would be considered helpful in guiding the physician's approach to the patient. Moreover, as the coronary care regimen was being implemented, the physician would also be closely monitoring the patient's reactions to the procedures. In Mr. Glover's case, this would be especially important in light of his documented reluctance to acknowledge a need for help. The difficulty with the arterial puncture would have been recognized early as a risk for the patient, not just a problem for the doctors. Mr. Glover's failure to complain would have been anticipated as consistent with his personality style and not interpreted as acquiescence to what was happening to him. Whether such an approach would in fact have averted the cardiac arrest is impossible to know. Certainly, sufficient experimental and clinical evidence exists linking the stress of a psychological impasse, as displayed by Mr. Glover, with increased risk of lethal arrhythmias, especially with preexisting myocardial electrical instability.

Cardiac arrest and successful defibrillation are illustrated in Figures 6 and 7, while what would have happened had resuscitation failed is diagramed in Figure 8. This sequence of diagrams demonstrates how higher system levels, e.g., family or community, may be affected by what is transpiring with the patient and how in turn they may then feed back to impinge on the patient with consequences for the stability of lower level systems. Indeed, sometimes the feedback from events involving the patient may contribute to morbidity, i.e., lower system destabilization, in close family members. I recently was involved in a dramatic example of such a situation.

> A 59-year-old man was hospitalized on March 18 with a massive myocardial infarction. Nineteen days later his very upset wife suffered a myocardial infarction while visiting her husband. For several days she had been having chest pains which she kept to herself lest she upset her husband. The latter had been recuperating and was to be discharged April 6, but early that morning he was found dead. His wife, who had anticipated his visit at 9:00 a.m. before he went home, died suddenly when she learned why he was not coming. Her final words were, "Oh, no, no, Doctor, why did it happen?" and then, "Oh, no, I'm going, too." She died of a ruptured ventricle.

Some argue that the biopsychosocial model imposes an impossible demand on the physician. That misses the point. The model does not add anything to what is not already involved in patient care. Rather, it provides a conceptual framework and encourages a way of thinking that enables the physician to act rationally in areas until now excluded from a rational approach. Furthermore, it motivates the physician to become more informed and skillful in the psychosocial areas, disciplines now

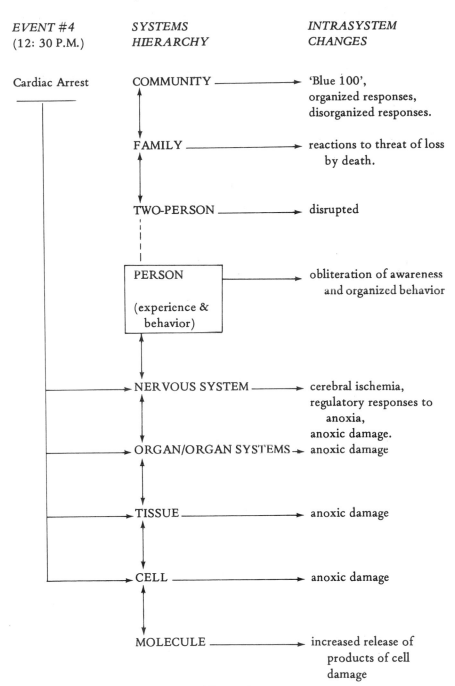

Figure 6.

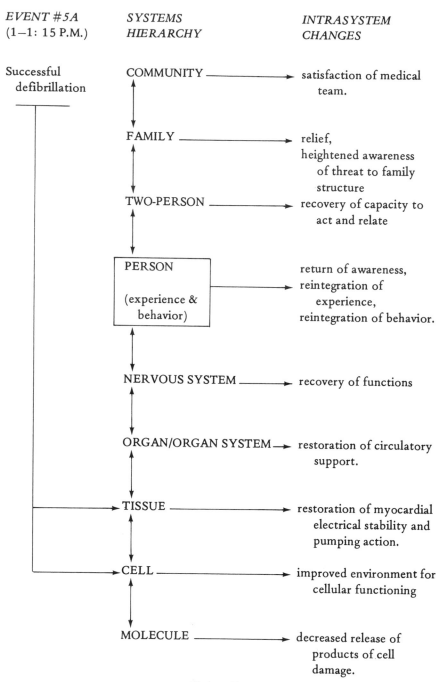

EVENT #5A
(1–1: 15 P.M.)

*SYSTEMS
HIERARCHY*

*INTRASYSTEM
CHANGES*

Successful
    defibrillation

COMMUNITY —————————————→ satisfaction of medical
                                                        team.

FAMILY —————————————→ relief,
                                          heightened awareness
                                              of threat to family
                                              structure

TWO-PERSON —————————→ recovery of capacity to
                                              act and relate

PERSON

(experience &
    behavior)
                                              return of awareness,
                                          reintegration of
                                              experience,
                                          reintegration of behavior.

NERVOUS SYSTEM ——————→ recovery of functions

ORGAN/ORGAN SYSTEM —→ restoration of circulatory
                                              support.

TISSUE —————————————→ restoration of myocardial
                                          electrical stability and
                                          pumping action.

CELL —————————————→ improved environment for
                                          cellular functioning

MOLECULE —————————→ decreased release of
                                          products of cell
                                          damage.

Figure 7.

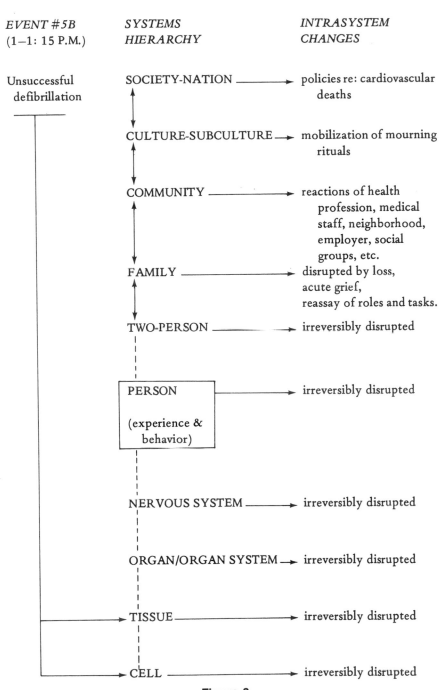

EVENT #5B
(1–1: 15 P.M.)

SYSTEMS
HIERARCHY

INTRASYSTEM
CHANGES

Unsuccessful
defibrillation

SOCIETY-NATION ⟶ policies re: cardiovascular deaths

CULTURE-SUBCULTURE ⟶ mobilization of mourning rituals

COMMUNITY ⟶ reactions of health profession, medical staff, neighborhood, employer, social groups, etc.

FAMILY ⟶ disrupted by loss, acute grief, reassay of roles and tasks.

TWO-PERSON ⟶ irreversibly disrupted

PERSON

(experience & behavior)

⟶ irreversibly disrupted

NERVOUS SYSTEM ⟶ irreversibly disrupted

ORGAN/ORGAN SYSTEM ⟶ irreversibly disrupted

TISSUE ⟶ irreversibly disrupted

CELL ⟶ irreversibly disrupted

Figure 8.

seen as alien and remote even by those who intuitively recognize their importance. The biopsychosocial physician is expected to have a working knowledge of the principles, language, and basic facts of each relevant discipline; he is not expected to be an expert at all.

The example of Mr. Glover, despite its oversimplification, indicates how the working conceptual model the physician uses can influence the approach to patient care. The biopsychosocial model is a scientific model. The biomedical model evolved as a scientific model, but by now it has become transformed into a folk model, actually the dominant folk model of the Western world. As such, it has come to constitute dogma. The hallmark of a scientific model is that it provides a framework within which the scientific method may be applied. The value of a scientific model is measured not by whether it is right or wrong but by how useful it is. It is modified or discarded when it no longer helps to generate and test new knowledge. Dogmas, in contrast, maintain their influence through authority and tradition. They resist change and hence tend to promote opposition and the promulgation of rival dogmas by dissident figures. The counter-dogmas being put forth these days in opposition to biomedical dogma are sometimes called "holistic" and "humanistic" medicine. They qualify as dogmas to the extent that they often eschew the scientific method and lean instead on faith and belief systems handed down from remote and obscure or charismatic authority figures. They tend to place science and humanism in opposition. However, as the history of the biomedical model itself has shown, progress is made only where the scientific method is applied. The triumphs of the biomedical model all have been in the areas for which the model has provided a suitable framework for scientific study. The biopsychosocial model extends that scientific framework to heretofore neglected areas.

Suggested Reading

Engel, G. L. 1971. Sudden and rapid death during psychological stress: Folklore or folkwisdom? Ann. Intern. Med. 74:771–782.

Engel, G. L. 1977. The need for a new medical model: A challenge for biomedicine. Science 196:129–136.

Peabody, F. W. 1927. The care of the patient. JAMA 88:877–882.

Von Bertalanffy, L. 1968. General System Theory. Braziller, New York.

Weiss, P. 1967. 1 + 1 = 2: When one plus one does not equal two. In: G. C. Quarton, T. Melnechuk, and F. O. Schmidt (eds): The Neurosciences: A Study Program, pp. 801–821. Rockefeller Univ. Press, New York.

Weiss, P. 1977. The system of nature and the nature of systems: empirical holism and practical reductionism harmonized. In: K. E. Schaefer, K. E. Hensel, and R. Bordy (eds): Toward a Man-Centered Medicine Science, pp. 17–64. Futura, Mt. Kisco, New York.

George L. Engel

3 Care of the Patient: Art or Science?

For centuries medicine has stubbornly clung to the view that the study of disease is a science while the care of the patient is an art. Because art is believed to be more dependent on personal qualities than on principles that can be examined and communicated, it is widely accepted that the art of medicine cannot be taught: At best it can be demonstrated only by precept and example. This dichotomous view that restricts science to disease while relegating the care of the patient to the "mystic" realm of art is the basis for the frequently voiced complaint that physicians have become too scientific and not sufficiently concerned with patients as human beings. Such complaints have been heard for more than 150 years. From time to time, however, a few have questioned if the reverse is not the case—if medicine's neglect of a scientific approach to its human side does not in fact mean that medicine has not yet become scientific enough.

In this chapter, I put forth the thesis that the care of the patient is as much a matter for science as is the study of disease, and that both involve art and require artistry as well. Behavior, feelings, human transactions, and relationships—and hence patient care—are indeed amenable to examination and study through application of the scientific method. It *is* possible to make precise observations of human behavior and to describe them verbally, to characterize and classify psychosocial data, to establish reliability, to draw inferences, and to develop testable hypotheses. It *is* possible to establish generalizations about patient care that have predictive value and provide reliable guides for how the physician should behave under particular circumstances. Once derived, such principles *can* be communicated, tested, refined, and applied by others.

Let us first specify that patient care encompasses all of the interpersonal and social transactions between the patient and the various health providers; it is not the responsibility of the physician alone, though this discussion is limited to the role of the physician. In practical terms, decisions concerning a patient's care are being made continually by the physician in the course of every transaction with a patient. Implementation of such decisions is accomplished through the doctor's behavior, by what is said or done—as well as by what is not said or done—and how it is or is not said or done. The ultimate goal of a scientific approach to patient care is that the basis for the decisions and the means of their implementation be rendered consciously rational and accessible to reporting. Decisions must not be personally idiosyncratic, mysteriously intuitive, or professionally ritualized—too often the manner in which physicians do make patient care decisions. They must be predicated on reliable data correctly interpreted and on principles amenable to scientific study and validation. Such standards must apply as much to minute-to-minute microdecisions as to more major decisions, e.g., whether to linger a moment longer at the bedside as well as when and how to propose open heart surgery.

In the treatment of disease, the time-honored precept has been: "Assist Nature and do no needless harm." For patient care a corresponding precept might be: "Assist Human Nature and provoke no needless upset." The doctor's task is to identify the patient's psychological strengths and social resources and help him make the best use of them. At the same time, the doctor must also provide the emotional and practical support needed to help compensate for existing weaknesses and deficits. The decisions made and the actions taken by the physician must as much as possible maximize confidence, hope, and equanimity and minimize needless emotional upset or social disruption.

To illustrate how Human Nature may be hindered, not assisted, and the patient unnecessarily upset, let us turn to an actual incident. From this we may consider how outcome may have been different had the doctor involved based his decision and behavior on a scientific understanding of human nature.

A middle-aged woman with a history of intermittent drinking and fatty liver had been abstemious for several years. She had been feeling relatively well until 6 weeks before admission when anorexia, fatigability, weakness, and loss of pep and interest abruptly developed. Her physician concurred with her concern that perhaps her liver trouble had flared up; he admitted her to the hospital for liver studies, including biopsy.

All the laboratory findings proved unremarkable, and her doctor was now coming to report the results of the biopsy. As a visitor I was accompanying my host on his morning rounds. Approaching the bedside together, he gave me a thumbnail sketch of the case, adding: "I am sure she will be glad to know the outcome of the liver biopsy." He greeted her with a cheerful smile and wave of his hand saying, "Good news, Mrs. Jones, the biopsy shows only a *little* fat in the liver, so you can leave the hospital in the morning. I'm sure you'll be glad to get home to your family."

The patient smiled faintly but said nothing as the doctor began efficiently to palpate her abdomen while asking, "And how *are* you today?" After momentary hesitation she responded rather wanly, "Pretty good, I guess," at the same time frowning slightly and raising, then letting fall, her right hand in a gesture of helplessness.

"Good," said the doctor, "I'm glad to hear that," and walked out of the room with a smile.

The patient looked so disconsolate that I lingered behind, commenting, "You don't seem so happy about this." She burst into tears. Encouraged by my interest, she readily reported that the anorexia, fatigability, weakness, and decrease in energy had begun abruptly when she learned that her husband of 25 years was leaving her for another woman. She acknowledged feeling rejected and hurt but denied that she had resumed drinking. She had hoped to be able to share this information with her doctor, but, she claimed, he gave her no opportunity. When I subsequently inquired of him, he expressed surprise at the information and amazement at how readily she had revealed it to me.

Our discussion here is limited to the decisions that bear on patient care which the doctor made during the few minutes at the bedside. As must be clear, they were predicated on both faulty information and poor observation. Indeed, they reflected more the physician's own needs and a ritualized pattern of behavior than they did a response to the patient's situation at the moment. The basic requirements of a scientific approach were ignored, presumably because the physician's education had not allowed him to appreciate that such was possible. We can be confident that his intentions were of the best—to make the patient feel better— and that he would no more knowingly and needlessly upset his patient than he would administer a drug contraindicated in liver disease. He was a clinician whose standards would not permit him to make decisions about the treatment of the liver disease without first establishing the pertinent facts. Yet he made decisions about her life without first investigating her current life situation and emotional status. Furthermore, he persisted in his decision in the face of a clear sign from the patient, the hesitant response and the gesture of helplessness, indicating that he had overlooked something. Such behavior on the part of the physician is equivalent to persisting in the administration of a drug contraindicated in liver disease in the face of jaundice and a palpable liver.

What, you may ask, does this have to do with science? Is this not merely an example of a physician singularly lacking in sensitivity, judgment, and common sense? (He was in fact a distinguished clinical teacher and investigator, greatly admired by his peers and his students.) The question may perhaps be answered best by reviewing how the scientific method was utilized to establish the meaning of the sign that the doctor had overlooked, i.e., the gesture that indicates a feeling of helplessness. By so doing, I hope to document that clinically relevant psychological phenomena are indeed amenable to scientific study.

Scientific Reading of Nonverbal Language

First, let us describe the gesture more fully: It is typically biphasic. When fully developed, both hands are raised fairly briskly to the level of the face, the elbows flexed, the palms facing each other and rotated slightly outward, the fingers spread, and the thumb and fingers slightly flexed as though preparing to grasp. This position is held for a second or less and then the hands fall limply with gravity. Abortive and incomplete gestures may also be seen. Thus the hands may be raised through only part of the arc, or only one hand may be lifted a few inches, rotated outward with fingers spread and then allowed to fall back. Sometimes the upward movement of the hands is accompanied by an upward glance, a slight elevation of the brow and lid, and a slight tilt backward of the head. As hands fall, the face may sag and the body slump as well.

Certainly this gesture must be familiar to all of you, but whether you consciously associate it with a feeling of helplessness, or even understand helplessness as an affect, is another matter. This is because nonverbal expressions of affects, e.g., gestures, postures, facial expressions, and tone of voice, evoke feelings more often than they stimulate a conscious intellectual response. Hence although we may differ in how sensitive we are to the emotional expressions of others, by and large most of us "feel" before we "know" what the other person is experiencing and communicating. Furthermore, we typically respond to and act on such feelings, at least initially, more in terms of our own emotional needs of the moment than in terms of the other person's situation. Thus a nonverbal expression that is threatening (e.g., anger) or demanding (e.g., helplessness or anxiety) may elicit overreaction or even be screened out altogether lest our own equanimity be threatened. As physicians committed to helping others in distress, however, we must go beyond our own feelings to understand what the patient is feeling and trying to communicate. This can be achieved through developing a scientific typology of gestures, postures, and facial expressions and establishing their relationship to the inner experiences being felt and expressed. Armed with such knowledge, a physician can regard such communications more objectively as signs as well as experience them empathically as feelings. How has this been accomplished with respect to the feeling of helplessness?

Schmale, in the course of his studies of psychological giving up, first formulated the concept of helplessness as an affect. Put into words, helplessness means, "I give up, there is nothing further I can do, no way I can cope by myself; only someone else or altered circumstances can help." Developmentally, Schmale relates the feeling of helplessness to that period from birth to 2 to 3 years when the child is totally or largely dependent on adults for even its most elementary needs.

The proof of the association between the gesture and the feeling derives from the following sources:

1. Verbal expression of helplessness and giving up often is accompanied by the gesture.
2. A familiar metaphor to express the inability to do anything further upon encountering a perceived impasse is "to throw up one's hands."
3. Volunteers directed under hypnosis to display through bodily expression the feeling of helplessness characteristically exhibited the gesture. They did not do so in response to the suggestion of 13 other affects.
4. For the small child, to be held in the parent's arms means comfort, security, and protection. When in distress, toddlers characteristically communicate their need for help by looking up and raising the hands, i.e., by signaling a wish to be picked up and held. This corresponds to the first phase of the helplessness gesture. Frame-by-frame analysis of motion pictures documents that the position of the upraised hands is the same as that of the toddler asking to be picked up. Thus to look up and to raise the hands are behaviors learned early in life to signal a need for help.
5. When active efforts to adjust to a changing environment prove to no avail, life may be preserved by withdrawal, inactivity, and disengagement, a biological regulatory process we have termed *conservation-withdrawal*. We suggest that the muscular hypotonia characterizing this process in primates accounts for the falling of arms with gravity that marks the second phase of the helplessness gesture.

Thus the helplessness gesture begins with the bodily communication of a wish to be picked up, only to be superseded by the hypotonia of conservation-withdrawal, as the very reaching for help emphasizes its futility at the moment. In the process, the need for help is communicated. The gesture is embedded in both the developmental biology of the infant-adult relationship and the biological regulatory processes of conservation-withdrawal. As far as we have been able to learn, it is a universal gesture.

Let us now turn to the clinical example that stimulated this discussion. I leave it to you to decide if the elucidation of the meaning of the gesture constitutes proper application of the scientific method. If you agree, then you must also agree that the doctor's failure to recognize and respond appropriately to the gesture was no more consistent with scientific medicine than would have been his failure to detect and respond appropriately to an enlarged liver. In this instance, the helplessness gesture not only indicated the unreliability of the patient's verbal response, "Pretty good, I guess," it also provided the physician with a second opportunity to consider another diagnosis, i.e., that the patient was feeling depressed. In light of this woman's propensity to resort to alcohol under such circumstances, his failure to correctly interpret and respond to his patient's behavior in fact placed her already damaged liver at greater risk. Clearly, to have assisted Human Nature here would also have assisted Nature.

Let us consider another example. The experienced scientific clinician, familiar with basic pathophysiological principles and how such processes are manifested in clinical terms, is often remarkably successful in drawing correct inferences from a relatively limited set of observations. This is because experience has documented for him a high probability that certain clinical phenomena relate to each other and in turn correlate with particular underlying pathophysiological processes. For example, when a clinician sees a patient propped up with pillows and gasping for breath, he immediately thinks of congestive heart failure. This constitutes a hypothesis, the correctness of which can quickly be tested by further history and examination. The ability to draw such high level inferences from relatively limited data and to know how to test them is indispensable for the successful identification and correct treatment of disease. The scientific physician is able at a glance to recognize cardinal manifestations, to derive from them plausible hypotheses, and to devise appropriate means to test such hypotheses. As a scientist, he is meticulous about the reliability and relevance of the methods he uses, diligent in verifying the validity of the data, and attentive to alternative hypotheses before he resolves on a course of action. Such commitment to the scientific method is by no means incompatible with the fact that clinical circumstances sometimes require the physician to make decisions and to act before all the facts are known or all the relevant hypotheses have been formulated and tested. Conscientious adherence to the scientific method is what differentiates the competent physician from the hack and the quack.

These principles are well recognized and observed in the diagnosis and treatment of disease. Do they not apply equally for the understanding and care of the patient? They do indeed, and it is only the widely held assumption that such matters are not amenable to a scientific approach that has prevented their inclusion in the education of medical students. Let me illustrate with an example of how bits of behavior may also justify drawing inferences pertinent to the care of the patient and how in turn the validity of such inferences can be tested.

While serving as visiting professor of medicine at another institution, I was asked at grand rounds to interview a man who 9 days earlier had suffered a cardiac arrest and been successfully resuscitated. The only information made available to me was that he was a retired businessman of 64 whose arrest had occurred in the parking lot of the hospital. Let us call him Mr. John.

The amphitheater was crowded, and there was barely enough room for the two of us when Mr. John, a somewhat portly, gray-haired, well-groomed man was wheeled in. In quick succession, the patient exhibited three telling bits of behavior. First, in a rapid yet nonetheless deliberate manner, he carefully scanned the auditorium, his expression changing from a slightly quizzical frown to a faint smile in the few seconds this took. Then apparently he noticed there was not room enough for both his wheelchair and my chair. As the house officer was attempting to maneuver the wheelchair into place and before I had even sized up what the difficulty was, the patient from his wheelchair began to move my chair. He ended up directing me and the resident until the two chairs were located to his satisfaction.

As the interview began I was holding a hand microphone which after my initial question I extended toward him for his response. Then came the third bit of behavior. Mr. John at once took the microphone from my hand and responded, gazing alternately from me to the audience. Thereafter it was he, not I, who controlled the microphone. When he had finished saying what he had to say, and only then, did he direct the microphone toward me for my next question.

What inferences, if any, may one draw from such a small sample? As with the example of the orthopneic patient referred to earlier, the answer depends on one's fund of knowledge, grasp of basic principles, and ability to make reliable observations—this time, however, in the realm of human behavior rather than pathophysiology. Few, I suspect, would disagree that this patient's behavior constituted an effort on his part to establish and maintain control in a new situation. However, such a formulation is a mere tautology, comparable to stating that our orthopneic patient was trying to get more air into his lungs.

Our scientific approach demands that we look much further. This patient's behavior, it seemed to me, was all the more remarkable considering the fact that it was displayed a mere 9 days after a cardiac arrest. Subdued, passive behavior might seem more plausible under such circumstances. Actually, this patient's behavior during the first minute of the interview immediately brings to mind the behavior and personality characteristics that many investigators, beginning with Osler in 1896, have reported among patients who develop coronary artery and cerebrovascular disease. Friedman and Roseman popularized this pattern as Type A.

For a physician to make such a generalization on the basis of merely 1 minute of observation is no different than would be his thinking of congestive heart failure and its pathogenesis upon observing a propped-up patient gasping for breath. In both examples the generalization also predetermines the questions to be asked and the strategies to be invoked to test its validity for the patient in question. In this case, we first needed to establish whether this behavior constituted a specific reaction to the situation of being presented at rounds or reflected a more enduring personality style. A mere 15 minutes of interviewing supported the latter. As Mr. John spoke about his hospital experience, the circumstances of his illness, his business career, his personal relationships and family life, his satisfactions and frustrations, and his life style, item after item emerged consistent with Type A personality. His personal account of himself and his life, comprised of incidents, experiences, relationships, and expressions of opinion, judgments, and self-characterizations, added up to the picture of an aggressive, ambitious man, always active, busy and planning, and preoccupied with deadlines, high standards of performance, and self-set goals; a man driven by an inner sense of time-pressure, and urgency; a man who basically felt he could depend only on himself to get the job done and to assure gratification of his own needs. To a remarkable degree, his behavior upon entering the amphitheatre accurately reflected many of these characteristics.

On the basis of our knowledge of psychological settings that seem especially conducive to sudden death, we entertained a second hypothesis. Experience has shown that the risk of cardiac arrest in the biologically vulnerable Type A person is greatest when the patient feels or actually is in danger of losing his sense of control over his environment, the more so if preceded by a period of discouragement and depression or accompanied by strong feelings of fear, anger, or excitement that culminate in a sense of futility or failure. In the case of this 64-year-old man, we learned that the patient's carefully laid plans to devote his retirement to "doing his own thing" had been thwarted by his daughter's divorcing and leaving the care of her 3- and 4-year-old children to Mr. John and his wife. To make matters worse, the older boy had then become ill. Rather than playing golf and cultivating his many new hobbies, Mr. John now felt burdened with these unwanted responsibilities as well as disappointed in his daughter. The cardiac arrest occurred on the way to the doctor's office with the 4-year-old when a parking space for which he had been patiently waiting was "stolen" by another motorist. He remembers angrily shaking his fist at the motorist, driving off, and nothing more. In the interview he described this episode as "the last straw." An acute myocardial infarction 5 years earlier placed him in the group at higher risk for cardiac arrest.

Biopsychosocial Model as Basis for Treatment Strategies

Perhaps you concede that this is interesting, maybe even persuasive, but the more skeptical among you may still be wondering how such information contributes to more effective patient care, in this case care of the Type A patient. The answer to that question requires a further step. If we are to assist Human Nature, as we earlier defined the goal of patient care, then we must know what these psychological characteristics, so readily established through proper observational and interview techniques, mean for the patient. Understanding this, we can also infer how the physician's approach to the patient may be adapted to minimize distress and encourage confidence and peace of mind. Scientifically, this requires a different level of conceptualization and a different strategy of investigation. It corresponds to *explaining* orthopnea rather than merely *recognizing* it as a cardinal manifestation of left ventricular failure. For orthopnea this requires elucidating the underlying pathophysiology; for Type A behavior it requires elucidating the underlying psychodynamics.

Basic knowledge of psychodynamics, like basic knowledge of pathophysiology, is best achieved through long-term or in-depth study of a few patients. Among persons exhibiting Type A behavior, a variety of unconscious determinants have been uncovered, the most critical of which is a deep-seated fear of being put in a passive, helpless, or dependent position. Typical Type A individuals exaggerate the opposite traits, striving always to be active, independent, and in control of the environment and the people in it. In the process they become their own most severe critics and exacting taskmasters. They continually set and then strive to fulfill higher and higher goals for themselves and others, thereby repetitively subjecting themselves to the risk of failure, a failure for which they characteristically take personal responsibility. By the same token, the deep fear of helplessness and passivity also makes it difficult for them to rest on their laurels; no matter how successful, they must constantly strive after more success, a situation both encouraged and aggravated by societies that place a high premium on performance and achievement as does our Western industrialized society. Suffice it to say, the physician's failure to take into account these underlying dynamics may have serious consequences for the patient, as the example of Mr. Glover in Chapter 2 illustrates.

Psychologically speaking, the circumstances under which Mr. Glover's cardiac arrest occurred—the emergency department—were not all that different from those in the parking lot where Mr. John experienced a similar life-threatening attack. Would the cardiac arrest have occurred had the cardiology team in the emergency department appreciated the psychodynamics underlying the Type A personality? Indeed, would not a more knowledgeable staff have been attentive to how the patient was responding to the events in the emergency room and made a more deliberate effort to deal with his feelings before the risk of precipitating a lethal arrhythmia had reached dangerous proportions? For such a risk is very real, as clinical study and animal experiments have shown.

The answer to both of these questions must, of course, be in the affirmative. Just as an understanding of the pathophysiology of left ventricular failure enables one to appreciate the risks of recumbency, physical exertion, or excessive sodium intake, so too does understanding the psychodynamics that underlie Type A personality enable one to recognize the risks of placing such a person in a passive, helpless position, subject to the domination or control of others. Furthermore, we can readily derive from these psychodynamics rational strategies that can minimize such risks. These in turn can be tested and refined in their application, as is the case with any therapeutic measure. Let me propose, from such principles, a strategy for the care of the Type A patient with a suspected myocardial infarction.

These two patients, Mr. John and Mr. Glover, clearly illustrate that Type A personality can be suspected from the patient's reported and observed behavior during the development of the attack and from his interactions with the doctor. Once the physician is satisfied with the reasonableness of such a personality diagnosis, the challenge becomes how to take the firm command that the seriousness of the situation calls for without, at the same time, mobilizing the patient's deep-seated fear of being helpless and dominated. Obviously this is not always easy, because somehow the patient must be convinced of the doctor's command of the situation and his competence and ability to provide the help he so desperately yearns for without threatening the patient's need to continue to feel in control. This can indeed be a delicate balance, especially when the doctor also is a Type A—as many of us are—who feels threatened by patients who resist submitting to professional control. I once asked a group of medical students how they would deal with the conflict of a Type A doctor trying to take care of a Type A patient. One proposed the following formula: In one way or another the doctor should communicate to the patient, "All my skills and all my knowledge are at your command." An elegant compromise! For thereby each preserves relative autonomy. For the patient it facilitates the illusion that he commands the doctor, while at the same time communicating the reality that it is the doctor (and surrogates) who is the sole possessor of the critical knowledge and skills.

In practice, care of the Type A patient requires monitoring of psychological processes, undertaken as carefully as one monitors cardiac rhythm on the EKG to assess the patient's continuing struggle to maintain autonomy while submitting to the demands of treatment. The very fact of the doctor's interest in the coronary patient's concerns over such issues, however expressed, can itself powerfully contribute to a growing sense of trust on the part of the patient, something not easily achieved by individuals with Type A personality traits. At the same time, the patient's awareness that the doctor is interested in and wants to understand whatever may be contributing to the patient's concerns enables the patient to feel progressively more relaxed in relinquishing some of his own needs to maintain control. Accordingly, judicious interventions (e.g., providing the patient with access to a phone or to a visitor, even in the Emergency Department, so that unfinished business can be resolved) may both relieve the patient's anxiety as well as provide assurance that he has not been capriciously stripped of all his command. Helpful too are trade-offs, the concession of lesser activities in place of more taxing ones, especially when done in such a way that the patient is given the feeling of participating in the decision to relinquish one activity in favor of another. The interactions between physician and patient, in the course of which information and concerns are shared and decisions agreed on, provide the matrix in which the patient eventually succeeds in identifying with the powerful doctor, thereby symbolically acquiring the doctor's strengths and sense of competence. In this way, the physician comes to be seen as a helpful surrogate rather than as a menacing adversary. The patient who says, "I discussed this with my doctor and *we* decided . . ." often is expressing such a successful identification.

The care of the patient, no less than the treatment of organ-level disease processes is a matter for science; excellence in both reflects the art with which the physician applies scientific knowledge. The power of dogma is great. More than a hundred years ago, Sir William Gull warned against the dogmatism of a too physiochemically oriented "Science, by throwing the light of particular inquiry full in our eyes blinds us for a time to that which lies beyond." The remarkable accomplishments of biomedical research and technology have had just such an unforeseen side effect. The challenge now is to expand our horizons and at long last begin to apply the scientific method with the same vigor to the understanding of human feelings and behavior as we have to the understanding of disease and pathophysiology. Enhancement of patient care and human well-being cannot help but follow.

Suggested Reading

Engel, G. L. 1971. Sudden and rapid death during psychological stress: Folklore or folkwisdom? Ann. Intern. Med. 74:771–782.

Engel, G. L. 1974. Signs of giving up. In: S. B. Troup and W. A. Greene (eds): The Patient, Death and the Family, pp. 45–72. Charles Scribner, New York.

Engel, G. L., and Schmale, A. H. 1972. Conservation-withdrawal: A primary
    regulatory process for organismic homeostasis. In: R. Porter and J. Knight
    (eds): Physiology, Emotion and Psychosomatic Illness, pp. 57–85. Ciba
    Foundation Symposium 8 (New Series). Elsevier-Excerpta Medica, Am-
    sterdam.
Friedman, M. 1969. Pathogenesis of Coronary Artery Disease, pp. 78–104.
    McGraw-Hill, New York.
Gull, W. W. 1976. Clinical observation in relation to medicine in modern times.
    In: T. D. Acland (ed): Collection of the Published Writings of William
    Withey Gull. Memoirs and Addresses, p. 38. The New Sydenham Society,
    London.
Schmale, A. H. 1962. Needs, gratifications and the vicissitudes of the self-repre-
    sentation: a developmental concept of psychic object relationships. Psy-
    choanal. Stud. Soc. 2:9–41.

4 The Doctor-Patient Relationship

The Language of Medicine

In this chapter and the one that follows we hope to convey to you some important notions about communicating with patients. We attempt to do so in simple English. We intend no disrespect for the often elegant, always parsimonious, and usually dispassionate language of medical science. Indeed, we were tempted to adopt a tone that was more traditional, and, if you will, "more uptown." A slew of possibilities for chapter titles came to mind—Facilitating Effective Communication Skills in the Doctor-Patient Relationship, Interviewing Skills for Health Professionals, and so on—but we refrained.

The reason we refrained has to do with the often unappreciated impact of languagae in the actual conduct of medicine. Let us illustrate this with a truism: The bulk of communication between doctors and patients occurs in language. We "speak," of course, in many ways but usually in words. Therefore giving some thought to the words we doctors and patients use to talk to each other may not be entirely trivial. Consider the doctor-patient relationship by means of simple analogy: Imagine a collaboration similar to that between a pair of mountain climbers. Their goal is to reach the top (develop an effective healing partnership). The route to the top is never entirely known in advance and requires ongoing cooperation and communication as the ascent proceeds. (The doctor-patient relationship is a process that evolves collaboratively over time.) In this analogy, we might add that one of the climbers is far more experienced in this sort of mountaineering: He has been on many similar climbs and thus often acts as an authority and guide. (The doctor has experience and expertise that the patient expects and relies on). Still, the climbers must tackle the mountain together, and their fates are fundamentally intertwined as they make their way up a sometimes treacherous and uncharted mountain face. Finally, these two climbers—whose roles are collaborative, though not isomorphic—are bound together by critical linkages: ropes, pitons, mutually understood signals, and other means of communication. In the doctor-patient relationship, our ability to talk with each other becomes our essential arsenal of ropes and pitons. We are linked not with hemp and metal but with words, empathy, respect, and mutual trust. To succeed, we must be able to communicate—we must be able to talk to each other and listen to each other. This is difficult at best. It becomes more so when a person is ill, frightened, and in pain. However, it becomes impossible only if doctor and patient cannot speak the same language at all! There is no substitute for it. No CAT scan or SMA-34 panel will ever be able to compensate. Thus we are not speaking here about niceties in "the bedside manner." We are talking about the success or failure of patient care.

How good are we doctors, then, at talking with patients? The answer would have to be—frequently terrible! Come with us for a moment on some imaginary rounds. They are taking place in a crowded, chaotic, city hospital at 7:00 a.m.

> A young doctor, Dr. Miles, is trying to tell his patient that he has inoperable, metastatic cancer. Dr. Miles is white, middle class, and 27 years old. He is very committed to being the best doctor he possibly can. The patient on the other hand, is a bit weary and worn down by life. His name is Ignacio Chavez. He is 58 years old, widowed, of Hispanic origin, and barely surviving financially on a small Medicare disability pension.

Some doctors would be able to communicate with Mr. Chavez beautifully. Given the lack of formal education in these skills that we provide, it is remarkable how often doctors manage to do so empathically and well. Alas, this is not so with Dr. Miles. Instead, we witness a painful series of halting stammers, equivocations, and bungled opportunities. Our young, bright doctor suddenly seems reduced to jargon and pathetic mumbles:

> "You have a primary CA," he says. "There may be metastases, little pieces of it, in your vertebral column . . . I mean in your spine . . . , you know, your backbone."

> Our patient, in turn, does not complain or protest. Rather, he nods and stares blankly, trying to be polite, pretending that he understands. Inside, he is also terrified, confused, and profoundly alone. These feelings will emerge only later, with his family, if he is lucky enough to have a family. Or perhaps they will not come out at all. Our morning rounds end thus:

> *Dr. Miles:* "Well, then, Mr. Chavez, so now you understand why I need to do the test on your spinal fluid."

> *Mr. Chavez:* "That's the one where you stick a needle into my back and take out some fluid?"

> *Dr. Miles:* "Right! It won't hurt much. Now roll over on your side and tuck up your knees to your chin."

> *Mr. Chavez:* (No verbal response, silently assumes position as instructed.)

> Our young doctor performs the lumbar puncture, collects the samples, and places a small Bandaid over Mr. Chavez' skin.

> "By the way," he adds on the way out the door, "you'll need to lie down for at least another 8 hours, and you may get a headache." Eight hours later Mr. Chavez is still lying in his bed, obedient and alone. He stares at the ceiling saying nothing. What is he thinking? It is difficult to know. His expression gives nothing away.

Is young Dr. Miles mean and callous? Is he hopeless? Of course not. He simply has never been helped to talk with patients effectively. Not only has Dr. Miles not been adequately trained in communication skills, he has concurrently been socialized into a frequently dehumanized system and inculcated with biases and narrow perspectives that have actually caused a deterioration in the native compassion and empathy he originally brought with him to medical school. Like most of us, Dr. Miles went into medicine because he wanted to take care of people. What happened? The answer is complex and multifaceted. One symptom of the problem shows up in his hopeless bungling when he needs to communicate: He reverts to a highly abstruse "technical" language that confuses the patient and leaves Dr. Miles feeling more than a little uneasy. On the other hand, it is this very language that Dr. Miles knows will score points with his attending physician on rounds. Quite a predicament!

It is often said that students like Dr. Miles learn 10,000 new words in medical school. This strikes us as a conservative estimate. Yet too often they still cannot talk to patients and, furthermore, do not know how to listen. Certainly the problem does not lie in mastery of a very precise technical jargon. For example, students learn that many anticancer agents, such as several that will be tried on Mr. Chavez, cause alopecia, ulcerative stomatitis, and desquamating intestinal enteritis. How different those words would sound, if one said: These drugs may cause my patient's hair to fall out. His mouth will become filled with painful, open sores. His intestinal lining may slough off, and he may bleed into his gut. The blood may come gushing out of his anus. He could bleed to death.

Despite the popular accusation, we personally do not believe that doctors fall back on excessively technical language with patients to appear pretentious, smart, or to lay verbal smoke screens. More likely, the problem occurs because young doctors are not helped to cope with the emotional impact of their work. On the contrary, they are encouraged by older house officers or professors who use similar defenses to twist language so that it denies the harsh emotional realities of what patients really face and doctors really do! How could a doctor so trained then be expected to communicate effectively with a suffering patient? In truth, it is ultimately impossible to imagine an effective doctor-patient relationship emerging from an educational system that ignores the feeling of the doctor, let alone those of the patient.

The biopsychosocial model, which forms the central theoretical foundation of this book, is a quantum leap forward in the right direction. It yanks the feelings and relationships in a patient's life out of the clichéd realm of "bedside manner" and plants them where they should be—in the hub of scientific medicine itself. The education of future physicians must also include helping the student to understand the biopsychosocial forces that he himself experiences so intensely; after all, he is half of the dyad and lives in that emotionally intense crucible as surely as his patient.

One final observation about the structure of our medical language: Repeatedly, we have been struck by the propensity of all physicians to gravitate in their speech toward highly action-oriented verbs. Listen to a group of doctors talking on work rounds. They will talk about "*doing* an LP." They will say they need to "*get* a urine sample." They will talk about "*ordering* a PA chest film." The words imply action, doing something to someone. They deny any notion of *interaction*. In one sense, this is perfectly logical. We doctors must constantly *do* things: We stick needles and cannulas into people's bodies; we withdraw fluids and tissues. Sometimes we cut bodies wide open to take out organs or even put them in. The active tone of our language thus reflects the active nature of so much that we do. Yet the procedures we "order" are seldom as one-sided as they at first might seem. For example, take a simple procedure—a doctor "orders" a barium enema. Yet anyone who has observed a patient undergoing this procedure—much less endured it himself—will appreciate how active the patient must also be. A day in advance, he is purged with harsh laxatives. He is then deprived of food. During the x-ray procedure, he must consciously squeeze his anus shut in order to keep a huge volume of fluid in his colon while he assumes awkward, embarrassing, and painful positions on a cold x-ray table! So the test we "ordered" is not so simple a matter as our language initially led us to think.

Imagine how different medical rounds would sound if doctors spoke like this "We'll need to get Mrs. Jones to our radiology technician in the morning for a really good upper GI." Or: "Mr. Smith and I are going to go to the examining room at 11:00 so that we can do a careful neurological—it's critical."

To some, these distinctions doubtless seem idle—the ruminations and quibblings of an obsessive lexicologist. Yet we argue the opposite. We think it is the *language* of doctors, perhaps more than any other aspect of their behavior, that betrays the difficulties they so often have dealing with powerful emotions. Over and over, physicians' choices of words reveal not only their awkwardness when they hear strong emotions in their patients but also their blindness to seeing the doctor-patient relationship as an interaction that involves both doctor and patient (not to mention the patient's family).

Our action-oriented, nonparticipatory verbs can actually mislead. Consider the phrase "getting a history." This language is common enough perhaps; but in a real sense, doctors do not *get* a history, or *take* a history, or *do* an interview. Rather, doctor and patient collaborate in an evolving, subtle, sometimes terrifying, but often joyous and always important process. The process is far from mystical and unscientific. Its goal is knowledge and understanding—the essential foundation for the diagnosis and management of all diseases—at least the ones that people come down with!

The Power of the Doctor-Patient Relationship

A highly respected, technically gifted, humane orthopedic surgeon once made a terrible mistake. He had treated an elderly woman for many years for an arthritic condition complicated by diabetes. She was very attached to him and trusted him implicitly. There came a point in her illness when the surgeon decided that she would have to have her left leg operated on. She readily assented and, in due course, the operation was performed. Then, while she was in the recovery room, a tragic error was realized. The wrong leg had been draped. The surgeon had operated on the wrong knee. After considerable personal anguish, he waited for her to stabilize postoperatively and then entered her room to tell her the truth.

"Mrs. Fenswald," he began. "I have to tell you that I have made a terrible mistake. Through a series of blunders, I operated on the wrong knee."

Mrs. Fenswald initially looked shocked, then pensive. For a moment, the two sat together in silence.

Then Mrs. Fenswald replied.

"You know, Dr. Jones," she stated, "I am obviously sorry that this has happened . . . but I'm really not that worried . . . you're such a good doctor. I'm quite sure that the other knee will get better anyway."

It did!

This vignette from Dr. Reiser's book *Patient Interviewing: The Human Dimension* is at once heartening and highly disturbing. Certainly it describes an iatrogenic catastrophe. Yet it also dramatically underscores the power of the doctor-patient relationship. It is this relationship that Balint has referred to as a "drug" for which "no pharmacology . . . exists yet." Whatever the metaphor one chooses, and there have been many eloquent ones over the years, it seems indisputable that the doctor-patient relationship is one of the most powerful human dyads that exists. It is as old as history, and it exists in every culture, however "advanced" or "primitive." Despite much current lamenting about the erosion of that relationship and the demoralization that has resulted, the dyad remains in many respects as durable and potent as ever. If one wishes anecdotal confirmation for this, witness how often people speak in disenchanted, even enraged tones about medicine in general yet refer in glowing terms to "my doctor." As Balint points out, however, this powerful drug is not without its side effects. If the strength of the relationship can cure, it also occasionally can cause great harm, and lesser disasters occur all the time. A patient who is treated rudely and unempathically by his physician may not die from the experience, but most assuredly he will suffer. Conversely, one who feels truly understood can sometimes face great pain, uncertainty, and even death in comfort and with serenity. If one thinks about it for a moment, it is the very power of the doctor-patient relationship that explains why so many Americans are currently, and most appropriately, angry with their healers. If doctors *were not* so important, it is unlikely that people would be so disappointed and angry.

Two final points about the doctor-patient relationship deserve mention. First, neither party is ever without conflict about being part of a relationship that is so intense and important. Doctors are understandably ambivalent about the power that is invested in them and the responsibility that goes with it. Almost without exception, patients are equally ambivalent about allowing someone to be so crucially important to them. Second, though we often talk about this relationship as though it were terribly mysterious, a scientific explanation that can account for some of its incredible power is both desirable and possible. Engel's biopsychosocial approach, explicated more fully in Chapters 2 and 3, points to such an explanation. As he observes, illness almost always evokes feelings of helplessness. Such feelings can, and often do, cause a patient—though he is in fact a full-grown adult—to feel very much the way he must have felt when he was a tiny, helpless baby. Being a patient can make one feel totally dependent again, like an infant forced to rely on his parents for emotional succor and even for survival. Hence the power of the doctor-patient relationship may derive in part from its symbolic connection to the earliest stages of life. This, of course, can be regarded only as a hypothesis, but it represents how one can use the biopsychosocial model to think scientifically about matters previously consigned to the realm of "art" and "intuition" alone. As Engel points out, people who feel that such considerations are beside the point completely miss the point. Perhaps scientifically informed inquiries will eventually lead to the elusive pharmacology that Balint laments still does not exist.

Doctor-Patient Dyad. I. The Student as a Person With Something To Offer

Medical training, from its first months to well into the house staff years, often seems diabolically contrived to make the student feel he is engaged in an interminable rite of passage. He sometimes fears that he is doomed to feel eternally inept, incompetent, and foolish. Students probably take little solace in reassurance that mastery and even wisdom do eventually come. For long years medical training feels too much like a harrowing twilight of incompetence in the face of overwhelming responsibilities and stress to permit students any optimism about the distant promised dawn.

Clichés do not mollify students on this point. It is often more helpful to suggest to these students, especially to those just beginning, that they actually have something to offer their patients.

A Biopsychosocial Perspective

To begin with and at the very least, students can offer their unbiased presence. There is some irony here. Very often, precisely because students have not yet grown excessively encumbered and narrowed by an exclusively biomedical viewpoint, they can actually interact with patients in some important and therapeutic ways that may be overlooked by their more medically jaded mentors. Students often dismiss this advantage as mere naiveté, "being a nice guy"—the bones students toss to patients in lieu of being able to do anything "real" for them. All this, they complain, is accompanied by the "fraudulent" donning of the white coat, the endless exploitation of patients as "guinea pigs." Reassurance alone does little to assuage most students' anxieties about these matters.

In fact, however, students are in an ideal position to approach patients from the perspective of the biopsychosocial model. Ironically, students may be the most free to see their patients as parts of a total system, from mitochondria to ministers, from white cells to wives. The student's relative freedom to learn and apply the biopsychosocial model to patient care can be an invaluable asset. This is one important reason why students, despite their relative technical inexperience, so often form relationships of such tremendous richness with their patients. Several eloquent examples of this can be found in John Rosenberg's account of his experiences as a medical student in this book's Prologue.

Curiosity

Students are usually curious. They are curious about the body and the mind, and about the ways in which the two interact. Though they fear asking something "dumb" on rounds, students in fact are encumbered by far fewer stereotypes than their mentors. Furthermore, their curiosity can be channeled and trained. With guidance, it can be honed from diffuse fascination to an astute capacity for accurate and detailed observation. The great diagnostic value of such observational skills are discussed more fully in the next chapter.

Compassion

Students occasionally find themselves mocked for their compassion by only slightly older peers. More egregious, perhaps, is the widespread folklore that depicts medical students as cut-throat, narrow-minded, and compulsive—survivors of the "dog-eat-dog" competitive system of premedical training that got them into medical school. Actually, nothing could be less true. Students rarely begin as the vicious connivers, grade grubbers, and compulsive zombies they are sometimes made out to be. If they finally end up that way, it is because they are made to fit that caricature by powerful, even irresistible pressures for social conformity that beset them during their medical training. In truth, medical schools are inundated with so many qualified applicants it is impossible to admit all of the intellectually superior, morally outstanding, *and* deeply sensitive young men and women who apply.

Students can and frequently do bring a capacity for concern and compassion to their patients. It is always welcome and occasionally vital to a patient's well-being. This is one of the ironic reasons that patients, especially at training hospitals, so often refer to the medical student assigned to them as "my real doctor." One student, for example, had this experience when he was still a freshman. He was working with a middle-aged woman who was dying of cancer. At a certain point, surgical removal of her ovaries seemed desirable as a palliative measure. The woman refused. Finally, the Chairman of the Department of Surgery attempted to prevail on her.

"Not until you get permission from my doctor!" she insisted. Ultimately, there was the whimsical spectacle of a prominent surgery professor being given "permission" by a freshman medical student to perform the operation. The incident cuts deeper than whimsy, however. In fact, this woman needed to trust in a doctor-patient relationship, and the task fell to one lowly freshman bedecked in his starched, uncomfortably new, "fraudulent" white coat.

Styles

Like patients, students have different styles. Some students are more assertive and action-oriented; some by nature are more contemplative and slower to act. Some tend to respond on an emotional and intuitive level; others rely on logic and cognition. There is plenty of room in medicine for such a variety of styles. One of the major tasks of medical education is to assist students to learn what their own style is and help them adapt it flexibly to a growing variety of complementary and divergent styles in their patients. Engel gives an example of this in Chapter 3, where he discusses the "Type A" physician taking care of a "Type A" patient.

Responsibility

Finally, the student quickly brings to his relationships with patients something very special and important—a deep sense of responsibility. From the outset of medical training, a sense of responsibility is literally pounded into the student. By the time he graduates, this sense has penetrated his very being. One can work at many jobs and leave the work behind at 5:00 p.m. when the whistle blows. Many chores and obligations can be hung like hats on pegs in a closet when the work week ends. This is not to be for physicians. Being a doctor is not a job. It is a state of being, it is a human experience. One is a physician 24 hours a day, 7 days a week, for the rest of one's life. It is a role that carries burdens as well as privileges.

Ironically, this deeply ingrained sense of responsibility—certainly among a physician's most noble traits—seems to be formed in part from the very same pressures in training that also promote callousness, dehumanization, and despair. To give only one example: There is no doubt that the rigorous, even savage, on-call schedule of the typical house officer, in which he is up all night every third night struggling with the nearly dead and pronouncing on the unquestionably dying, is a process which forges in some way the deeply internalized sense of responsibility that good physicians feel. Such a sense, of course, is not restricted to physicians, and many other individuals in other vocations also possess it. Yet it remains one of the most important gifts that the medical student, even the greenest student, has to offer his patients.

Doctor-Patient Dyad. II. The Patient as a Person With a Problem

Biopsychosocial Model

In the words of Sir William Osler, "It is more important to know what kind of patient has the disease than what kind of disease the patient has." A group of junior medical students and their preceptor found this out:

They were conducting an interview at the bedside with a 58-year-old man who weighed 430 pounds. When the group of seven entered the room, they found the huge man poised on the edge of the bed with almost gelatinous precariousness. Gigantic rolls of fat plunged pendulously to his knees. His night shirt was mostly unbuttoned, and his pajama bottoms had slipped down below his thighs, exposing pubic hair and genitalia. Still he beckoned the students in with a hearty laugh and showed no obvious embarrassment. His wife, a heavy-set woman herself, wore thick glasses and labored at a piece of crochet work in her lap. She blushed faintly when the group entered. She had been sitting opposite her husband. Now she hurriedly pushed her chair up against the far wall, nearer to his head yet out of his line of vision. She then proceeded to watch the interview very intently but said nothing.

The student who was conducting the interview tried valiantly to ask open-ended, empathic, and appropriately leading questions—ones that would encourage the patient to open up about why he was, literally, eating himself to death. From the medical chart the group knew that he had been gaining weight since his retirement as a truck driver 10 years before. His obesity had not exploded, however, until 4 years previously, after his 24-year-old son committed suicide, leaving two young children. The patient mentioned none of this spontaneously. Rather, he seemed to prefer to joke cavalierly about politics and the like. Several times he said he "loved to swim." He planned to go swimming with his wife that summer, but caustically referred to her as "a hunk of blubber in the water." At one point, the wife started to interject something about the son's suicide, but he quickly cut her off. Despite the obvious drama of the events, the interview itself was a bore. The patient managed to stonewall everyone. Students yawned, looked repeatedly at their watches, fidgeted, and dreamed about dinner. The preceptor stifled a yawn. When the interview finally ended 5 minutes early, all departed with a sense of relief.

The group then huddled. What had "gone wrong"? Their main data came from detailed observation, and, above all, the students' ability to heed their own feelings. (This second matter is discussed further below.) As the students conversed and conjectured, the preceptor encouraged them to delineate strictly observable data. A number of things stood out. For one, the patient seemed utterly oblivious to even the most basic amenities, apparently betraying no shame for exposing his genitals. Furthermore, he appeared mysteriously indifferent about several catastrophes in his life: his obesity, a serious urinary tract infection, and finally his son's suicide. Then there was the wife, who never said a word, except once only to be cut off, who sat neither in nor out of the scene, vigilantly overseeing every nuance but never herself plunging in.

The students' ultimate formulation is discussed below, under Feelings. Here, simply observe that the biopsychosocial components of this man's illness were overwhelmingly obvious. This had not, incidentally, seemed so obvious before the group went to the bedside. In fact, the student who selected the patient had originally thought he only wanted the preceptor to decide if the patient was "pickwickian." He had also anticipated a discussion of the pros and cons of gastric stapling procedures in the treatment of obesity.

By the end of the interview, however, it was abundantly clear that this man, with kidneys inflamed at the parenchymal level, was also shockingly emotionally disturbed; and—most troubling—he seemed to be reacting to all of the tragedy with complete noblesse oblige and jocularity. Finally, this dying, infected fat man had a wife and an extended family. Somehow they had to be part of this morbid process too.

As one student exclaimed, "This man is eating himself to death! He's killing himself! Why isn't anyone stopping him?" Clearly the answer to this question lay in an understanding of the forces that went beyond parenchyma and calories alone.

Empathizing with the Patient's Anxieties about Meeting the Doctor

Typically, beginning students are so apprehensive about their own shortcomings and inexperience that they understandably focus largely on themselves. Will they "blow" the interview? Will they miss getting that arterial puncture? Will the patient complain about their looking so young? Although such apprehensions are inevitable, it is often helpful for students to consciously draw a parallel: As apprehensive as the student may be, imagine how anxious the *patient* may be. The patient doubtless expects to see a young doctor, a concerned person, but one in a hurry, who will ask many questions. Will this young doctor approve of him? The last one got impatient when he could not recall the exact date his symptoms started, when he did not stick to the "important" details of his left lower quadrant pain. Will the student become physically disgusted by the smell from his infection? What will he think of the urine bag dangling there below the sheets? If a student can empathize with the enormous apprehensions a patient has about meeting a new doctor, some of the student's own self-consciousness may decrease. Furthermore, the appearance of anomalous reactions in such a setting can also be telling. As Engel pointed out in Chapter 3, the patient who is *not* anxious, who immediately takes the offensive, or does not even seem to care—this patient is revealing important information about himself.

Developmental Stages

Erik Erikson was one of the first to state what now seems so very obvious, i.e., that development and change do not cease at puberty. Rather, people undergo major developmental changes throughout their adult life. Since Erikson, important research has been done by Levinson and Vaillant. Much of this pioneering scientific work has also been incor-

porated into an excellent popular book by Gale Sheehy entitled *Passages*.
It is extremely useful to familiarize oneself with this body of literature.
Most students *are* young. Most of their patients *are* older. Although
empathy, rapport, and understanding can bridge most gaps, a student is
helped immeasurably when he has some cognitive handles to help him
understand what developmental issues a 40-year old, a 60-year old, or
an 80-year-old faces. "Will the 50-year-old woman whom I am about to
interview suffer from the 'empty nest syndrome'?" "Will the high level
executive who is 48 and in the hospital for his first myocardial infarction
be asking himself what he has really done with his life?" People are
almost always more complex than the paradigms we invoke to describe
them. Nobody progresses predictably through rigidly predetermined
life stages like a ship advancing through locks in a canal. Nevertheless,
there are normative stages that have now been well delineated, and
applied flexibly they can be very useful. Knowledge of these can be
especially valuable to a student who wishes to form an empathic alliance
with his patient—a person so often different from the student in background and age. Still, even in the early, often awkward moments when
doctor and patient are trying to form a bridge, they have the most
critical element of all in common: Despite differences in age, socioeco-
nomic background, and life experience, both are human beings. Both
know what it means to suffer; and whether either admits it or not, both
know, deep down, what it means to fear loneliness. The psychiatrist,
Harry Stack Sullivan, once said, "We are all more human than anything
else." This is true. A 25-year-old woman medical student raised in Massachusetts may be very surprised to discover how much she *can* understand about a 70-year-old Filipino immigrant dying of prostatic cancer,
how much more than she might have imagined she possibly could. Our
human capacity for empathy can be awesome and sometimes even a little
frightening.

The Patient Has a Life

Even the most isolated, down-and-out skid row derelict has a life.
He must have a place somewhere where he hangs out, and usually there
are people he hangs out with; moreover, there are assuredly things that
matter to him—maybe just a soiled snapshot or a tattered address book.
Above all, everyone has memories and a past. Everyone had a mother
and father—once. Everyone also has a future—hopes, aspirations,
dreams—these as well as illnesses and fears. Even our most anonymous
patients have a life. Students should never forget that hospitals are very
artificial environments. Hospitalized patients are stripped of their cloth-
ing, their wallets, and their jewelry. Favorite pipes and pictures are gone.
We dress them in gowns and tell them to lie down flat. We isolate them
from so much that makes each of them a person. Why we routinely do

this to people is both curious and complex. In some ways it seems necessary. Sometimes one wonders, though, if we perhaps do it also to protect ourselves emotionally. Maybe it is just too wrenching and frightening to see people so very sick in the full torrent of their humanness, and to think—they could be us. Whatever the reasons for our rituals, remember that the supine figure you see on a gurney under a sheet has a life, as surely as you or I. It is always worth inquiring into, for it is virtually impossible to treat someone despicably whom one understands, and sometimes our understanding itself can help immeasurably.

Feelings

What do we do about feelings? In medicine they are all over the place. Patients are having them, and we are having them. Generally we do not talk about them much. When they erupt, their occurrence often seems awkward, even guilt-laden—witness the savage nursing-station humor of house officers complaining on admitting night about getting another "hit." Similarly, patients may erupt suddenly into uncontrollable sobbing or rage. Are feelings "scientific?" What do they have to do with medicine? Engel addresses this question in Chapters 2 and 3 and concludes persuasively that understanding the feelings of doctor and patient is essential and amenable to scientific study.

Allow us to take the whole matter one step further. We propose that the doctor who understands feelings—both his own and his patient's—is a better doctor. He is better because he is able to comprehend what is truly important and therefore can provide more effective help. Empathy for our patients' feelings and insight into our own are not frivolous "window dressing," as some educators have tried to make them out to be. We go even further: The failure of contemporary medical education to help students integrate their affect with their intellect may prove to be its greatest failing. Our profession is littered with casualties: doctors who are addicted, alcoholic, and divorced or else deeply depressed, disillusioned, and alone. For rare individuals, the apparent opportunity to deny all emotion may seem a welcome relief, but it is a dangerous denial and one most of us do not welcome anyhow. For the vast majority of us, being in touch with our feelings and coming to peace with them is essential to our well-being. There is good evidence that patients are much more vulnerable to disease if they are not in touch with their feelings. We believe that doctors too are at greater risk and for the same reason. We cannot continue to treat ourselves, much less our patients, like insensate machines. As educators, we have an absolute and urgent obligation to help physicians handle feelings—in their patients and in themselves. The evidence is already piling up that we have failed in this area, and we risk continuing to do so only at the greatest peril.

Feelings Are Useful

Feelings provide us with vital clinical data. To begin with, feelings are biologically very old, both phylogenetically and ontogenetically. They are the essential matrix for human bonding and socialization in our species, as essential to life as protoplasm. Phylogenetically and onto-genetically feelings originate first in lower mammalian forms and in the infant. Ideas became attached to them later in evolution and develop-ment with the emergence of the neocortex. Contrary to medical folk-lore, the scientific study of feelings is possible. It is, in fact, essential. On a more day-to-day basis, each of us must come to grips with our own feelings if we hope to be effective as well as professionally satisfied. Above all, the clinician who is in good touch with his feelings possesses a most wondrous and reliable diagnostic tool. Let us return at this point to the case of the 430-pound man cited earlier. Recall that the students saw how many biopsychosocial influences were affecting this man. Yet the situation remained very puzzling. Where were the feelings? He did not seem depressed, when he should have been. Where was the anxiety? After the interview, the students sat around a conference table yawning, cracking cynical jokes, saying they wanted to knock off early that day. The preceptor began to put up a list on the blackboard, a list of feelings the students were having. Among the feelings: hopelessness, despair, remoteness, and boredom. Above all, the feeling tone among the stu-dents was unmistakably depressed. Why?

It began to dawn on the students that they were having the feelings the *patient* should have been having. This discovery led to an interesting notion. The notion went: This man's entire family never recovered from the suicide of the 24-year-old son 4 years before. Instead of grieving or feeling depressed, the family's feelings seemingly went underground. In some complex way, the depression was hidden and then divided up among the whole extended family. The father got fat. The mother said nothing. The students could only speculate about the family's many children, including the surviving children of the suicide, but by the end of the discussion a lot more was known. Using the data of their own feelings, the students were able to construct a decent, testable hypothesis to explain the bio-, psycho-, and social sequelae of this tragedy.

Transference and Countertransference

Transference and countertransference, two rather lofty and for-midable sounding words, have suffered over the years from misuse and overuse. The terms originated in psychoanalytic theory, where they have specific definitions and applications. Currently they have degenerated into little better than jargon. The concepts are nonetheless very useful, even if the argot has grown confusing. Rather than adding to the mess, consider a definition that is brief and intentionally quite simple: All

human beings *transfer* things—feelings, attitudes, and expectations—
that they once had toward important people from their childhood, typically parents and siblings. Such transfers are probably ubiquitous but
often become highly prominent in the doctor-patient relationship, especially as it develops over time. Sometimes such transferences are prob-
lematic. Often they are not. Usually, however, it helps if they are understood. Some kinds of psychotherapy deliberately foster and then
examine transferences as a major focus of treatment. This usually does
not occur, however, in the typical doctor-patient relationship.

Here is an extremely simple example of transference:

> A man of 36 grew up in a family where he felt his father was harsh and
> critical of everything he did. When this man, now an adult, began to
> develop signs of chronic obstructive pulmonary disease, his physician (a
> man his father's age) counseled him to stop smoking. When the patient
> did not do so, the physician admonished him about how really
> important this was for his health. The patient exploded angrily and
> berated his surprised physician for nagging and belittling him, and not
> appreciating his efforts to stop.

This was *transference*—the patient acted as though the doctor were his
father. In turn the physician found *himself* reacting.

Countertransference, strictly defined, is the reaction of a doctor to his
patient's transference. In this case, the doctor had a reaction. He found
himself disgruntled with his patient, even a bit disgusted. He complained to a colleague about the patient's stubborn ingratitude and, especially, the patient's unwillingness to let him be of help. This was countertransference; the doctor actually felt toward his patient like a
disgruntled father. Many transference-countertransference reactions
are far more complicated and subtle. Furthermore, it is quite possible
for a physician to have a *transference* to a patient. For example, if a young
man is treating an older woman who reminds him of his mother, he may
form a transference to *her.*

Students often quite properly protest the hazards of pseudopsy-
chologizing. Sometimes, students correctly assert, feelings are straightforward and real and belong in the present. One student expressed the
skepticism well: "Just because I was bored and grumpy today doesn't
automatically prove that I'm having some kind of countertransference to
my patient. Maybe I'm just in a bad mood. Maybe I was on call last night
and didn't sleep. Maybe I had a fight with my wife."

Quite true! Yet it is still surprising how often these straightforward
feelings can also originate in response to a person's *transference.* Of all his
patients that day, for instance, why did the student get grumpy with *this*
one? In any event, the most important skill involves being aware that
transference often does occur. Patients are especially prone to developing strong transference feelings toward their doctors. Knowing that such

feelings can and do happen, and having some notion that they might be transference, is more important than definition and jargon.

Medical Slang

"Turkeys," "crocks," and "gomers." Let us be truthful—at some point, the most well-intentioned among us may conceivably use these denigrating terms or their equivalents, outrageous as that is. Thus it is impossible to conclude a discussion of feelings in the doctor-patient relationship without talking about the frustrated, angry feelings medical students and house officers inevitably experience in the training hospitals where they spend so many crucial years. Typically this training occurs in large public hospitals, VA hospitals, jails, and city wards. Students are told that they will have to take a lot of responsibility in these settings and see a lot of "pathology." Both statements are true. Frequently, however, students and young doctors are also assailed by a grim, raw, desperate, even hopeless side of human existence that they were hardly prepared for. Their sensibilities are shattered and overwhelmed by the seemingly endless procession of overcrowded wards, dilapidated and inadequate equipment, haggard and overworked staff. Into these nightmarish environments flow severely ill people—people who are not just medically ill but physically burnt out, psychologically crushed, defeated by life itself. In they pour like an interminable deluge—cases of hopeless alcoholism, drug addiction, brain damage, knife and gunshot wounds.

What one witnesses in these settings is *not* all of medicine or indeed all of life but it is what the young doctor sees day after day and night after night. Sometimes a benumbed feeling of nihilism sets in, even in the most sensitive of us. Very few of us can forebear endlessly or be so saintly that we never once call a patient a gomer.

Still, we must ask why. As difficult as things may get, when we find ourselves hating or mocking patients we must ask why—not to try to be saints but because the insight often helps. When we hate a patient, usually something specific has gone wrong, beyond the general frustrations. Somehow doctor and patient are failing to understand or empathize with each other at all. This is not always easy. Sometimes it may feel nearly impossible. Some patients *are* very far gone. Nevertheless, we have repeatedly seen instances in which a student or house officer expressed hatred for a patient not from nihilism but because it seemed too painful to feel otherwise. The anguish seemed just too deep to bear and the reward for recognizing such feelings too miniscule, far too remote. Similarly, over and over we have witnessed patients suffering in these settings. More than a few are rude and hostile because underneath this they are too terrified to hope, too frightened to reach out just one more time, to show their humanity, only to have it crushed again.

When you call someone a turkey, ask yourself why. It is almost impossible to hate someone you understand.

Denial of Death

In Chapter 3 Engel observes that much of what we call "art," "intuition," and "bedside manner" are actually essential to the proper understanding of patients. He argues persuasively that in this area we probably have not been scientific enough. Yet there is a widespread mythology that such matters are not amenable to scientific scrutiny. This mythology, coupled with our failure to effect such study, has had a disastrous effect on medical education. Engel believes that this narrowness has evolved from the scientific model of Western medicine itself, which for centuries has been based on reductionism and the Cartesian mind-body dualism.

Yet could there still be another level to the problem? Why has modern medicine seemed so entrenched, at times so stubborn? We personally suspect it has something to do with our inevitable proximity to what is most disturbing, mysterious, and impenetrable in life itself. Doctors are present when life is born. We are there when sane people go mad. We are there when death comes. By the nature of what we do, we are inevitably, inexorably tangled up with our patients in the crucible of life's most painful and agonizing questions. Above all, as mortal human beings ourselves, we doctors must nonetheless confront daily the most unimaginable yet undeniable truth of all—we all die. Without doubt, when we confront this reality in our patients, we are forced to make certain unavoidable inferences about ourselves.

Centuries ago, before medicine was based on science, doctors were priests, shamans, and medicine men—witch doctors. Though they were endowed with the special respect due to those who have commerce with the ultimate mysteries of life and death, they were also lonely and set apart. In Keniston's words, they were members of a "feared and powerful guild."

Times have changed, centuries have passed. Though some have wondered if a field can change so rapidly and constantly and still call itself a science, modern medicine is indisputably based on science and the scientific method. The dazzling technology that now surrounds us is not in itself dehumanizing. It is a monument to science and to the scientific method itself.

Yet for all of this, some things have not changed. People still die. Though we have advanced with astounding alacrity and success scientifically, we inevitably remain just as helpless, frightened, and befuddled as ever by mortality—life's cruelest hoax! For all our knowledge, we still do the work of shamans; it is noble work and, like them, we are treated as special—but we too remain deeply uncertain and alone.

We do not like this one bit, of course, and attempt with all our might to deny it. Probably the shamans and witch doctors did too. The causal connections our ancestors invoked had to do with angry gods and dangerous alignments of the moon and stars. Nowadays, we speak far more accurately of pathogeneses that originate in immune complexes, anaplasty, and genetic markers. We *are* much closer to the truth. We *are* being more scientific, but the ultimate riddle still eludes and torments us. The most unbearable truth has not changed. Maybe we doctors, if we are to become truly wise and truly at peace, must learn to accept that our intimate involvement with life's greatest mystery, death, commingles dramatically with the triumph of our advancing technology and expanding knowledge. We can do more and we know more, yet control of life's ultimate riddle remains beyond our grasp. We remain the descendants of shamans, and perhaps we should accept this and be proud.

Possibly, then, we can free ourselves and our students from the shackles of a narrow dehumanizing view of man—a view that both denigrates science and ignores the existential curse and blessing of our calling. In the future we will learn more and more about how people regenerate and degenerate, how they come into being and how they die. We will keep advancing on the truth—humane scientists, scientific human beings. However, we will all die, and our work has to do with this too. The renal failure in room 407 is you, me, all of us. If we are to achieve our ultimate stature as the noble profession we can be, we must strive to study and learn always; but we must realize that the very nature of our calling puts us in the eye of the hurricane. We deal with life's most inevitable, ineffaceable truth, our mortality. This is as true for us as it was for our noble shaman predecessors who rubbed herbs in their hands, sang incantations, and searched for the answers that never came from dim and distant stars. We are closer, but still we search. By the very nature of science, there will always be this excruciating paradox. As doctors, the farther we push the ocean of our ignorance back, the more we will find ourselves still standing at the very edge of an unutterably beautiful and terrifying shore.

Suggested Reading

Balint, M. 1964. The Doctor, the Patient, and the Illness, 2nd ed. International Universities Press, New York.

Becker, E. 1973. The Denial of Death. Free Press, New York.

Cassell, E. J. 1979. The Healer's Art: A New Approach to the Doctor-Patient Relationship. Penguin Books, New York.

Erikson, E. H. 1963. Childhood and Society, 2nd. ed. Norton, New York.

Keniston, K. 1967. The medical student. Yale J. Biol. Med. 39:356.

Levinson, D. S. 1978. The Seasons of a Man's Life. Knopf, New York.

Quill, T. 1983. Partnerships in patient care: a contractual approach. Ann. Intern. Med. 98:228–234.

Reiser, D. E., and Schroder, A. K. 1980. Patient Interviewing: The Human Dimension. Williams & Wilkins, Baltimore.

Sheehy, G. 1976. Passages. Dutton, New York.

Vaillant, G. 1977. Adaptation to Life. Little, Brown, Boston.

5 The Patient-Centered Interview

The purpose of this chapter is to describe an approach to talking with patients, one derived from principles inherent in the biopsychosocial model. What follows is not a lexicon of foolproof rules and techniques. In fact, the biopsychosocial model, by its nature, encourages a far more flexible approach to patients. It may be difficult to define precisely what constitutes a "biopsychosocial" interview, but a compendium of rote questions and rigid techniques it clearly is not; too often the latter is what students are accustomed to learning in its place. One should also realize that a chapter such as this is only an overview and cannot be fully comprehensive. Given these constraints, we attempt to delineate four key approaches to patient interviewing, approaches we view as fundamental to a full and effective understanding of all patients. Specifically, these four are the *science of observation, following the affect, the concept of process,* and the *"A.R.T." of interviewing.* With some apprehension, we offer a section entitled "Strategies," "Hip-Pocket Standbys," and "Pearls." Though we are wary of oversimplifications, we see the need to provide at least some tricks of the trade. Finally, we offer a brief summation of what interviewing is and, just as important, what it is not.

The Science of Observation

As Engel points out in Chapter 3, skills of observation can be greatly refined through education and practice. The fruits of such skills are valuable clinical data, part of science, not "art." He also makes a related point and a very important one: Observational skills should not be mystified or romanticized as products of intuition or as a "knack with patients." They can be taught, and they can be learned.

Despite this logic, medical students are often astonished when an experienced interviewer draws conclusions from data that passed them by unnoticed. "How'd he figure that out!?" Yet, nine times out of ten, such students have actually managed to overlook evidence that lay conspicuously before them. The problem is not simply faulty memory. When students are reminded of a key observation that seemed to have eluded them, they typically respond with immediate recognition. They do turn out to have seen the critical incident. Somehow, though, they "forgot" it. Most likely they forget because, lacking experience, they do not yet have a context into which the data fit, thus making them meaningful. As Engel points out, an experienced internist immediately knows what the sight of a patient sitting bolt upright in bed struggling to breathe usually portends: "congestive heart failure"—the thought is almost a reflex. Less experienced students naturally lack such a matrix of repeated observation and experience and therefore have more trouble anchoring the observable data to organizing concepts.

Still, everyone has to begin somewhere, and we urge students to heed this nostrum: Pay scrupulous, even compulsive attention to what happens *first*. The crucial significance of how interactions begin seems to be a highly replicable, indeed almost irresistible, human phenomenon. With astonishing predictability, patients reveal some of the most essential truths about themselves during the first minute or two of a new interaction with their doctor. Dr. Engel gives a beautiful example of this in Chapter 3: Recall the case of the retired businessman in a wheelchair who took over the seating arrangement and control of the microphone within the first few seconds of the interview. Engel remarks, "In this case, we first needed to establish whether this behavior constituted a specific reaction to the situation of being presented at rounds or if it reflected a more enduring personality style." Further inquiry supported the latter. As he described his hospital experience, the circumstances of his illness, his business career, his personal relations and family life, his satisfactions and frustrations, and his life style, item after item emerged consistent with such a formulation (i.e., the importance of control in this man's psychological functioning).

Like Dr. Engel, we should all be cautious of making too much out of too little. Students are especially leery of this danger and display appropriate skepticism toward those prone to "speculate." Still, with uncanny consistency, one finds that the behavior of patients in the early moments of an interview often does seem to predict and even summarize their general coping styles. That is in part because being interviewed is a challenge that demands coping. Therefore make every effort to scrutinize all details of what transpires at the start. One cannot overestimate their value and importance. One clarification is required, however. Be aware that the interview does not actually begin with the doctor's formal invitation to start talking. Critical data, indeed often the *most* critical data, typically unfold before the interview has "officially" started. Keep your eyes peeled from the instant the patient comes into view.

Developing observational skills is actually not as formidable as one might think. Ultimately, all observable data must enter through one or more of the five senses. Physicians depend primarily on what they hear and see. Perhaps one also gets a "feeling" from time to time; and if such hunches are analyzed carefully, it becomes clear that these "feelings" do not materialize from thin air. They are the product of a complex synthesis the doctor effects almost instantaneously from the data of the patient's expressions, sighs, body language, and other cues. It is true that increasing experience augments this ability to synthesize. Herein lie the rewards of sustained effort and clinical experience; but even a beginner can learn much if he pays attention.

Take in everything. What happened during the crucial first minute? Was the patient sitting or lying? Did she lean forward or remain positioned as she was? What was the book that lay open on the man's lap? What did he do with it when he saw the interviewer first enter the room? How was the room decorated? What was the expression on the patient's face? How did it change? Were there any unusual odors?

Does the patient have any get well cards on his bedside table? Photographs of family? No? Why not? So much of importance is embedded in what people commonly pass off as trivial. If you were a novelist, you would invoke just such external details to symbolize the inner landscape of a character's mind. In reality, patients are not so different. They too reveal much in what seems to be commonplace. People classically reveal their more critical secrets in what is apparently trivial, habitual, and apt to go unnoticed. Look for these nuggets, and you will find them. Above all, what *exactly* are the first bits of casual banter? These are always tipoffs. One patient assented to be interviewed by remarking, "Sure, you can ask me anything you want except my bank balance!" Just a joke? It turns out not. Subsequent inquiry soon revealed that the most dramatic events in this patient's childhood had been his father's death when he was six. It occurred during the Depression, and severe poverty followed.

It turned out that the patient currently was deeply chagrined because he had to be a patient in a public ward. In the past, he had been able to afford private care. Now again he was impoverished, just as he had been as a child. The tipoff was there—in his opening "joke."

After an initial period of vigilance, we then suggest a change in posture, one that may at first seem paradoxical. We will explain its rationale under the A.R.T. of Interviewing, below. Let go, adopt an even-hovering attention, allow your thoughts and emotions (and those of your patient) to wander where they will. Trust in where such receptivity takes you. Students often ask, "How will I remember what happened?" In fact, if one has paid careful attention to the interactions at the beginning, the rest can usually be recalled without difficulty.

Following the Affect

Early in training, before a matrix of conceptual and clinical experience has been fully developed, the affect displayed by the patient is the student's most reliable organizer: Directing one's comments in relation to what the patient is feeling usually keeps patient and student on the right track and also lends coherence to the student's own perception of the interview. Without attention to affect, interviews often seem fragmented, disjointed, and difficult to follow. Themes emerge, disappear, and reemerge. One minute the patient is talking about her liver. The next she is discussing a relative in Portland, Maine. The beginning interviewer understandably has trouble following these various threads. Almost always, however, an interviewer can perceive a distinct emotional tone that is fairly consistent throughout: depressed, anxious, reserved, seductive, etc. In addition, more rapid variations oscillate within the overall tone, similar to a brief series of musical notes played over the lingering resonance of a predominant chord. Both the chord and the notes are worth heeding. Also, the central emotional chord is usually sounded clearly and unequivocally during the first moments of the interview. Still, the notes that follow may range considerably. In a depressed patient, for example, one sometimes discerns shifts from anxiety to calm, from elation to despair, from hope to dejection.

The student's ability to keep track of his *own* feelings is equally crucial. The student also usually has a predominant emotional response to an interview—occasionally even the same thoughts and fantasies as his patient. Not long ago a group of students observed an interview with a dreadfully depressed dying man. All five quickly tuned out and indulged in essentially the same fantasy, i.e., getting out of the room. One daydreamed about dinner. Another thought about riding his bicycle. A third reminisced about a recent vacation. The content of the fantasies varied, but the theme was astonishingly consistent. Everyone felt restless and wanted to escape. By anchoring subsequent group discussion to these important data, we were able to develop a plausible hypothesis that explained the patient's severe isolation from his own feelings and experiences. The students had wanted to escape from the room because the patient had, in effect, already escaped—to some place very far away. Indeed, in his own mind, he was already gone . . . before the students had even gotten there! This dreadful truth was only accessible through an examination of the student's own feelings. This patient, in a sense, had already died.

Following the affect is also an effective way to keep an interview moving. The student who can stay with the patient emotionally by remarking from time to time, "That must have been sad," or "Boy, I bet *that* was frustrating," is usually able to help the patient get to his most important concerns. Very often this intervention alone can bring insight and relief that are very therapeutic.

Students should also try to work up the nerve to *say* what the patient must be feeling, rather than beating around the bush. Do not ask a patient what he feels when you know. Usually students are empathically correct far more often than they give themselves credit for. Identifying an affect is almost always perceived by the patient as supportive, not intrusive. Still, there seems to be a widespread myth to the contrary, that the "analytically proper" interviewer remains utterly neutral, open-ended, and completely unrevealing. Students must sometimes be helped to see past such clichés. Ponder the matter for a moment. If *your* mother had just died, which remark would *you* prefer: "You must be devastated!" or "Tell me, how did her death affect you exactly?" Even if the student is wrong, the patient can always say, "No." When students are right, the patient usually responds first with a "yes," "no," or "maybe." It is in what follows this initial hedge that the student's correctness is actually affirmed or negated.

An inexplicable lack of affect on the patient's part is also important to keep track of. Why is a feeling *not* there when it should be? The same holds true for the student as well. Why *does* the student feel bored when he "should" feel sad. This phenomenon is illustrated in Chapter 4 in the case of the 430-pound man.

Finally, though it may seem thoroughly obvious to experienced interviewers, students must be reassured that it is all right for them to *have* feelings! It is not easy for a beginning student to acknowledge boredom, disgruntlement, or dislike—much less sexual feelings, revulsion, or sadistic impulses. Usually, however, once students are reassured that such feelings are permissible (and come to appreciate that they may indeed disclose more about the patient than the student), the typical student quickly becomes able to identify and even delight in the broad range of emotions he experiences during an interview. The key lies in assisting students to see that these emotions provide *valuable data about the patient,* not embarrassing revelations about the student.

Interview Process

The concept of *process* is essential to all good interviewing. This complex subject can be touched on only briefly here, and the explanation that follows must be regarded as introductory. There is a *process level* to *all* communication between people. It involves the rhythm, timing, and order in which themes, affects, ideas, and behavior arise during an interaction. An analogy to masonry is helpful. If the *content* of what a patient says forms the "bricks" of communication, then the *process* forms the mortar. Process is always present. In every interchange, people talk and listen; but as they do so, an endless series of silent questions, associations, and thoughts run through their minds, some at a more conscious level than others.

A useful analogy is to imagine that you are at a cocktail party. For didactic purposes, imagine specifically that you are conversing with an interesting but unfamiliar stranger. You are curious, so you begin to make small talk. You talk about sports, current events, the weather. You ask each other about your interests. This is the surface of your interchange—the content. It is obvious, however, that something else is unfolding between the two of you below the surface. Behind the small talk, you are actively sizing each other up, revealing things about yourselves in some ways of which you are aware and, very possibly, in others of which you are not. What is going on between you at this level is *process*. You may be silently asking yourself, "Is this person intelligent?" "Is he or she a good listener?" "What does he or she think of me?" In such a social situation you are not apt to pay too much attention to process, though it is there.

However, when doctor meets patient, the process level of communications between them becomes extremely important, a matter that goes far beyond a social interchange. So much of what is important to a patient is communicated in process, not content. A person who falls ill feels anxious, depressed, angry, irritable, hypersensitive, and frightened, among a host of other emotions that inevitably accompany significant illness. Often, however, the patient is not aware of these feelings, and just as often he is unable to express them to his doctor, at least not initially or straight out. The patient often has no choice but to communicate these vital concerns only at the process level. For instance, the following vignette illustrates a concern that is almost universal in patients: "Can this doctor take care of me? Can I trust myself to be in his hands? Will he understand me?" Sometimes patients are aware of these concerns, more often not. Frequently they are just too afraid to admit them, even to themselves. Thus such thoughts almost never come up directly. They are communicated instead in process:

> A first-year psychiatry resident ushered his new patient down the hall to his freshly painted office for their first interview. The resident was

clean but shaggy; he sported a full, reddish growth of beard and longish, though neatly trimmed hair. He wore corduroy pants and looked, at best, 23. Money was tight at the time and, though he was impeccably clean, the back pockets of his Levi's were beginning to reveal holes. The soles of his boots had begun to wear through. They creaked with every step.

The patient was 60—a meticulous man with silver-gray hair. He had paid scrupulous attention to all details of his dress. Even his shoes sparkled from a new shine. He had clearly gussied up for this occasion.

As the patient followed his resident down the hall to the office, he remarked, "Hey, Doc! I think your back pockets are about to fall through. Your wallet's hanging halfway out!"

The resident was initially tempted to go on the defensive, but he refrained. Once in the office, he waited for an opportune and tactful moment, and then remarked, "Bad enough to get a resident, huh? Now a threadbare one to boot! Maybe you think I'm a green apple!"

"Nah," the patient replied initially, but soon he began to discuss his apprehensions. The resident was so *young*. The patient, on the other hand, was getting on. How *could* the resident truly understand his plight?

"I can see your point," the resident observed. "You're wondering if you've landed someone totally wet behind the ears. How *could* such a person understand the problems you face, especially those involved in a generation gap? I can see why you'd be feeling concerned."

"Well . . . yes and no." The patient finally responded. "The fact is, my wife and I have this problem. . . ."

The interview proceeded from that point quite smoothly.

The resident was no Svengali. What he *did* do was to listen accurately to the interchange's process. Instead of reacting defensively to the content and its unmistakable accusation, he tuned in to the underlying concerns expressed in the process. He did so by heeding the following three questions:

1. Why is the patient telling me this *now?*
2. What is the patient telling me about his feelings *now?*
3. What is the patient telling me about his feelings regarding the relationship *between him and me now?*

A more extensive discussion of the interview process is beyond the scope of this text, but the concept is an important one. Understanding process takes practice, experience, and time. Still, students who do not master every nuance of the concept of process should not feel unduly discouraged. Usually the mastery of precise observational skills, coupled with an awareness of affect (in both the patient and the student), enable most doctors and patients to communicate quite effectively. For students who wish to pursue the concept, a more detailed explanation is provided in Reiser and Schroder, *Patient Interviewing: The Human Dimension* (see Suggested Reading.)

The "A.R.T." of Interviewing

Consider for a moment the real implications of the biopsychosocial model, and something important becomes apparent: Despite the importance of interviewing to patient care and despite a proliferation of interviewing texts and courses, none quite manages to capture the spirit and letter of the model we so readily pay lip service to. The student, however open-minded, is beset with a bewildering array of quasisolutions. Some texts and courses offer narrow biomedical schemata. These provide often useful outlines for obtaining important details about signs and symptoms, but they leave the person out. Other texts and courses emphasize, almost exclusively, the psychosocial aspects of medicine, thus speaking eloquently of heartache but ignoring heart failure. Too often students respond in suit, by dichotomizing instead of integrating. We have observed students respond to these courses and books, and their responses do indeed reveal a troubling bias. Students frequently end up regarding open-ended, psychologically oriented interviews as "my psychiatry course." One even called it "learning analysis." Conversely, they refer to their biomedical training as "medicine." It is sad and destructive polarization but understandable given the current circumstances.

A very pointed example of this transpired recently when we consulted with a junior medical student interested in Family Practice. He began by introducing his patient to us in the following manner: "Mr. Bartholomew," he began, "I hope you don't mind if we interview you for our psychiatry course." Thus this student quite inadvertently betrayed the dichotomy in his thinking that Dr. Engel discussed earlier in Chapter 2 of this book. It is a false and highly destructive yet prevalent dichotomy: the "scientific" versus the "intuitive," "medical" versus "psychiatric."

Trends in medical education come and go, but currently there is quite an interesting one. Most medical schools in the United States have some kind of interviewing course. Typically it is taught early, during the preclinical years, and often it is dominated, if not exclusively run, by psychiatrists and mental health professionals. The intent of such courses is most surely noble. The idea originated in the reasonable wish to expose students to clinical contact with patients early in training; above all, such courses are meant to instill a humanistic appreciation for the patient as a person, not just as a vessel containing an interesting disease. Yet our latest educational tactic may have backfired. Too often students begin to associate humane, empathic attention to patients with "psychiatry." It is only a small step from this assumption to the conclusion that understanding the patient as a person has little to do with "real medicine" but is the province of "psychiatry"—just the opposite of what we educators intend. Furthermore, this very polarization is rife not only in the student's formal education but in most of the textbooks that are available.

Repeatedly we have observed the results of this polarization in the apparent existence of an almost dual clinical personality among medical students. When many students are on rounds with "psychiatric" types, they adopt, indeed find value in, the apparently more open-minded and holistic approach that psychiatrists take to patients. Hours or even minutes later these same students go on rounds with their surgery or internal medicine team and revert with equal facility and conviction to a highly content-oriented, symptom-focused view of the same patient lying in the same bed. Why this occurs is addressed more fully in Chapter 2. What does it really mean? Suffice it to say that students are not acting as conniving double agents willing to go with one perspective at this instant, then attaching readily to another the next. Rather, it seems more likely that both approaches, in their commonly polarized forms, fail to help students integrate the benefits of each perspective into a unifying approach for interacting with patients. Platitudes aside, this integration is really not so simple. On the one hand, a good doctor must be reflective, receptive, and sufficiently open and nondirective. He must allow the patient to open up. On the other hand, pressures of time and, more important, the need for specific data pertinent to diagnosis require that the doctor bird-dog certain paths of inquiry with rigor and specificity if he hopes to arrive at an accurate diagnosis. Both tasks, broadly construed, are essential to adequate and comprehensive management of any patient. Yet effecting a bridge between interviewing process and content turns out to be one of the most difficult, though unquestionably one of the most important, skills a clinician has to master.

We cannot hope to redress this imbalance here. What we do hope to do in the following section is to review briefly the conceptual bridge that we have found helpful in integrating these apparently disparate concepts—The A.R.T. of interviewing. The mnemonic device refers to three components of all good biopsychosocial interviewing: assessment, ranking, and transition. These terms are an attempt to offer a conceptual link between content and process in the clinical interview. Like all conceptual frameworks, this one should be viewed as a guideline and not as a set of rigid rules and nostrums. Really, there are no magical formulas in medicine, as much as we might wish them.

Assessment

Because most doctor-patient interactions begin with a period of mutual assessment, how the doctor and patient size each other up is based on a host of factors ranging from past experiences to the sense of intuition and "chemistry" that occurs the moment these two critical partners in the dyad first meet.

The patient begins to assess the doctor from the moment he walks in the door. Is he young? Is he old? Does he look stern or kind? Is he clean-shaven and youthful or long-haired and bearded? Each of these clues filter through a matrix of past biases and experiences. For instance, a young patient who is a member of the counterculture is apt to react far differently to a long-haired resident than to a staunch-looking conservative, and so on. The factors that go into assessment are instantaneous, inevitable, and highly complex. To a large extent, these factors are initially nonverbal.

For the doctor, assessment is more complex. He too has all the initial gut level responses to his patient. In addition, he draws on the memory of many other patients whom he has seen before. From the beginning, his assessment is based on clinical experience and personal memory. Is the patient cyanotic? Does she appear pale? Does he show visible pain? Is he moving all extremities? Finally, of course, an astute clinician keeps in mind the kind of impressions he is making on his new patient. What does the subtlety in a patient's mannerism and expression reveal about how the patient is assessing the doctor?

Doctors are accustomed to a very focused and goal-directed approach to history taking. They try to go after the facts, to pursue a line of inquiry that will yield the most data as quickly as possible. This is the reason why, traditionally, the chief complaint and identifying data come first and why the doctor then uses these data as guidelines. At first glance, it hardly seems worthwhile to pursue an extensive history of joint distress in a patient whose chief complaint is chest pain. Still, the key to effective assessment is the clinician's ability to maintain a relaxed and open-minded receptiveness. After all, the chest pain might be due to costochondritis or osteoarthritis of the spine. This is what Freud long ago called an "even-hovering attention." Such a stance is far less active than clinicians are accustomed to, and many doctors at all levels of experience find the restraint involved in this stance difficult. Yet it is critical. An experienced clinician is alert yet quiet and receptive. Especially during the initial phases of the interview, he must be vigilant yet allow his mind to wander where it will. He may be struck by a smell or an unusual color in the patient's hair. He might find himself curious about something he sees at the patient's bedside. As the patient's story begins to unfold, many thoughts cross the clinician's mind. He associates to other patients and to diseases he has seen in the past, journal articles he recalls, and syndromes he remembers from grand rounds. Hypotheses begin to form, and his attention becomes progressively more active and directed. Obviously this process depends on the extent of clinical and factual background the clinician possesses.

A beginning student cannot expect to "zero in" with the homing instincts of a highly experienced clinician. Yet with increasing experience, hypotheses begin to enter the student's mind during the assessment phase, and his attention begins to focus with increasing specificity and intensity. Obviously, this process of narrowing-in accurately improves with clinical experience, which brings to the advanced clinician a rich matrix of memories, cases, and factual knowledge. Regardless of one's level of experience, however, the diagnostic process should always begin with this phase of maximum open receptivity.

Perhaps it is partly a beginning student's lack of clinical experience that leads him early in training to focus in too fast, resorting to lists and specific questions—fired at the patient like shotgun blasts in every direction. Understandably, students may feel they have to shut their eyes, pull the trigger, and hope that with enough shots something will eventually fall out of the trees. Yet even the beginning student can learn the process of assessment. It is not a mysterious or an arcane art known only to the most advanced clinicians. Rather, it is a different way of being receptive to the empirical data of one's own observations, an approach that trusts the integrative abilities of the mind to sort through what is extraneous and begin to discern the figure from the background of a clinical problem. Although experience and knowledge are crucial, even beginning students have a far richer matrix of memory and logic to work from than they credit themselves with early in their training.

As we have suggested, assessment soon leads to an increased focusing-in as specific hypotheses are defined and refined and rapidly zeroed in on. However, this is not truly a linear process in any simple sense. Even at a very advanced stage of the clinical interview, a skilled physician keeps at least one part of his mind open. Even as he interrogates for the pertinent specifics, another part of his mind hovers freely, still relaxed and ready to be taken by surprise. Assessment is a process that occurs continuously throughout the diagnostic process with the patient, from beginning to end.

The highly nondirective stance of the assessment phase is also designed to ensure in the patient a sense of openness and trust. It encourages him to express any and all of his concerns, regardless of how trivial they might seem to him. For years psychiatrists have known the importance of beginning an interview with open-ended, nonleading remarks. This is important in any interview, whether "psychiatric" or "medical," terms we put in quotes because the biopsychosocial model views these as part of a continuum.

The extreme open-endedness of the initial assessment phase serves two purposes. It opens the clinician's mind to all data and possibilities. It permits the integrative and synthetic capacities of the clinician's own mind to begin to delineate critical features from a total gestalt. Secondly, it encourages the patient to bring up whatever seems important. Sometimes this is an emotional concern; but not infrequently it reveals an important physiological symptom that the patient might have dismissed as too trivial to warrant mention. Often these are the data that alert the clinician to where he should focus his attention.

Finally, though this hardly needs repeating, starting with an extremely open-ended question such as, "What sort of troubles have you been having?"; or with merely a simple inviting gesture of the hand that tells the patient to commence, communicates the most important message of all: *"You are my patient but you are a person before you are a patient, and it is you, the total human being, who concerns me, not just your disease."*

Ranking

As we suggested above, ranking of hunches, hypotheses, and priorities occurs rapidly during the diagnostic interview. Though it is often not a conscious process in the minds of many clinicians, it goes on constantly. Ranking—zeroing in the lens from wide angle to a focused close-up—is a skill that increases with experience the clinician's assessment of a problem's medical urgency and, finally, the clinician's personal style. We feel that too many doctors tend automatically to rank biomedical problems at the top of every list. In doing so, they not only miss important biomedical data the patient may think "too trivial" or "unrelated" to bring up but also risk communicating to the patient that they are interested only in the physiology and organ systems affected by the disease.

There are, of course, medical emergencies in which a thorough medical history—at times even a true emergency triage—must be preempted by the immediate need for medical intervention. For instance, a patient with a possible myocardial infarction or one suspected of having a subarachnoid hemorrhage must be assessed rapidly from a biomedical perspective. A more holistic approach to the total person may have to wait, but not for long. Remember Mr. Glover's arterial puncture and cardiac arrest in Chapter 2.

Actually, such situations are far less common than is sometimes thought. Most patients do not present in a state of extreme medical or surgical emergency. Almost always there is time for an initial phase of open-ended assessment—a warm and inviting gesture of the hand that says, "Tell me your story. I'm interested. I will look you in the eye and care about whatever you bring up. It is *you* I wish to understand."

Transition

Of the three skills contained in the mnemonic device, transitions are the easiest for even the beginning student to effect. Smooth transitions are critical to a good interview and make the difference between a bewildering and even frightening experience for the patient and one where a sense of collaboration and trust begins to grow. Despite this, surprisingly few clinicians effect transitions with clarity, reassurance, and a clear sense of purpose that the patient can grasp. Effecting transitions is really a matter of remembering to do it. We believe the reason clinicians often fail to do so is because they too often forget how terrified and "in the dark" a patient feels about his illness. For example, a clinician who suspects peptic ulcer disease but whose patient is currently talking about his fear of missing work may suddenly ask, "Have your stools ever turned black with this—black like tar?" The logic of such a question is obvious to the clinician, but the already frightened and bewildered patient may read far more ominous and confusing messages into such a radical shift. "The doctor is linking *my* problem, how can I manage to stay at work, with *black stools* . . . Does that mean I have *cancer?* . . . Is it a sign that I may not live?" Obviously, these apprehensions are always present. This is the reason why a good clinician must always pay attention to all of his patient and not just to a part of him. Smooth transitions can help. For instance, the doctor cited in this hypothetical example could have changed the subject by saying, "I'm sure you are concerned about getting back to work without jeopardizing the project you're working on. Let's get back to that, but I would like to turn my attention now more specifically to this pain you've been having in your abdomen, where you pointed a few moments ago. Let me ask you some specific questions that may help me understand the nature of the problem. Have you ever noticed any change in the color of your stools . . . " etcetera.

The real trick to effecting transitions is to remember that a patient is not a physician and cannot read your mind. Therefore when you shift lenses, whether it be to zoom in or pan out, share these transitions with the patient: Explain why you are shifting your line of inquiry at that particular point. It sounds simple, and it is, yet it is frequently overlooked at the expense of needless patient suffering.

Comments on A.R.T.

We have invoked the A.R.T. mnemonic device to delineate the three phases that we believe occur in all doctor-patient interactions. We feel there is considerable conceptual advantage in discussing them separately. The student should remember, however, that these three phases do not proceed in any simple lock-step fashion, with one phase leading neatly to the next. Actually, all three processes go on constantly and indeed simultaneously.

The A.R.T. paradigm was developed to help the interviewer establish an alliance with his patient that permits him to obtain important data in all three sectors of the biopsychosocial sphere. Its usefulness naturally increases with growing clinical knowledge and sophistication; but we believe the framework may be useful from the onset of clinical learning. Above all, the goal of this and kindred paradigms should be viewed as heuristic rather than prescriptive. The beginning student, especially, should not expect of himself a matrix of clinical experience that is not yet there. Beyond this, we believe that translating the biopsychosocial model into a readily applicable method of ongoing patient care has not yet been fully achieved. The field awaits further synthesis, a synthesis we are sure will come.

"Strategies," "Hip-Pocket Standbys," and "Pearls"

Every patient is different, and every doctor-patient relationship is unique. Most students appreciate this, but they also want answers—pearls, mnemonics, and tricks of the trade. Clinically, all students get into jams, and they want to know methods for getting out of them. Understanding is great, students say, but they also want some specific plans of attack and ways to get out of a pickle. Fair enough. But students must also remember that there are no foolproof tricks. From their own experience, they know full well that the very worst doctors are the ones who have memorized a dozen "tricks" and proceed to apply them with procrustean monotony to every patient. Still, there are some tricks of the trade; and with these cautionary observations, we offer some "pearls." Remember, though, they are not foolproof, nor are they ever a substitute for understanding.

1. *Wear a white coat.* We know it is not in vogue. We also know that students are very resistant to calling themselves "Doctor" before they actually receive their M.D. degree. Times and fashions change, for when one of the authors (DER) was a medical student (a scant 15 years ago), all students were admonished to call themselves "Doctor" from the time they were freshmen. Call yourself what you will, but for goodness sake wear a white coat! It is a courtesy to your patient. It also reduces the disadvantage your relative youth sometimes imposes. Patients feel reassured, not deceived, by the white coat. It identifies you as being associated with the health care professionals, not as a visitor, or heaven knows what! More generally, do not insult yourself and your patients by dressing like a slob. We need not spell out the specifics. Anyone with the intelligence and psychological resources to get into medical school can figure out what constitutes dress.

2. *Respect confidentiality.* You will see occasions when your professors and peers do not. Do not succumb to this debasing and unethical behavior. Confidentiality is stressed in the Hippocratic oath, and you will feel better when you practice it. You will feel like a doctor! Choose other ways to assert your individuality. That is your right—and patients are too vulnerable to be harmed in any way.

3. *Do not be afraid to be yourself.* Do not inhibit yourself by trying to imitate some caricature of a pseudo-Freudian statue. If patients joke and the joke is funny, laugh! Telling a patient a detail or two about yourself does not necessarily spell catastrophe. There are times

when it is appropriate, even indicated, to touch a patient or hold his hand. If you are naturally reserved, do not be phony, but do not be afraid to reach out and be human either. Remember, however, that physical contact is a very potent "drug" with huge side effects. It takes experience to know when to touch and when not to. However, you will never learn if you always keep your hands in your pockets. Remember also, though, that an understanding expression and kind word, spoken softly with empathy, can also "touch" a patient, sometimes far more deeply than any pat on the back. Always guide yourself by asking: Am I doing this for me or my patient?

4. *Be warm but not contrived.* Express your warmth in a way that sincerely reflects your own personality. Do not develop a repartee of cocktail-party jokes and glib social patter. Do not talk baseball scores and tennis strokes as a substitute for real warmth and interest in your patient. He has entrusted himself to your care. The matters he faces are very serious. The latest football scores are irrelevant.

5. *Let patients cry.* They do it all the time. Especially if your empathy has helped them to feel understood. Crying helps. Patients feel better. No one ever died of tears, and no one ever cries forever. If you were a patient, you might cry, too—alone in the hospital, sick, confused, in tremendous pain. A patient's tears often represent the highest tribute he can pay you. He would not cry in your presence if he did not feel understood and safe. Do not cut it off with jokes or banter. The same general principle applies to other strong affects—rage, fear, love. In general, words are preferable to actions, but all principles have exceptions. The expression "handholder" has fallen into undeserved disrepute. Generally, if feelings are being expressed at a reasonable decibel level and do not lead to furniture throwing, let your patients get their feelings out! Who knows? You might even find yourself holding a patient now and then. That is where it all began: The child's cry meant "hold me!"

6. *Think of your patient in developmental terms.* Read Levinson's book *The Seasons of a Man's Life* or Sheehy's *Passages.* It is difficult to know at 25 what it must be like to be 60. It helps to learn, and there are some good books to help you out.

7. *Remember that the patient is more scared than you are.* He is nervous about meeting you, and, remarkable as this may seem, he is even more self-conscious than you are. He *needs* you. Never forget for a minute how important it is for him to make a good impression on you. Do not let your own self-consciousness blind you to your patient's.

8. *Pay attention to feelings.* Pay attention to your patient's and *your* feelings. They are the best compass you have. You will get better at this as you mature clinically, but, at worst, you will probably turn out to be better at it than you think. Rest assured, the patient will tell you if you are wrong.

9. *Tell a patient what you think he is feeling.* Do not play "20 Questions." This is one of the most common errors made by beginning clinicians, including beginning psychiatrists. Think of yourself for a moment: Imagine that you are in the hospital for an exploratory laparotomy. You might have cancer. Which would be more helpful for you? A physician who says to you with an expression of concern, "It must be scary for you!" or a physician who rubs his perfectly manicured beard and with an expressionless face says, "How do you feel about your upcoming operation?" Over the years, fewer scenes have been more painful to us than the spectacle of a young psychiatrist asking a visibly suffering patient, "How do you feel?" This "neutrality" is one of several utterly stupid mythologies about relating to patients that somehow has gained widespread and undeserved credulity.

10. *Share your joys, and your pain, with a friend.* Without breaching patient confidentiality, reach out to your husband, wife, lover, friend, support group. If you need a psychotherapist, see one. Do not be a "lone soldier." Medicine is an incredibly intense undertaking. Doctors who end up killing themselves are usually the ones who tried to endure the pain alone. It just is not necessary—do not let deluded "stalwarts" convince you otherwise.

11. *With patients, who you are is far more important than the act you put on.* By and large, patients are not dumb. They know if you care about them or if you do not. You can be an absolute bumbler during interviews, during the performance of new procedures. In fact, we guarantee it—you *will* be! This is not license to subject your patient to excessive emotional or physical pain. Tell your resident or intern "No!" if they try to make you do something you cannot, but do not kid yourself—a patient will trust you and respect you even if you stumble over your questions and shine the ophthalmoscope in your own eyes—if he senses that you care. It is true that more-experienced clinicians can often instill greater confidence in their patients. Medicine is a field where one does get progressively better. Still, most of your patients will know what really matters and let you be their doctor even if you do stumble on your own shoelaces a time or two. They are nervous too.

12. *When an interview bogs down, try repeating the patient's last words.* The psychologist Carl Rogers first introduced the technique of repeating the last few words a patient says to encourage the patient to open up. Some interviewers try to get away with doing nothing *but* this, which is obnoxious and ridiculous. However, repeating the patient's words *can* be remarkably effective. It is as close as you will come in interviewing to a sure-fire trick. However, do not keep hitting the patient over the head with it. An attentive silence can also accomplish the same thing (see No. 14 below).

13. *Go ahead and ask the "unaskable."* If you are in touch with your own feelings and those of your patient, you may realize that a patient is

very scared or depressed. It may even occur to you that he is thinking about killing himself. Tragically, some patients do. Most do not,
but the real tragedy is aloneness—many think about death but feel
they cannot tell anybody. It is a devastating, guilty loneliness. Go
ahead and ask. Do not mince around. The same thing applies if you
suspect alcoholism, drug abuse, child-battering, and other socially
"delicate" areas. Yes, you will occasionally offend, but less often than
you think. Naturally, in giving this advice we are assuming that you
possess some sensitivity and tact. If you find yourself repeatedly
offending patients, get some help with what you are doing wrong.
Nine times out of ten, however, the opposite problem occurs.
Highly empathic students are afraid to say what the patient is already thinking anyway. Go ahead and say it.

Special note should be made here of sexuality. Despite our
"liberated" times, it is surprising—and suspicious—how often doctors "forget" to inquire about a patient's sexual concerns. Yet clearly
sex is part of being human, and it is frequently affected by illness.
Usually, however, the physician must inquire if he hopes to contribute to this aspect of the patient's care. Students sometimes fear that
they will probe or intrude where they do not belong. In fact, when
patients are given the opportunity to discuss sex, 50% raise concerns
with both gratitude and relief. By contrast, only 10% of patients
bring the matter up spontaneously. It is not just sex, but all taboos,
to which this admonition applies—fear of death, mutilation, sexual
dysfunction, cancer, suicide. Patients experience these concerns but
are afraid to say so. Ask! Be tactful, but ask. A patient lets you know
if you should back off. Usually, he opens up with tremendous gratitude and relief.

14. *Learn to be quiet.* When patients come to a point in their discussion
with you where they are getting to uncomfortable material, often
they fall silent. Silence is socially awkward, but as a professional you
can learn to use it. When a patient falls silent, go ahead and be silent
too! Yes, the pressure *does build.* It feels awkward. Seconds feel like
hours. Soon enough, however, the patient goes on, and usually he
goes on to tell you what really hurts him. People make fun of psychiatrists for their legendary silences. Sometimes psychiatrists do
overdo it, but generally the psychiatrist is on to something. The
taboos of normal social intercourse affect us all, and we all share the
impulse to avoid silence. Observe, for example, the rapidity with
which someone always jumps in at a dinner party with idle chitchat
or other banter the moment a group falls silent. The doctor-patient
relationship is no Sunday brunch. True—repeated, sadistically protracted silences reflect serious insensitivity, but most doctors would
do well to listen more and talk less. Allow a silence to occur. Try it!

15. *Pay attention to body language.* Body language is one of many avenues
that patients use to communicate. Recently this subject has received
considerable attention in both medical and lay publications, proba-

bly more than it deserves. Serious medical books try to explicate the way a person "speaks" through his body. Overnight, "experts" publish paperbacks and show up on TV talkshows promising to teach one how to reach another's innermost thoughts, fears, conflicts, and desires. In short, "body language" has become something of a fad. Yet, it *is* a very important way in which patients (and doctors) express themselves. Unlike the tongue, the body seldom lies.

Body language at the beginning of an interview is particularly revealing. Observe how a patient positions himself and moves at the outset of the interview. Watch the way he sits or stands, the way he seeks or avoids direct eye contact. Despite the proliferation of books on the topic, most students know innately what one posture is "saying" in contrast to another. Phylogenetically, body language is an old and highly reliable form of communication. We still use it. The trick, as with other observational skills, lies in being *conscious* of what we observe and in allowing ourselves to *think* about it.

As a student advances, especially if he learns how to listen to the process of communication as well as the content, body language becomes simply one of the many avenues through which patients communicate their concerns. However, it remains a perfectly reliable and legitimate source of understanding. It is a language that is always present and, by its nature, one incapable of dissembling.

16. *Start broadly and gradually focus in.* At the outset, it is rarely necessary or wise, to focus narrowly on any predetermined agenda. Allow the patient a few minutes to bring up whatever is on his mind. Listen. There is ample time to focus in on specifics as the interview proceeds. This concept is amplified in the discussion of A.R.T. above. The only possible exception to this principle is a medical emergency where rapid assessment of worsening physical symptoms is imperative.

17. *"The customer is always right."* Much has been written about the so-called "difficult" patient. Typologies have been developed to differentiate these types and strategies developed for managing them. These categories can be very helpful, though people are always more complicated than our most elegant schemata. Actually, there is one thing these very different and difficult patients share. In one way or another, they all faze the interviewer and, in some way, knock him off balance. The form of the attack can vary greatly—an impossible request, a refusal to cooperate, seductiveness, monotonous complaining. Whatever the specific form of the assault, however, the effect is always to disarm and put the interviewer on the defensive. This can lead to some terrific impasses and occasionally to no-win situations between doctor and patient. The interviewer often feels trapped by two impossible choices, neither of which will work. On the one hand, he can get defensive, which simply inflames the patient. On the other, he can try to be conciliatory and give in to the

demand, but this invariably leads to the demand's being repeated again in an escalated way. A better approach, odd as it may seem at first, is to agree with the patient. Let us take a simple example to illustrate:

> Mr. Penderhughes is a hostile 50-year-old senior department store manager who never seems to stop complaining about something being wrong with the way the hospital is treating him. When the student approaches him to request an interview, Mr. Penderhughes barks, "You're another one of those medical students, aren't you? I'll be damned if I'm going to be a guinea pig in this hospital!"

Clearly, arguing back is not going to work. Obsequious apologizing will not work either, for Mr. Penderhughes will stonewall the student anyway. Of course, the student—in some settings at least—can back off and forget the whole mess. Let the intern take care of it! However, the time comes, soon enough, when the student *is* in charge. A better approach with Mr. Penderhughes is to *agree*. "You're right, Mr. Penderhughes!" the student might respond. "We've all been using you to help us learn from the time you were admitted, haven't we?"

Another simple example: A sullen, depressed woman with Crohn's disease who says, "Why should I talk to *you?* It won't do any good." The student might consider saying, "Sounds like *nobody* here has been doing you much good. So maybe you're right—why should *I* be any different?"

Some people call this technique "going with the resistance," or "paradoxical intention." We personally prefer just to say: "The customer is always right." We may not always understand his complaint or the reasons for it, but surely he *has* them. So go ahead and agree!

This technique is by no means foolproof, but in a surprising number of instances the patient begins to talk. Mr. Penderhughes may begin, albeit angrily, to tell the student about all the people who promised him help, only to fail him in the end. Our depressed lady with Crohn's disease may sigh wearily and begin to speak of the numerous doctors and treatments that have already failed, as her disease is "hopeless anyway." Such talk may not be pleasant stuff, but at least the doctor-patient interaction has begun. This approach works far more often than one might imagine.

There Is No Such Thing as "Doing" or "Taking" an Interview in Medicine

The discussion of interviewing technique in this chapter is far from complete. We have only touched on a few highlights and thrown in 17 "pearls" that may occasionally help out in a pinch. However, even if the discussion were definitive, let us share with you a secret. We do not think there is any such thing as "doing" a medical interview, at least in any simple sense. Admittedly, it is a little brazen to say this in a chapter devoted to interviewing, but we say it. Our objection to the whole business of what people call interviewing goes back to the discussion about language in Chapter 4. Let us illustrate: A newspaper reporter can *do* an interview with a politician. A boss can *take* an interview from a job applicant. In such instances, one person is expected to get information, and the other is expected to provide it. This is just not how the doctor-patient relationship works. The doctor does not *take, administer,* or *perform* an interview on a patient. Likewise, the patient does not *give* a history, *provide* data, or *disclose* a 20-year drinking history. The doctor-patient relationship can seldom be reduced to give and get, do and be done to, administer and receive—at least not in any simple sense. Of course, all of these verbs apply at points, but only at some points. Szasz and Hollender, for example, have shown that the doctor-patient relationship can vary greatly in the type and extent of activity involved, especially the degree of mutual participation. At heart, it seems to us that the doctor-patient relationship is always precisely that—a *relationship,* a mutual process, a sharing that is both intimate and complex. Yet how consistently our choice of words betrays the ways we ignore this. We constantly talk of *ordering* a test, *taking* a history, *doing* a procedure. We so seldom speak of mutuality, so rarely acknowledge that we and our patients are actually in the same boat. Let us face the truth: We are, in fact, constantly collaborating with our patients, whether it is to obtain a history, treat an illness, or find the courage to face life's most cruel and puzzling mysteries. Yet so often we talk and act as though doctors were somehow themselves exempt from the very laws of nature—spared the vicissitudes of life and death. We pretend, instead, to be distant gods. We like to hover, curious and inquisitive but detached, over the petri dish of life, occasionally adding a drop from the end of our very long emotional pipettes. Why do we pretend that we are so different from our patients? Is it possible that at times we deny our humanness because our work exposes us to a side of humanness that can frighten us desperately? We think so. This is all terribly hard to admit, and to admit so relentlessly, so endlessly, so daily. We too get sick, go mad, grow old. We die. Perhaps this sounds morose, but we personally view the matter very differently. We believe that doctors can find the greatest meaning and joy in life when they admit that they too are a part of the most fascinating, terrifying, and unexplored continent of all—the human continent.

Hopefully, we will become ever more scientific in the study of our own humanness. Hopefully also, the power and the beauty of our calling will come from the humility and compassion we bring to that quest.

Suggested Reading

Binger, C. 1947. Why the professor fell out of bed. Harpers 195:337–342.

Levinson, D. J. 1978. The Seasons of a Man's Life. Knopf, New York.

Morgan, W. L., and Engel, G. L. 1969. The Clinical Approach to the Patient. W. B. Saunders, Philadelphia.

Reiser, D. E., and Schroder, A. K. 1980. Patient Interviewing: The Human Dimension. Williams & Wilkins, Baltimore.

Sheehy, G. 1976. Passages. Dutton, New York.

Snow, C. P. 1961. The Two Cultures and the Scientific Revolution. Cambridge University Press, New York.

Szasz, T. S., and Hollender, M. H. 1975. A contribution to the philosophy of medicine: the basic models of the doctor-patient relationship. In: T. Millon (ed): Medical Behavioral Science. Saunders, Philadelphia.

6 The Experience of Illness and Hospitalization

To become ill, even slightly so, is always disruptive. We forget just how disruptive, of course, as soon as we recover; but think back and recall how troublesome your last cold actually was. A cold is trivial enough, yet at the infection's height you probably could not think clearly and felt too uncomfortable to enjoy reading, music, friendship, or even food—and this was just a cold! When a person enters the realm of more serious illness, wrenching disruptions and profound feelings of anxiety and loss are inevitable. Moreover, illness forces change in a person: altered expectations, dashed hopes, and a fragmented self-image. The ill person does not choose to change—he must. Yet just as the Chinese symbol for crisis represents both danger and opportunity, illness can be an important, though unwelcome opportunity for new strength and inner growth, as well as a terrible threat. In this chapter we cover in broad overview some of the key concepts involved in understanding how a patient experiences illness and hospitalization. These include the stages of illness; the experience of illness depending on who the person is; the challenges of illness; coping mechanisms; and so-called "problem patients."

Stages of Illness

Much attention has been given recently to the phenomenon of health-seeking behavior. What are the factors that lead a person to identify himself as a patient? What motivates someone to call a doctor for an appointment or to drive to an emergency room and actively seek medical care? Obviously, the answer is multifaceted and based on much more than the mere presence or absence of a given symptom. *Who* the person is becomes critical, as do his previous experiences with illness, his perception of doctors, the reactions and pressures of his family, and the symbolism of the symptom—these and many other influences go into any person's decision to seek help. To give just one example: An otherwise healthy adolescent might well be apt to ignore increasing thirst and a pressure to urinate unless he knew from what had happened to his sister previously how diabetes can first present. Conversely, few people would ignore the appearance of blood in their urine. The cause of the blood in the urine might, or might not, be as ominous as the appearance of thirst and urinary frequency. Yet here the symbolism of the symptom becomes very potent. Few people could see blood in their urine without becoming alarmed. In most cases this alarm would drive them to seek medical attention, even if the ultimate cause of the hematuria turned out to be less serious than the discovery of juvenile-onset diabetes.

Health-seeking behavior is also greatly affected by the emotional, psychological, and social context in which physical symptoms appear. As we have emphasized so many times in this book, a complete and thorough physician *must* include an assessment of these as part of the evaluation of any patient. Consider, for example, the hypothetical case of two young mothers. Both are 26 years old and both have 5-month-old nursing infants. Let us assume also that both have "identical" headaches located in the same place, with attributes that are completely alike. Yet the headaches turn out to be vastly different for each when we consider the life setting in which they occur. Mother A. feels overwhelmed currently and terrified. At times she has felt suicidal. This is something that she has not told anyone and does not voluntarily tell her doctor unless he discerns how distraught she is and tactfully, but firmly, inquires into her depression. This mother will tell her physician (*if* she is asked) how every day she struggles with an urge to beat her screaming, colicky infant. On several occasions, in fact, she has come close. She is terrified that the urge will get out of hand. Nor would such an occurrence be foreign for her. As a young child she was beaten repeatedly and severely by her own mother. When she calls her physician for an appointment, however, she reports only "headaches."

Mother B., our other woman with headaches, can fortunately be dealt with more briefly. Her life is reasonably happy; her family setting is safe and secure; and she is well integrated psychologically, with a stable sense of self-esteem. She does not, in fact, think to call the doctor. Two aspirin tablets seem to do the trick, and she never actually picks up the phone.

Identical headaches, but vastly different problems. To discern this, however, the physician must appreciate his patient's difficulty at different levels of the systems hierarchy. A note in the chart that reads "tension headaches likely, rule out CNS tumor or migraine" is just not adequate. Yet some physicians limit the focus of their inquiry to just this degree. If a doctor were to put on such blinders in his assessment of Mother A., she would doubtless leave the office with a muttered, "Thank you, doctor," most likely with a prescription in her hand (that may never be filled, much less taken). She will have left with her real pain unexpressed, possibly to go home and explode. And the doctor might well believe that he has a satisfied patient and has done a competent job.

Finally, we wish to emphasize one subtle, yet critical point regarding the management of these "identical" headaches. The proper intervention is derived from an understanding of systems theory—it is not a matter of "bedside manner" or "clinical intuition." A nonsystems-oriented physician might or might not see value in inquiring about a patient's circumstances and life. He might think of this as interpersonal warmth, humanism, viewing the patient "holistically," or some other phrase that is currently popular—or he might consider such matters basically trivial. A physician who understands systems theory knows differently; viewed from this perspective, understanding a patient comprehensively is not *nice* or optional—it is essential. A systems approach makes it clear that Mother A's headache is affected, possibly even precipitated, by the emotional stresses she faces. To inquire of her about these is not being "kind" or "sensitive," it is being diagnostically complete. To reiterate: changes at any one level of the systems hierarchy invariably affect the functioning of systems at many other levels of the hierarchy. The rage, frustration, and despair that Mother A. feels at the level of the two-person system (she and the child) and at the family level of the system (Where is her husband? What roles has her own child abuse played in her life?) have *effects* at the organ system level. The precise nature of these effects has yet to be well delineated, though promising research is appearing. For example, it seems likely that psychosocial stresses, such as the ones Mother A. is experiencing, have an impact at the neuroendocrine level with resultant pathophysiological, including immunological, changes.

The reason why it is so critical to grasp the highly interactive nature of different levels in the systems hierarchy is because without such an understanding the physician is not able to prescribe the best treatment for the patient. For Mother A., this treatment obviously involves more than the prescription of pain tablets. It is true that Valium may relieve her muscle spasm and codeine, the subjective experience of pain, but these interventions do nothing to alter the disturbances at higher levels in the systems hierarchy that are precipitating the problem. The physician must help Mother A. to deal with her concerns about her parenting capacities and the current relationship with her husband and child. This is not being "nice" or "holistic." It is the only rational treatment strategy to be applied in this case. Finally, a physician who truly understands systems theory is not prone to say when the woman experiences relief from the headaches (after proper diagnosis and treatment at all levels of the system) that she was "just being hysterical" or "using the headaches as a ticket of admission." He does understand *why* the headaches got better, and why the 20-minute counseling session that he conducted with Mother A. and her husband was a potent therapeutic intervention resulting in effective treatment of her headaches and painful situation.

Given the contextual nature of illness and the importance of viewing it from a systems perspective, it should be possible to conceptualize an evolving illness broadly, encompassing more than pathophysiology alone. Reiser and Schroder proposed that one way to conceptualize reactions to illness is to view serious illness as a *developmental crisis,* occurring within the overall context of a person's life. From such a perspective, illness may be viewed as a new, and sometimes critical, challenge to a person's homeostasis and sense of identity. As this crisis evolves, three important stages in that evolution may commonly be discerned: *awareness, disorganization,* and *reorganization.* In the discussion that follows, we attempt to delineate some important characteristics of each of these stages. The reader should bear in mind, however, that people are inevitably more complicated than the schemata we invent to categorize them. Our own cubbyholes are no exception to this limitation. Still, there may be some value in recognizing that illness is an evolving process with often critical implications for human development, and not just some unfortunate moment frozen in time, quickly to be forgotten.

Awareness

Awareness, above all, is characterized by *ambivalence.* As it begins to dawn on a person that something is wrong, whether it be in his body or his mind, a terrible conflict sets in: Does one struggle to deny the problem and pretend that nothing has changed? Or does one acknowledge the dreaded truth and begin to seek answers? Reason and logic notwithstanding, most people seem to do both, either simultaneously or in rapid succession. One moment the typical patient dismisses the problem altogether, "It's just a cold." The next he is convinced of the worst, "I know it's cancer." This is a period of great anxiety and bewilderment. Often it is mercifully brief. The symptoms abate, normal functioning returns, and the person "forgets" that anything ever was, or could be, seriously wrong. Fortunately, it did turn out to be just a cold! Some illnesses, however, are more serious and do not go away. People so beset, so frightened and conflicted, soon become our patients—a role transition that is far from painless or simple.

Why not use the simpler and more common term "denial" in place of the concept of *awareness* and *ambivalence* about knowing the truth? After all, we commonly hear that people early in an illness use "denial"—and indeed, they do! The problem with the term is its static, nondynamic connotation. When people use denial, they never do so completely or with total success. This is because denial is only *half* the patient's conflict. A person *wishes* to know the truth, even as he fights to *deny* the truth. The concept of denial is ultimately too simplistic to describe what a patient experiences at this stage of illness. During the stage of awareness, one part of the person *needs* to know, *craves* to know, and *prays* to know. Simultaneously, another part of the person needs *not* to know, craves *not* to know, and prays *not* to know. Both parts are equally intense and during the stage of awareness find themselves in active conflict with each other.

Most readers can appreciate what the stage of awareness is like for a seriously ill person by recalling the fleeting health worries that we all have had at one time or another when some "trivial" symptom has appeared. Medical students reading this book especially should have no trouble understanding this state. For a period in their education, every new disease that students learn about tends to induce in them the very understandable fear that they might now get it. Although this is sometimes laughingly called the medical student's "hypochondriasis," it is actually a painful and frequently inevitable part of learning to be a physician. Students so beset can understand the patient's ambivalence. "That bump on the elbow *probably* is just a bump"—but still, the thought intrudes, "it could be *cancer*." "That nosebleed I got doesn't mean I have leukemia—after all, I've gotten nosebleeds like this since I was a kid." Yet, then, the more dreaded thought—"leukemia!" To empathize fully with the patient's experience, the student must only imagine that the bump does not go away but grows bigger, that the nosebleeds become more intense and frequent. Now denial begins to fail. Something *is* amiss! Something is very wrong! The intense anxiety and marked ambivalence a patient experiences during this stage clearly can become quite excruciating. Finally sometimes the struggle to continue to deny can have tragic consequences, as in the patient who denies symptoms of a myocardial infarction and fails to get to the hospital on time or the patient who fails to get a mass biopsied before it metastasizes and spreads.

Disorganization

The stage called *disorganization* is a highly traumatic period for virtually everyone who experiences it. It is typically, though not universally, heralded by intense confusion, despair, and anxiety as coping mechanisms the patient had invoked during the stage of Awareness begin to crumble. At this stage, the patient finally realizes, often with a sudden shock of conviction, that something really is wrong with him, a realization beyond any possibility for rationalization or denial. It is no longer possible to deny or hope that the problem will somehow disappear. The ECG is confirmatory. It *is* a heart attack! The blood count comes back grossly leukemoid. It *is* leukemia! In some patients the moment of truth comes long before official pronouncements or confirmatory laboratory tests. For others, it may be forestalled, as the patient continues to protest even in the face of hard evidence, "That just *can't* be right!" When the realization occurs, however, a profound disruption in functioning results. Suddenly everything has changed, leaving the patient feeling overwhelmed, powerless, helpless, and shattered. Hopes, dreams, plans for the future may no longer pertain. Important relationships are suddenly altered. The patient's relationship to his own *body* is dramatically altered. Above all, the patient now experiences a *shattering of omnipotence.*

When a person finds it impossible to deny any longer that something is seriously wrong, a universal human defense is demolished—the magical belief that "It could never happen to me." Disease, disfigurement, death—these things happen to *someone else, not to me.* This is obviously a preposterous bit of human hubris and self-deception, yet it is one we engage in, so long as we are healthy, virtually 100% of the time. Indeed, the deception seems to be almost integral to normal functioning, and when this defense goes an individual's reality changes radically. One reason, we believe, that physicians and other caretakers often shun dying patients has to do with this defense. The undisputable *truth* of death is embodied too vividly in the sight of a suffering, terminal patient. The most dedicated among us may be tempted to back away to preserve *our* illusion of omnipotence.

During this stage patients feel cut off, and indeed they are. The sick person is severed from all of his usual connection to everyday life—schedules, habits, activities, friends, family, and work as well as hobbies, TV shows, favorite pipes, coffee mugs, and slippers. He is trundled down tiled corridors through doors that say "No Admittance." Naked, he is dressed in a hospital gown. He is deposited in an unfamiliar hospital bed, dependent on anonymous if well-intentioned strangers. No wonder such a person feels isolated, depressed, and demoralized—cut off not only from his routine and people but from his very sense of self. There are accompanying distortions in thinking that occur during this stage—increasingly idiosyncratic, superstitious, and self-centered preoccupations that the ill person abhors, yet cannot help. Strangely, perhaps, there is often guilt. Many patients believe at some level that their illness is a punishment for some transgression. For others, illness invokes a sense of helpless rage. Like Job, they ask bitterly, "Why me?"

That this period of crisis is profoundly painful for a patient should be obvious. To be effective a physician must have empathy for the turmoil the patient is suffering; he must be able to reach out across that chasm of terror, isolation, and loneliness as best he can. To do this, the physician has to have done some serious introspecting of his own and come to some inner peace about his own mortality. If he has not, he will defensively back away just when the patient needs him most. The physician should also recognize that although no patient would ever invite such a crisis, the radical introspection it forces on a person can lead to increased wisdom and new life perspectives. Illness always seems to yield a bitter harvest, but sometimes it has an unanticipated fruit—the opportunity to expand as a person, to change, and to grow.

During this stage of Disorganization, some people progress rapidly to death. Many more, mercifully, go on to recovery. Usually they too try to "forget"—but really there can be no forgetting. Once a person has been seriously ill, he *has* changed. A man who has had a heart attack is not the same man who has *not* had a heart attack. His cardiac enzymes may be back to normal. His ECG may look good. He may take up jogging and achieve a robust new sense of health. Whatever he does or does not do, however, he is, forever after, a man who has had a heart attack. In life, the moving hand does indeed write. Whatever the eventual outcome of a specific illness, that hand moves continuously on. A heart attack or a bout with cancer can never be undone, washed out, cancelled from memory. We can excise a tumor from a person's body, but we cannot abate the meaning of that experience from a patient's life. Above all, we believe that the shattering of omnipotence changes a person from then on. Of course, the terror recedes and the defenses return, but at some level a person who has been seriously ill has seen his own mortality. Such a person is altered—wiser on occasion, often not—but not the same. By the nature of the work, a similar transformation also occurs in most doctors.

Reorganization

Though the reality of illness seems overwhelming at first—imagine what it would be like to suddenly have cancer—the stage of Disorganization is usually surprisingly brief. Somehow the unbearable is borne, the unthinkable is assimilated—and all this with an alacrity that is sometimes astonishing. At some point, and usually sooner than later, the ill person begins to accept the reality of his disease and to grasp the changes it has wrought, the tasks in the future that must be faced. The ill person begins to acknowledge, in one form or another, that the illness is no longer something foreign that "has happened to me." Rather, he realizes, "It *is* me." . . . "I have not been *attacked* by diabetes, I am a person *with* diabetes." Typically a patient's emergence from Disorganization into Reorganization is heralded by statements such as: "You've got to go on" or "You can't lay around feeling sorry for yourself forever" or "What's done is done; you've got to accept and get on." These and similar expressions convey two essential features of the stage of Reorganization: (1) the *recognition* that one cannot stop time or turn back the clock ("You have to go on"), and (2) *acceptance* (the patient no longer fights or denies the reality of his condition).

For a patient and his family, the phase of Reorganization is the most important part of the illness. For example, if you were to ask a woman who has undergone a radical mastectomy for breast cancer to describe her experience, chances are she would dwell primarily on concerns that pertain to the Reorganization phase—living with the disfigurement, the fears of recurrence, worries about the reaction of her husband, where to get mastectomy brassieres—all the things that would matter to any person facing life with a recent diagnosis of cancer and the hasty amputation of one of her breasts. Contrast this picture, however, with what her *physician* would likely say were *he* asked to describe Mrs. Smith's bout with breast cancer. Very likely, he would launch into a discussion of diagnosis, staging, pathology reports, questions of radiation therapy versus chemotherapy, and whether a mastectomy or a lumpectomy was indicated. This is perfectly understandable. Such technical considerations are a large part of what every physician thinks about and does. Yet we can also see that the physician's concerns are very much out of harmony with his patient's. In contrast to her concerns, most of which have to do with the phase of Reorganization, the physician is primarily concerned with the Disorganization phase of illness. Clearly, this can be a serious problem. From the outset of their education, medical students are exposed almost exclusively to people in the stage of Disorganization, hospitalized patients who are in the most acute stages of illness. As soon as the patient is stable enough to leave the hospital, he is discharged from the student's care and all too often from the student's mind. Experienced physicians in primary care who see such patients year after year know reality is far different; but the young physician in training tends to view the experience of illness and the scope of his responsibilities as being limited to the phase of Disorganization. Nothing could be more misleading, for from the patient's perspective and his family's, when the time for discharge from the hospital arrives, the illness process has barely just *begun*.

A better understanding of what a patient faces during Reorganization is far from trivial. It is here that a physician can often make a real difference. This phase contains great opportunities for growth, increased wisdom, a deeper sense of love, and enhanced spiritual meaning. It also contains the equally real potential for human failure. A patient may give up, withdraw, and become embittered and defeated for the rest of his life.

We are all moved by sagas of heroism, stamina, and grace displayed by the gravely ill. Helen Keller's courage has moved people for generations and will doubtless continue to do so. We all admire the rectitude and forbearance of Franklin Delano Roosevelt, who conducted the presidency from his wheelchair. Lou Gehrig died of amyotrophic lateral sclerosis (since then called Lou Gehrig's disease), but the nation remembers him most for the dignity he displayed to the very end.

By contrast, we are considerably less comfortable with Reorganization's darker side. Many physicians feel highly uncomfortable when confronted by patients who *fail to* "get better," "take care of themselves," or "do their part." Permit an example: A formerly successful businessman has a myocardial infarction and then becomes a "cardiac cripple." A year later his myocardium has mended, but he has resigned his employment and lives on disability insurance. His wife is distraught and on the verge of divorcing him because of his brooding self-preoccupation and refusal to initiate any sexual activity whatsoever. He has given up all hobbies, sports, and interests. Most days he just sits, watches television, and broods. He laments, with melancholic self-pity, that his life is "over." Initially, perhaps, a physician has sympathy for such a patient. He may exhort him to try harder, reminding him that the prognosis is much better than he seems to believe. Sooner or later, though, the physician is apt to grow weary, defeated, and ultimately disgusted by this patient's stonewalling and ultimate failure to surmount his illness and go on with life. Finally, such patients get labeled. They are called "crocks," "chronics," "hypochondriacs," or "psych cases." These cruel and casually misapplied epithets refer, of course, to human beings, and their use should always be discouraged. When they are used in this context, however, the doctor is communicating something very specific. He is saying, "I can't stand the sight of helplessness, passivity, dependence, depression, and giving up. These are all experiences that I would fight in myself and would dread ever succumbing to. Therefore when I see a patient succumbing to them, I feel threatened and back away defensively, experiencing, instead of empathy, contempt and disgust."

Many factors ultimately determine whether a patient grows or regresses during this stage. They include: (1) the patient's personality and previous experience with illness and doctors; (2) the meaning of the illness to the patient; (3) the patient's support system; (4) the environment; (5) the severity and nature of the disease process (e.g., a malignant and disfiguring illness may be especially devastating); and (6) the effectiveness of medical care, including that given by the patient's doctor.

Sometimes, it is true, we doctors have a perception of ourselves that is grandiose and inflated. Here, however, the problem is actually the opposite: For many of us it is difficult to acknowledge that we matter so much. Patients who are brave, dignified, and successful are obviously going to be easier for us to deal with than those who are frightened, regressed, angry, and inconsolable. Yet the latter comprise many of our patients. They need us, too. Sometimes they need us the most desperately of all. Could it be that our "cardiac cripple" might have been helped, might *still* be helped, by a physician who took the time—not to give more lectures of stiff-upper-lip pep talks, but to form an empathic alliance where the patient felt supported and understood. Perhaps with such an alliance he still might feel safe enough to face what frightens him. Possibly. We should also consider the worst. It is possible that this patient, even with the best of support from his physician, will *still* fail to bounce back. These depressing outcomes can and do occur in medicine—all the time. Even with this, is he our patient any the less? Does he need us any the less? To the contrary, it is this patient who needs us most! Isolated, rigid, unable to change, such patients experience profound loneliness and suffering. Eventually they drive everyone away, psychologically if not literally. They grow to be shunned by society and held in contempt (something they are aware of). Perhaps *only* a physician can transcend these prejudices and manage to view his suffering patient in an accepting and nonjudgmental manner. Surely the patient is in pain. Even if we cannot cure him of the corrosive nihilism that is eating away at his soul, we can still soothe him. We can reassure him that we will not abandon him. As doctors, we can attempt as best we can to ease his pain and suffering—one of our most ancient and fundamental responsibilities.

In closing this section, we wish to repeat what we said earlier: This view of illness as a developmental process is only a model. Like any model, it can be useful if it provides a foundation for increased conceptual clarity and understanding. It can remain useful so long as it remains heuristic and is not applied mindlessly, uncritically. Unfortunately, models have a considerable tendency to degenerate into nostrums and "gospel truths," at which point they lose their usefulness. The advantage of viewing illness as development, so long as we heed the above warning, may be twofold. First, modern medicine has tended to forget that people are part of a rich and complicated life setting, a context in which all of them fall ill. Doctors trained in contemporary medical institutions too often seem to regard the world as though it were a huge admissions area, depositing endless legions of sick people at the physician's doorstep to be examined and studied. Actually, doctors and hospitals are threads woven through the fabric of a person's experience, not the warp and weft of life itself. Second, exphasizing illness as development does draw our attention to another neglected area—the importance of the physician *throughout* a patient's illness. Too often doctors come to think of themselves as responsible for patients only during the most acute phase of illness, a problem we discussed above. The current structure of medical education, in fact, makes this therapeutic astigmatism almost inevitable. Yet the bulk of our patients are people with life-long disease. The afflictions may vary—from arthritis to diabetes, from heart disease to schizophrenia. What they all have in common is that they do not go away. By thinking of illness as development, it may be easier for doctors to begin to understand what it would be like to be someone with a chronic illness, a life-long illness—what it would really mean to walk in that person's shoes, not for a few yards or quarter of a mile, but for the distance, mile upon mile, year stretching into year. We doctors are needed along that pathway, too.

The Experience of Illness Depends on Who the Person Is

In large measure, the experience of illness depends on who the person is. It is for this reason that we must heed our patient's personality and coping style, not simply because we wish to psychologize. How the individual handles being sick reflects his attitudes, defenses, strengths, weaknesses, and philosophy of life. If the sick person is a "fighter," for example, one who always seems to bounce back from adversity, this style may well predict how he will cope with serious illness. A superb example of such a fighter is depicted in *Heartsounds* by Martha Weinman Lear. This book is a very moving account of a doctor's own cardiac illness as it progresses through acute and chronic stages and finally ends in death. The book was written by his wife with much input from the physician himself and maintains an intensely personal tone throughout. It is eminently readable and richly instructive, a book difficult to put down once you begin. The account begins with Dr. Harold Lear's first heart attack and his initial adjustment to that sudden illness. Eventually he undergoes open heart surgery and as a result tragically succumbs to organic brain damage. Yet right up to his death he remains a fighter. His will to live is truly astounding and inspiring.

Dr. Lear expresses how he felt when he realized that modern technological medicine had nothing to offer him and he was going to die. His reflections also illustrate a positive outcome in the transition from Disorganization to Reorganization. He faces his reality, but he does not give up.

> I am not losing hope . . . I know I'm not going to get any better. That's hard to take. What always helped me in the past was thinking, later I'll be better. I don't think that any more—wiping his eyes—but I'm not giving up. I'm simply accepting my realities. I may challenge them sporadically, but my denial is much less now. The closer people can be to their realities, the better off they are.

> The paradox is that in many ways I'm happier now than I've ever been. I never thought about how I might cope with sickness. I was the doctor.

Now I look back at all these things that happened to me, emerging from these experiences with holes in my head, and I wonder how I was able to cope. What was there in me that allowed me to survive as well as I did emotionally? Why aren't I in a deep depression? I don't know. I guess it's still my father. 'You've got to make the best of it.' That's what he always told me. And I try to, and I'll never give up. [p. 371]

The profound, critical importance of this—not giving up—is also expressed by the young physician who cared for Harold Lear during the last months of his life. Dr. Fried gave this eulogy at Dr. Lear's funeral:

. . . Since the way a man dies, just as the way he lives, is often a solid measure of his spirit, it is appropriate that we share perceptions of his very last days. . . Harold Lear was a physician who understood every detail of his pathology and prognosis. He knew exactly the conditions of battle, he was not awed, and he fought like hell. . . . [p. 498]

It is clear that Dr. Fried fought like hell too. Like his physician-patient, Dr. Fried also did not give up. Along with Dr. Lear's own family, the young physician stood by him with unwavering support.

Dr. Lear wanted *Heartsounds* to be written because he felt that if physicians knew what it is really like to be profoundly ill they would treat their patients far differently, with much greater sensitivity and empathy, perhaps also with more courage and a sense of pride and hope. Read it—we think you will agree.

Elsewhere in the book, Lear's wife cries out in consternation, lamenting a physician who, she felt, abandoned her husband at a critical point in his care. He is referred to as Moses, or Moe, in the text, and in the passage below, she castigates him for transferring her husband's care to his younger associate just when the going got rough:

. . . You do not do such a thing, Moses, to such a patient who comes to you at such a time, humbled by disease. You perhaps have never been deeply and chronically ill; you perhaps do not know from within how sickness humbles—how it clouds and corrodes and befouls the sense of self. I do not know why this should be so, that physical disease plays such cruel vanquishing tricks upon the ego, even the sturdiest ego, given time enough. But I have seen it happen here, to this fine strong man, and I have read a bit about such things and I know that this is classic in long chronic disease; this is what the failures of the body do unerringly to the soul. And I know this much, Moses, surely you know it too. And you are neither an unkind nor an uncaring man. So why do you reject him now, when his ego is so fragile? Could it be that yours is not fragile enough? Too thick a hide, eh? Or that you are angry at this sick patient for remaining so intransigently sick? Or—this being my darkest suspicion—that you can do nothing more for him and so choose, in subliminal ways, to wash your hands? Not that I wish illness upon you, Moses, may you never have illness, but perhaps it would teach doctors something they do not know. Or know only theoretically, which is not enough. Perhaps there should be a way to induce illness, pseudo-illness, something dreadful but safe, with clear parameters, that would last, say, for a year and wreak all due havoc upon the body and spirit before it disappeared. A required course at all medical schools; no one graduates without two consecutive semesters of chronic, debilitating sickness. What do you think, Moe, old friend, old eminence: would that make better doctors? [pp. 272–273]

Mrs. Lear is obviously very angry and understandably so, but she raises a key question: What enabled Dr. Fried to care and remain attached when Moses could not? She ventures a plausible guess: Moe fled not because he was callous but because Lear's dying hurt too much. Though her anger at Moe is understandable, we should not follow suit. Instead, we should try to understand. It is difficult to remain committed to suffering, dying patients, especially when they are doctors like ourselves. For Moe, older and more vulnerable, it might have been too much like looking in a mirror. Moe, in fact, attended the funeral visibly in pain. This was not the act of a cold and indifferent man. Like Chiron, of Greek legend, Moe had been wounded—a wounded healer.

Dr. Lear's heroism is inspiring. Yet we must also be prepared for patients who respond very differently—who regress, fall apart, give up. These people, too, have their reasons. No one consciously chooses to fail, and often there are discernible reasons why people do. How would Dr. Lear have fared, for instance, without his wife's tremendous love and support? Our empathy must go out all the more to those patients who are not so brave, who are "difficult" or "weak." Doctors are often surprisingly, and disturbingly, angered by these so-called "problem patients." We believe that part of the difficulty may come from the physician's own fears of regressing and losing control. Few prospects frighten doctors more.

We have been talking, of course, about the pivotal importance of hope. Over and over, our patients teach us that hope is crucial and sometimes highly predictive of prognosis as well. We cannot measure hope, unfortunately, the way we can stage lymphomas. Yet its vicissitudes are just as important and its effects just as powerful. With relentless regularity, patients who give up quickly deteriorate. The phenomenon cannot be explained by levels of organ impairment alone. The matter is still more complex: Just as the physically afflicted go downhill once they give up, somatic illness itself is often heralded by circumstances in life where a physically healthy person gives up hope. This surrender can take many forms. A classic one is severe grief. It is well illustrated by the case of a woman we shall simply call Mrs. Smith. The story begins with the husband.

Mr. Smith, a 68-year-old man with metastatic bronchogenic carcinoma, was admitted to the hospital because of marked difficulty breathing.

Examination disclosed large bilateral pleural effusions. Mrs. Smith was 67 years old and required daily insulin for her diabetes. During Mr. Smith's hospitalization, she was constantly at his bedside, day and night. On the third hospital day Mr. Smith began coughing up massive amounts of blood and died. Mrs. Smith was briefly comforted and then asked to give permission for the autopsy. She assented. The busy physician in charge of the case then had no further contact with Mrs. Smith, nor did he expect to. Ten days later, Mrs. Smith was back all too forcefully. She came in comatose—her diagnosis severe diabetic ketoacidosis. With rapid and appropriate management, she soon regained consciousness. When queried about what had transpired, she lucidly described a deep feeling of exhaustion. She just could not muster the energy to give herself her insulin injections after her husband's death. Yes, she said she understood the consequences of this inaction but had felt totally paralyzed and inert.

Over the course of her hospitalization, with the assistance of a sensitive medical student, she began to express her profound sorrow and sense of loss since her husband's death. When she was discharged, she still grieved but was able to manage her insulin and diet once again. In a real sense, helping her to begin the grief process permitted her to resume control over her diabetes and her life.

Engel also illustrates the giving-up response dramatically in his paper, "Giving-up/Given-up Complex."

. . . This concerns a couple, Charlie and Josephine, who had been inseparable companions for 13 years. In a senseless act of violence Charlie, in full view of Josephine, was shot and killed in a melee with the police. Josephine first stood motionless, then slowly approached his prostrate form, sunk to her knees, and silently rested her head on the dead and bloody body. Concerned persons attempted to help her away, but she refused to move. Hoping she would soon surmount her overwhelming grief, they let her be. But she never rose again; in 15 minutes she was dead.

Now the remarkable part of the story is that Charlie and Josephine were llamas in the zoo! They had escaped from their pen during a snow storm and Charlie, a mean animal to begin with, was shot when he proved unmanageable. I was able to establish from the zoo keeper that to all intents and purposes Josephine had been normally frisky and healthy right up to the moment of the tragic event. No autopsy was performed, so we can go no further in explaining the death.

Engel cites this example not simply for drama but to underscore the fact that we are dealing with an evolutionarily deep, essentially mammalian phenomenon. Devastating, even fatal grief is not simply a quirk of "neurotic" and "oversensitive" human beings—attachment is rooted in biology, and loss really can break a heart and end a life.

Schmale and Engel outline five characteristics of a condition they call the giving-up/given-up complex and which seems to be associated with the onset of illness: (1) feelings of helplessness and/or hopelessness; (2) a depreciated self-image; (3) a loss of pleasure and meaning normally derived from important relationships and roles in life; (4) a disrupted sense of the vital continuity in one's life that links past, present, and future; and (5) a reactivation of memories of earlier periods of giving up. It seems to constitute a psychological state in which vulnerability to pathogenic factors is increased.

The myriad ways in which people respond to illness are naturally as varied as people are themselves. Although it is useful to delineate some general principles about how patients respond to illness, people are just too rich, complex, and innately resilient to fit into any neat schemata. Generalities help but do not suffice when we face the person in that bed who is sick and needs our help.

To assist our patients as individuals is possible. Although people cannot be neatly categorized, approaches to understanding people can. A few of the important ones are learning about a person's personality structure or style, his usual coping mechanisms, the adaptive and mal-adaptive experiences in his life, his past experiences with illness, his family relationships and circumstances, his personal attitudes. The su-perordinating principle is to attempt to understand each person as the unique individual he is, and this is not impossible. Given the chance to talk about himself, provided by the patient-centered interview approach described in Chapter 5, he usually tells you what is important about himself, and these disclosures have a value that goes far beyond estab-lishing rapport. If you can find out from a person who he is and who he has been, you will have a good chance to know who he is about to be— and you do not have to be a genius. He will tell you, if only you will listen! And watch! And feel! This knowledge will obviously have imme-diate and compelling relevance to one's treatment approach, one's style of supporting the patient's own strengths, and one's sense of the mal-adaptive behaviors to look out for in a particular patient. Recall Ms. Johnson (Johnnie) and Mr. Glover in Chapters 1 and 2.

Challenges of Illness

Illness—any illness—disrupts. It poses serious and sometimes horren-dous challenges. Some of these have been described by Moos and Tsu. The list is vivid, but we should heed it for it is also very accurate, though inevitably incomplete.

1. *Dealing with pain, discomfort, and incapacitation.* These are a part of every illness. The amount of pain and its intensity vary with each

patient. All pain is real, and understanding the patient's perception of his pain is critical to effective care. Also, understanding the patient's view of his illness and the accompanying incapacitation or disability is essential to helping each patient recover from acute illness or to accept limitations in function associated with chronic illness.

2. *Dealing with the problems posed by treatment procedures themselves* and the actual hospital environment (e.g., the special concerns imposed by invasive diagnostic tests and by the ICU or CCU experience). Patients undergoing technical procedures and treatments with real risks and in strange hospital environments cry out for helpful information, understanding, and human support.

3. *Developing positive relationships with caregivers.* For example, dealing with conflicting information, staff styles, covert and overt disagreements can be not merely bothersome but terrifying. To take a common example, many patients find it difficult to engage their physicians in a true partnership, one where the patient feels his preferences about treatment are respected and heeded. Breakdowns in the therapeutic relationship may arise from shortcomings on either side of that critical dyad. Yet when these occur, it is all too tempting for the doctor to blame his patient, attributing the patient's apparent intransigence to "neurosis" or a bad attitude. Sometimes physicians retaliate; ironically, the "punishment" is occasionally a psychiatry consult. By contrast, the astute clinician continually strives to monitor and understand his own reactions to his patients. There is actually a gold mine of information about difficulties the patient is having—not the frustration that is so often perceived. Some patients, of course, do have difficult and even contratherapeutic character styles. They cannot help it, and such patients challenge the wisest, kindest, cleverest, and most tolerant among us. How ironic that these very people are so typically thrust on impressionable young students and house officers as their first learning cases! Yet the rewards of making a difference in the lives of such people—even a small one— can be immeasurable. More often than one might think, students turn out to be the very best physicians for these "impossible patients" whom others have written off.

4. *Dealing with upsetting feelings.* As great as the physical discomfort can be, the mental pain of illness is often even worse. Patients suffer feelings of grief over physical loss or incapacitation, apprehension about the future, self-blame, failure, and isolation from people who are healthy. Such feelings are always difficult. Nor is the absence of feeling in patients at all reassuring. Most likely, they are denying, failing to deal with the realities they face. Some degree of denial is inevitable and in fact healthy ("I know I'll come through—my surgeon's the greatest!"). Yet too often we see something palpably different from healthy denial: the suffering patient who withdraws, refuses to comply or perhaps drinks, and ultimately gives up all feelings of

connectedness and hope. Such despair, and it is common, militates against natural healing processes. For the physician true to his profession, the restoration of hope to such patients should be paramount.

5. *Maintaining an acceptable self-image.* We all need a sense of independence, integrity of identity, and autonomy in life. Illness, with its inevitable tug toward regression and dependence, can be devastating. To survive is one thing—to be truly alive we must preserve our sense of self-worth. Illness can challenge this in ways that are utterly malicious. Consider the patient whose face is burned or whose breast has been amputated or whose testicles have been removed. These are visible kinds of insult. Think of a college professor with dementia who cannot remember the date. The assault on one's self-esteem can be savage, deeply poignant, bitterly unfair.

6. *Preserving satisfying relationships with family, friends, and co-workers.* Beyond the literal physical separation caused by illness and hospitalization, being sick effects subtler forms of alienation. Almost universally, an emotional separation from other people sets in as well. An invisible yet impenetrable barrier separates the sick from the well—indeed, the sick person from himself. As doctors, we can reach out and ease the loneliness, but we cannot take it away. The sick person faces his fate, in some ways, alone. We can help more by empathizing with this truth than by trying to be facile and denying it. Illness is always a harbinger of life's inevitable experience—death itself—and this we all will face, and face alone.

Coping

Once a person becomes ill, he must adapt, for better or worse. Those who love and depend on him must also adjust. No one welcomes such change. It is simply inescapable. Therefore major illness poses a serious, totally uninvited developmental crisis: One's dreams, self-image, and plans must all be reconsidered or even abandoned. It is no small undertaking.

The ability of the patient and his family to cope with this challenge determines not only the course of the illness itself but the quality of life that is to follow. Helping to maximize our patients' success in this momentous struggle is also part of our responsibility as doctors. Attempts by physicians to deny this are as common as they are absurd. Yet we believe such denials are not born of callousness but from puzzlement. Most physicians have not been helped in their education to help their patients in just these ways. Within medical education, lack of such a perspective remains a glaring deficiency, though one that is increasingly being addressed. There is much cause for optimism. Yet, many students would add, much potential for rhetoric, moralizing, and vagueness lurks here. Treating the whole patient sounds fine—but how? In a real sense this whole text evolved as a response to just this question—"but how?" How, without mysticism, clichés, or platitudes, can we take care of the total human being?

The reader must indulge us here and permit a brief explanation of what is essentially a teaching problem. We explicate it at this point because we believe clarification will help the student to understand better the dilemmas faced by those who wish to teach this broad perspective of patient care. Essentially, the risks in teaching this subject run to unhelpful pigeon-holing at one extreme and excessive vagueness and ambiguity at the other. All students no doubt have encountered educators who commit one error or the other, perhaps even both. Yet how to convey this material effectively is not so obvious or easy, especially when confronted with a subject as complicated as a human being. Discussions of patient "types," "classic" defenses, and "typical" problems are rife in the literature. They offer the allure of apparent neatness and order—"the seven patient types" and even lists to be committed to memory. Patients, by their sheer diversity, outfox us, however. Inevitably they wiggle free from our neat pigeon-holes. At the other extreme, generalizing about how "everyone is unique" and caring for the "whole person" does not help either. Such admonitions arm the student with little that is applicable or useful, full as they may be of indisputably noble sentiments.

In what follows we try to offer some frameworks and categories, maybe even a pigeon-hole or two! The reader must remember that we are attempting to provide tools for understanding, not conceptual chains and shackles. One must bear in mind that these concepts, like all tools, are there to help us understand our patients better and not to carve them up into some predetermined shape. These frameworks, within the limits imposed by individual complexity and sheer variety, can offer a doctor some handles—attitudes and approaches that may ease the suffering that our patients so often endure. The concept of "coping with illness," no matter how acute or cataclysmic, is always, in some way and to some extent, made to mesh with the basic and enduring themes of a patient's life. Put another way: in time, illness becomes an integrated part of the process of that person's life. How we manage the vicissitudes of that process can be critical in a patient's life—for good or ill.

Ways of coping are sometimes called defense mechanisms. We prefer the less glamorous term because it emphasizes the universality and often nonpathological nature of these mechanisms. When threatened, we all experience anxiety and try to reduce it. To do this, typically we invoke the mental and physical tricks that have worked in the past. For example, the intellectual attempts to cope by reasoning, the athlete by "working out," etc.—if of course one can perform such tasks, for illness often plays cruel tricks. Typically, coping mechanisms contain within them a considerable range of extremes and can be understood from the perspective of dichotomies. Here are some of the more common ones:

Inward turning versus outward turning: Some people seem to retreat "in-side" when sick; others seek increased interaction with friends, family, and even strangers.

Organized versus unorganized: Some gain strength by focusing on details, order, and regularity. Others abandon efforts to keep things "straight" and in order.

Confrontation versus avoidance: Some need "to know" and seem most comfortable when they are kept fully informed of all aspects of their situation. Others seem to avoid knowing (at least consciously) and may "forget" or deny truths.

Dominant versus submissive: In the face of illness, some people find it helpful to maximize their control and mastery over as many areas of their lives as they can. Others regress and yearn for others to "take over for a while."

Several observations must be made here. These guidelines do have important implications for caring for patients: To which patient do we tell the bold truth? Who needs a lot of control over his own treatment? Who requires that we take over? Who needs to be comforted; who left alone? Our ability to identify these trends correctly in our patients can enhance their comfort and occasionally head off disaster. Remember also, though, they are just trends. In truth, we feel both ways at different times, perhaps even at the same time. The stoic who says, "Tell it like it is," may nonetheless experience terrible dread. The woman who says, "Leave me alone," may yet long for closeness and comfort. We must learn to diagnose changing trends and watch for shifting vectors of these polarities over time. Never assume that patients remain fixed along this continuum over time.

It should also be clear that such coping mechanisms are not pathological per se. They can be, of course, but often the trick for a skilled clinician involves helping a patient use the coping methods he already has to his best advantage: Allow Mr. Adams to be involved with decisions regarding his treatment; let Mrs. Jones leave matters "in your hands, doctor."

Above all, help the patient not to give up. Moos and Tsu have identified several indicators that a patient is coping effectively with his illness. These generally include: minimizing or even denying the seriousness of the illness; seeking relevant information, particularly about the illness and the medical procedures or interventions that will affect him; seeking reassurance and emotional support; setting limited yet realistic and concrete goals; rehearsing alternative outcomes; and last but not least, seeking to derive new purpose, meaning, and direction in life despite the illness experience. Conversely, the absence of these signs should be regarded as ominous.

This, of course, does not exhaust the repertoire of coping styles and skills in our patients, but it hopefully provides guideposts. Pay attention to the "track record." The way a person has coped with other serious stresses in his life is an excellent predictor of how he will cope now. No pat generalizations about the "ulcer personality" or "migraine personality" can replace a thorough understanding of how any particular patient is apt to react when he is frightened, uncertain, and in pain.

The following case exemplifies how recognition and understanding of coping styles can contribute to improved patient care:

Ms. S, a 26-year-old woman, was admitted to the hospital because of acute bacterial endocarditis. Although this was her second hospitalization for the same condition, she seemed guarded and distrustful, able to confide only in one particular nurse and her own personal attending physician. For the rest of the staff, she remained very aloof. It would have been tempting for the rest of the staff to dismiss her—"an unappreciative patient"—but they did not.

For all her aloofness, she was repeatedly overheard expressing anguished concerns that she "look well" for her boyfriend. She was keenly aware of his visits and became visibly distraught when he failed to appear.

As the staff accepted and did not reject or overpersonalize her discomfort with strangers, it became easier for them to tolerate her tendency toward emotional distance. Yet they did not abandon her in response to this. Instead the staff made a special effort to provide regular, consistent people to work with her. Consistency seemed important, and trust, though hard won, continued to be a goal the staff had working with this patient. Respecting her need for distance did not consequently become carte blanche for her caretakers to abdicate responsibility for this woman.

Especially, the staff wanted to do something about her obviously agonizing dread that she might lose her boyfriend. He was strongly encouraged to visit predictably. The staff encouraged him to discuss plans for their future together—one beyond her illness. The realistically predictable course of the illness and its possible complications were reviewed with the patient exactingly. Every attempt was made to dispel frightening distortions that she harbored about a bleak future and, most especially, her fears that her illness would destroy her relationship with her boyfriend beyond salvageability.

Never did she become overtly tearful or emotionally effusive. The staff was able to appreciate that this was her way of coping. In fact, when she did become visibly upset, she asked to be "left alone." Even her few select confidants on the staff were not welcome at such times. When she was highly distressed she would withdraw into a flurry of "housekeeping." She would tidy her hospital room, for example, in a meticulous, yet driven and stereotyped fashion. The staff saw this for what it was—not "pathology" but this particular woman's inevitable attempt to cope with the threat of possible loss and emotional chaos by maintaining a tight web of superficial control as best she could. This was *her* way. The staff was sensitive and wise enough to understand and accept that she preferred it to *"our"* way."

During the hospitalization, she was immensely comforted and helped. Imagine how different the outcome might have been if the staff had insisted that she "open up" and do it "our way"—or worse—had simply written her off as too remote and distant to be bothered with at all.

"Problem Patients"

No one can be long in a hospital or clinic without learning that some persons are labeled "problem patients." Nevertheless, we discourage reductionistic, cookbook typologies that promise magical techniques for approaching "the seven kinds of problem patients." Closer scrutiny usually reveals that these are patients who are coping with their illness in ways the doctor does not approve of or understand—not some candidates for pigeon-holes or recipes of patient "types." The coping styles of such patients often serve the patient and his family well, but they collide with hospital routine, orderly operation, and, above all, the doctor's own belief about how a sick person should act and behave. When this occurs, sparks fly, and we have as often as not "a problem patient." Yet it is useful to step back at such times and ask: Why is the patient behaving so? From his perspective, after all, there must be a reason. Above all, it is always worth asking: Does this patient's behavior disrupt him, or does it nettle us and our own values? Is this the actual problem that leads us to feel such a patient is "sabotaging" the treatment and fighting against the therapy? As often as not, such a query leads to an obvious, yet important recognition. The patient is not usually fighting what is "good" for him—he simply has an entirely different view of what this "good" might be.

Kleinman, Eisenberg, and Good have called this the problem of discrepant "explanatory models." An awareness of this extremely common phenomenon is important. It leads to a reduction in futile angry finger-pointing and encourages in its place an open-minded inquiry about where the discrepancy lies. This is well illustrated by these authors' own clinical vignette from their article in *Annals of Internal Medicine:*

> Mrs. F. is a 60-year old white Protestant grandmother who is recovering on one of the medical wards from pulmonary edema, atherosclerotic cardiovascular disease, and chronic congestive heart failure. Her behavior in the recovery phase of her illness is described as strange and annoying by the house staff and nurses. While her cardiac status has greatly improved and she has become virtually asymptomatic, she nevertheless repeatedly induces vomiting and urinates frequently into her bed. And she becomes very angry when told to stop. Psychiatric consultation is quickly requested. Review of her lengthy medical record reveals nothing about the personal significance of this bizarre behavior.

When queried about it, however, and encouraged to explain why she is doing what she is, her response is most revealing. She begins by reminding the doctor that she is the wife and daughter of plumbers.

Furthermore, she reminds the consultant that she was told that she had "water in the lungs." She goes on to report that her understanding of anatomy is equally hydraulic: The human body has a chest hooked up to two pipes, namely, the mouth and the urethra. Consequently, she has been trying to be helpful by removing as much water from her chest as possible through self-induced vomiting and frequent urination. She analogizes the latter to the work of the "water pills" that she is taking, which indeed the doctors told her were for getting rid of the water in her chest. Logic is logic! She concludes: "I can't understand why people are angry at me." After appropriate explanations, along with diagrams, she was eventually able to understand that the "plumbing" of the body was quite different from her conception. Her unusual behavior ended at that time. A "problem patient" also vanished.

Certainly, patients can be obnoxious and act "crazy," but usually, with effort, we can understand their "folly." Keep in mind that as humans we are all highly diverse and endlessly creative beings, always looking for ways to turn difficult events to our own uses, even when the events are profound disruptions, such as illness. Apart from the fact that certain kinds of psychological situations seem to predispose people to illness onset, the illness itself can and indeed must be integrated into a person's life. Often this unappreciated creativity, in which patients turn undesirable afflictions into avenues to achieve desirable ends, is pejoratively labeled "secondary gain." However, it is more complex than that. Patients do learn the ropes and often make almost exasperating use of the bureaucratic and institutional red tape that we have created in the first place. It is easy to pejoratively label such people "manipulators." A few are, but more are not. They are adapting creatively—albeit with sometimes pungent irony—to the circumstances we have placed in their paths. "Compensation medicine" is fraught with these issues, and there are a host of publications about the "accident process" and the "illness process." Yet when we confront such apparent monsters as the "compensation patient," we should not, as Dr. Frankenstein did, forget too quickly who actually yanked the lever on the transformer that supplied the juice. In fact, studies of such patients usually show that they are behaving in ways entirely consistent with their prior life experience. They are coping as life and the system have taught them to. We can intervene effectively, but not if we hastily condemn. If you search in such patients' behavior for what is *creative* and even ingenious, you will usually find it. This is a general principle, of which the so-called "compensation neurotic" is only an extreme instance. Most "problem patients" are coping with problems. Most "crazy" behavior turns out to make sense, given the patient's experiences and beliefs. His attempts are usually efforts at self-cure; self-healing attempts to understand and improve aspects of life that are unsatisfactory, painful, and frightening. These attempts are not always rational or wise, but as caretakers we cannot assist if we condemn before we attempt to understand.

Suggested Reading

Engel, G. 1968. A life setting conducive to illness: the giving-up/given-up complex. Ann. Intern. Med. 679:293–300.

Groves, J. E. 1978. Taking care of the hateful patient. N. Engl. J. Med. 298:883–887.

Kleinman, A., Eisenberg, L., and Good, B. 1975. Culture, illness and care: clinical lessons from anthropologic and cross-cultural research. Ann. Intern. Med. 88:251–258.

Lear, M. W. 1981. Heartsounds. Pocket Books, New York.

Lipp, M. R. 1977. Respectful Treatment: The Human Side of Medical Care. Harper & Row, Hagerstown, Maryland.

Moos, R. H., and Tsu, V. D. 1977. Crisis of physical illness. In: R. H. Moos (ed.): Coping with Physical Illness, pp. 3–21. Plenum, New York.

Reiser, D. E., and Schroder, A. K. 1980. Patient Interviewing: The Human Dimension. Williams & Wilkins, Baltimore.

Schmale, A. H. 1972. Giving up as a final common pathway to changes in health. In: Psychosocial Aspects of Physical Illness (Vol. 8, Advances in Psychosomatic Medicine). Karger, Basel, pp. 20–40.

7 On the Nature of the Healing Process

The main reason for healing is love.

—PARACELSUS

Healing and Natural Systems: The Distinction between Curing and Healing

Every so often one hears about some "miraculous recovery" in medicine. A man with advanced metastatic cancer suddenly goes into remission and all traces of malignancy seem to have vanished. A woman with a terminal brain tumor defies the odds and continues to live. And so on. Often such stories have the potential for sensationalism and are reported in the popular media for dramatic effect. At times they are exaggerated. Yet, such "spontaneous" remissions, though rare, do occur. They have been described in the scientific literature and are not well understood. Furthermore, less extreme forms of psychological control over physical processes abound—we all know of the dying man who "made it" to his birthday; of the mother who "held on" until she was reunited with her child. The fact that such phenomena have been regarded more from the perspective of sentiment than science should not discourage our curiosity and willingness to wonder about such things rationally and scientifically. Perhaps if we could stop applying such terms as "miraculous" and "astonishing" to natural phenomena involving healing (extreme and not so extreme), we would begin to understand them better. And really we should not be so astonished. Healing is basic, a natural, integral aspect of all living systems. In truth, what should amaze us is only the extent to which this has been forgotten. As doctors, we too often tend to overestimate our power, to assume that we always can and should act. Too quickly we reach for drugs, defibrillators, and Teflon grafts. Too frequently we forget that all such devices—no matter how wonderful in the right context—are only adjuncts to, or substitutes for, natural healing. Healing is an intrinsic activity in all natural systems. Utilizing a general systems approach, we know that it takes place on all levels of the hierarchy, and that every level or part influences that whole and vice versa. Unless we have become totally benumbed, we also see the poetry inherent in this truth and stand in awe of the mysterious forces that spark life and promote healing. This is true whether it occurs on a subcellular level with replicating DNA; a cellular level with billions of new cells replacing dead cells every day; or an organ tissue level with the regeneration of vital functioning and wound healing. On a personal level we know how important the human spirit and will to live are to a patient recovering from an illness. We are aware of the immensely healing properties of human relationships in their own right, whether they are the bond between mother and child, compassion toward a patient, or the love of a suffering person's family. Beyond this, we recognize that cultures, nations, societies, and the biosphere itself can promote healing by facilitating harmony, or destroy it by fomenting fragmentation and chaos. On a world scale, there is nuclear madness. Currently, there is a growing concern among physicians about the threat of nuclear extinction. This is not simply political, it is compellingly sensible and indeed inevitable. Increasingly, physicians are perceiving their responsibility to protest this trend. The fate of the biosphere itself depends on nuclear restraint. Physicians who recognize this are being professional and acting logically on conclusions that a systems perspective forces all of us to reach.

To many, our injunctions to this point may seem obvious. Still, the history of contemporary medicine and our current practices make it very clear that we are not always doing what seems obvious. Far from it! Just look at our language, at the metaphors we so often choose. Too often we view ourselves as medical soldiers of a sort, waging war against disease. We speak of *combating* an infection. We *attack* the problem of heart disease. We try to *conquer* cancer. In short, medicine is a battle. It is war. Disease is an evil invader that has landed on the patient's shores from some remote and barbarous region. When the patient begins to lose the battle against this invader he calls the doctor in. Like a hired gunslinger or Samurai warrior, the doctor takes up the fray.

Of course, reality is very different. Illness always occurs in the *context* of a person's life. The settings in which illness emerges has much to do with a person's life—his relationships, work, setbacks, triumphs, hopes, defeats, dreams, and struggles. Naturally, one should never be simplistic about this. It would be far too reductionistic to say, "He got cancer because he worried about his son" or "Her thyroid disease came about because the marriage was breaking up." It is equally foolish to deny all such connections and insist that illness is simply a random statistical event.

How such a narrowing perspective became so pervasive in medicine is complex. Regardless, the effects of this perspective have been troubling. What does such a perspective do, for example, to the doctor-patient relationship? The answer has to be a great deal of harm. Viewing medicine as a battle too often reduces the patient to an object—a fragile boat, a rudderless frigate, a hapless barge of statistical misfortune tossed upon the stormy seas of illness. The doctor, in turn, views his responsibilities as a naval skirmish—a confrontation to be prepared for, fought, and won. The patient in this perspective is entirely passive. He hopes only to be saved. The doctor sends in his armada and tries to occupy disease's strategic islands; or occasionally he has to retreat. What he does not do is relate well to his patient. The family of the patient is also relegated to the role of helpless bystander—worried figures huddling outside the patient's room, clutching hats and purses, waiting, hoping, praying for the doctor to perform his miracle. With distressing regularity, families are excluded from any substantive involvement with the physician. Too often they are shunted aside, pushed into the corners of waiting rooms. There they are expected to wait, drink tepid coffee from vending machines, peruse old magazines, and comply with the rules. They hover compliantly in the background while physicians, medicine's gladiators, unsheathe their swords and do battle with disease. What a waste of powerful, and potentially healing, resources!

Beyond the damage all this does to the patient and his family, all the opportunities for healing that are missed, what is just as troubling is the discouragement this promotes in physicians. Doctors, conceptualizing their efforts too exclusively in terms of absolute cure, have inadvertently relinquished critical roles, responsibilities, and opportunities that could bring considerable reward and meaning. This may be the saddest consequence of all. In our experience, the young physician who thinks solely in terms of cure risks terrible discouragement. It is *this* doctor people refer to when they speak of "burnout." Currently, there is an epidemic of such malaise among physicians. Everywhere we hear of such burnout, "identity diffusion," and "job stress." Medicine *is* stressful; it always will be—but some of the stress is actually the disheartenment that comes from misdirected energy, futile attempts to cure accompanied by an equally unfortunate failure to see the splendor and meaning in the healing work we really can do.

Doctors thus discouraged naturally try to compensate, but vacation homes, trips to Europe, six-figure incomes, and fancy German automobiles do little to soften the core existential pain that results from a crisis of purpose and meaning. Medicine *is* a highly existential undertaking. As physicians, we confront life's greatest challenges—its highest joys, horrors, and mysteries. Above all, we confront mortality, our own as well as our patients'. This is truly a rare opportunity. It is also a stress. The practice of medicine is at the heart and soul of human realities that cannot be avoided, denied, or cast aside. As physicians, we *must* come to terms with life and death; and though it is unquestionably a rare opportunity, young doctors need guidance and support if they are to master the pain and realize the opportunities. Too often medical education has failed to meet this challenge.

Finally, even if we physicians ignore the existential core of what we are engaged in, our patients cannot. Think about it! Patients today are clearly searching for something. Just look at the proliferation of self-help books, holistic health movements, acupuncture, acupressure, naturopathy, irridology, Rolfing, and chiropracty. Many physicians look down their noses at all of this. They view patients attracted to such trends as dupes, the naive victims of charlatans and quacks. However, such a sanctimonious and judgmental view is far too short-sighted. These patients, however misguided, are clearly seeking something. Instead of feeling smug, physicians should be asking: *What* are my patients seeking? Could the holistic health movement, despite its portion of demigods and quacks, be a response to important, valid human needs? Could these be needs that contemporary medicine has ignored? Most of these newer movements emphasize the *human* needs of patients, including their spiritual and existential longings. We believe that until physicians take these matters seriously people will continue to turn to those who do meet these needs, sometimes to demigods and quacks, with adverse consequences to their health.

Three Patients

In this section we discuss three patients who were trying to heal. In all of these cases, opportunities were missed, not because people did not care but because the physicians involved viewed their tasks too narrowly. With all of these patients we believe that a healing partnership could have been possible had the doctors been able to see beyond the confines of a strictly biomedical perspective.

Some readers will notice something else. In all three cases it was a medical student who first sensed that something was wrong with the care each patient was receiving. Some will find this ironic, but no one should really be surprised. In truth, it takes years of formal education to expunge broad-minded, humanistic attitudes out of students. Fortunately for these patients, the "training" of their student-doctors apparently was not complete.

Mrs. Dunbarton

Mrs. Dunbarton was a frail 82-year-old widow living in a pensioners' hotel near the Tenderloin District of San Francisco. A thin, wrenlike woman, she tended to wave her hands a great deal whenever she became excited, upset, or confused. At these times, her bony fingers would flutter like the wings of birds. The hand-waving occurred more often nowadays, for she was becoming increasingly forgetful and confused. By now she was also quite deaf. Despite these infirmities, however, she remained a pleasant, even-tempered woman, who always had a smile for people, including her nurses and doctors. Generally, she greeted the world with compliance and trust, even when this was hardly warranted. Had she been wealthy, some con man no doubt would have taken advantage of her. In truth, she did not have a dime. Often when Mrs. Dunbarton did not comprehend something, she would fake it. At these times, she would cock her head to one side, look up at the ceiling, and adopt a sage expression. At such moments she appeared on the verge of saying something astonishing or profound, but the pronouncement never came. Instead, her mind just drifted off again.

Mrs. Dunbarton was in the hospital for the third time in 6 months, with pneumonia. The senior resident told Alice, the junior medical student taking care of Mrs. Dunbarton that recurrences of pneumonia were not uncommon, but he also exhorted her to do a really good work-up, "just to be sure." This work-up turned out to be both exhaustive and exhausting. They got more than enough sputum samples for culture and sensitivity. There were x-rays of her chest, tomograms, and numerous skin tests for tuberculosis, coccidiomycosis, and histoplasmosis. Many tubes of blood were drawn. Mrs. Dunbarton was definitely getting a "million dollar work-up."

Ultimately, the investigation was negative. Her x-rays showed the same degree of emphysema present on the previous admissions. Her cardiac silhouette was small. Her ECG revealed low voltage but was otherwise normal. All cultures came back negative for any organism other than pneumococci. Thus the medical team confidently concluded that this was again simply a case of pneumonia and left Mrs. Dunbarton's care to Alice, the medical student.

Quickly, the penicillin did its magic. Mrs. Dunbarton's fever came down. Her white count dropped once again below 10,000. Within a week, she was ready for discharge.

One morning, however, as Alice approached her bedside at a later hour than she ordinarily did, something caught her eye. Mrs. Dunbarton had a visitor. This was the first time Alice had ever seen Mrs. Dunbarton with anyone. Her visitor was a middle-aged black woman who exuded enthusiasm, vitality, and strength. When Alice approached the bedside, the woman extended her hand and clasped Alice's firmly. She seemed eager to talk.

Mrs. Montgomery was her name. She was a volunteer from Mrs. Dunbarton's neighborhood church. During all three hospitalizations, Mrs. Montgomery had visited faithfully. For the first time, Alice learned the actual details of Mrs. Dunbarton's life outside the hospital. The old woman lived in poverty and squalor, spending her days in the lobby of a decaying downtown hotel where she and other pensioners rented small, peeling rooms. The tenants rarely went outside—there were too many muggings and everyone was in terror of venturing out. During the winter there were months without heat or hot water. Mrs. Montgomery tried as often as she could to visit her friend. On each trip she would bring Mrs. Dunbarton a boiled egg and a roll. Many Sundays she walked with her to church.

Learning of this stirred Alice deeply. She was shocked and unsettled by the stark reality of Mrs. Dunbarton's plight. That afternoon, Alice called the hospital social worker. It was the first time in Mrs. Dunbarton's three hospitalizations that Social Services had been contacted. A case worker was assigned. They began to inquire about obtaining additional Social Security benefits. They explored whether there might be a better place where Mrs. Dunbarton could live. Arrangements were made to have a daily hot meal brought to Mrs. Dunbarton by "Meals on Wheels" after her discharge.

Why had all of these remedies been so long in coming? After all, Mrs. Dunbarton had been a patient in a topnotch teaching hospital where the house staff worked hard and really cared. The problem lay not in anyone's intentions but in the failure of her doctors to see beyond the organic part of her illness. Ironically, it had probably been the fact that Mrs. Dunbarton's disease was so *curable* which delayed and prevented proper comprehensive care: pneumococcal pneumonia—it seemed so simple. An infection, an organism visualized, a drug to treat it, and a grateful patient who responded promptly. Unfortunately, until the third admission her doctors each time had returned Mrs. Dunbarton to the same grim and depressing environment that may have contributed to compromising her resistance to developing pneumonia in the first place.

Mrs. Vincent

Back in her teens, Bonnie Vincent had looked forward to a promising future as a fashion model. Now, 10 years later, only traces of that halcyon time remain. On the mantle over the fireplace in her small meticulously swept apartment there is a picture—a framed reproduction of a *Seventeen* magazine cover. Bonnie poses in the center, flanked by other lovely long-legged, willowy girls with sparkling eyes and insouciant smiles. Seven ingenues have been posed together, winners of the magazine's beauty search. Bonnie is especially stunning—the tallest by several inches and also the only black. Ten years later, Mrs. Vincent is

27, harder, perhaps wiser. The insouciance is gone. When people allude to that earlier time, she waves it away with a gesture of her hand and admonishes people that "all that was ages ago."

It *was* long ago. The present finds Mrs. Vincent thinner, wan, and visibly in pain. She is propped up in a hospital bed on three pillows. Yet she is still very attractive, and if one looks closely there are traces even now of a more innocent past. Her huge brown eyes are still strikingly beautiful, though they are now webbed with shadows and deep, furrowed lines. At 17, she was light complected and slender. Now, she is ashen in color and profoundly gaunt. She is dying.

Mrs. Vincent has an extremely malignant type of leukemia from which there is almost never a successful recovery. At this precise moment, however, and despite her deteriorating condition, she is trying to pack her overnight case. She is scheduled for discharge in 2 hours, "Against Medical Advice." She still insists that she does not want to leave the hospital, but she silently accepts her fate. Her expression is cryptic. As she packs various items on her nightstand, she bites her lip, shrugs her shoulders, and perhaps reveals the faintest hint of a forming tear. There are no two ways about it—sick or not, dejected or not, the staff wants Mrs. Vincent out. She has definitely become *persona non grata* on ward 7-North.

In order to understand how this sorry state of affairs came about, one must go back 4 months to when Mrs. Vincent was first admitted to 7-North with the diagnosis of acute granulocytic leukemia. At the time, she had been extremely ill with a high white count comprised almost exclusively of immature cells. She also had severe anemia. The residents treated her with transfusions of packed red cells, prednisone, IV antibiotics, and an aggressive course of chemotherapy. Mrs. Vincent had responded quickly. The treatment had also caused her considerable suffering. During chemotherapy, she lost nearly all of her hair and developed painful ulcerations in her mouth. It became almost impossible for a time to swallow and even attempting to eat became torture. She suffered severe shooting pains down her arms and legs and was racked by uncontrollable nausea and vomiting. Nevertheless, she had cooperated with her treatment completely. She believed in the doctors who told her, "This will get you better."

Though she was always cooperative, from the outset she had not seemed especially warm or open. She tended to be standoffish and exceedingly shy, responding to the staff's attempts at friendliness by pursing her lips, shrugging her shoulders, and looking away. At Mrs. Vincent's bedside, morning rounds would often go something like this:

Resident:	"How are you feeling this morning?"
Mrs. Vincent:	(Purses lips, looks away, and shrugs).
Resident:	"We're going to be giving you another course of the vincristine today? Is that ok? Do you feel up to it?"

Mrs. Vincent:　(Purses lips, looks away, and shrugs. . . . Then, after a
　　　　　　　 long pause, nods faintly).

It was difficult to know whether her icy countenance reflected hostility,
fear, or depression, but overall the residents found her to be a difficult
patient to warm up to. They performed their duties conscientiously but
without much sense of satisfaction or joy.

Frequently Mrs. Vincent had a visitor—a burly, bearded black man
in a peacoat who always wore dark sunglasses. He was totally unfriendly,
and when he visited everyone steered clear of them both. Often they
argued, quarrels that ended with the man storming out and Mrs. Vincent in tears. Mrs. Vincent also had two young daughters, 2 and 5 years
old, but hospital policy prohibited their visiting. She kept pictures of
them on her nightstand.

After the chemotherapy, Mrs Vincent went into remission and was
discharged. She declined follow-up in the outpatient clinic, stating that
she preferred to see her own doctor. As time passed, Mrs. Vincent was
forgotten. Then, 4 months later, she was readmitted to 7-North, in
severe relapse. Nobody was overjoyed. The rapidity and severity of her
relapse spelled trouble. Everyone dreaded the next round of chemotherapy on this silent, emotionally inaccessible patient. Nevertheless, as
duty required, they prepared to treat Mrs. Vincent once again. Only this
time, they did not get very far.

"She's refusing chemotherapy," the intern told his senior resident.
"She says she's willing to take the transfusions and antibiotics, but she
doesn't want any more chemotherapy."

"We'll see about that," the resident replied. Now it was the resident's turn to strike out.

"She says she doesn't want to *leave* the hospital," the resident later
told his attending, "but she refuses any more chemotherapy . . . she
says if God wants to take her, then let God do his work."

"I'll talk with her about that," said the attending.

He did. Mrs. Vincent refused to budge. Negotiations continued for
the next couple of days but without progress.

"I am prepared to die," the patient kept repeating.

Finally, house staff and attending all agreed. If Mrs. Vincent
refused to accept appropriate medical treatment, they would discharge
her, Against Medical Advice.

It was in this context that Joe, the medical student on the team,
became concerned about his stoic patient's feelings and welfare. He
asked us to visit Mrs. Vincent as part of a "Psychiatric Aspects of Medicine" course. [See reference by Rosen and Blackwell in Suggested Reading.] Joe had become alarmed when Mrs. Vincent refused a second
course of chemotherapy but even more alarmed when the medical team
decided to begin forcing her to sign out Against Medical Advice. He

feared that such a drastic measure would only compound her current suffering.

We talked with Mrs. Vincent at some length. Though she was not effusive, she was open and honest. We learned that since the last hospitalization she had separated from her husband, the sullen man in the peacoat. She said she was fed up with his infidelity, alcoholic excesses, and abusiveness toward her and the children. Yet regarding her current situation, she was adamant.

"No," she said to us, "no more chemotherapy. Absolutely not."

She wanted the doctors to treat her as best they could. To make her comfortable. But not if that meant she would have to endure the "living hell" of chemotherapy again. She wanted to live, but added, "I'm not afraid to die."

Toward the end of our discussion, Mrs. Vincent revealed a cherished personal goal. She wanted to live long enough—just about 3 weeks—to complete divorce proceedings. This would ensure that her daughters were safely in the custody of her mother, legally protected from the abusive father.

With tears flooding her eyes, she said, "This is really all I want."

"I'm not afraid of death," she said again.

She told us that she was greatly comforted by her religious beliefs. Indeed, she had a theory about her own passing: God wanted children and beautiful young people in heaven too, so that it would not be filled just with people who were old and debilitated.

With our support Joe presented his findings to the rest of the team. He was inclined to think that Mrs. Vincent was depressed. He urged the house staff and attending physician to give him more time to form an alliance with the patient. Then, perhaps, he could convince Mrs. Vincent to be rational about accepting chemotherapy. During this discussion, the idea was never seriously entertained that Mrs. Vincent might have a right to refuse the treatment.

The medical team agreed to an extension, but 2 days later Mrs. Vincent still had not budged. She had several more affable conversations with Joe in the interim and expressed increasing confidence that her life had not been in vain—but on the matter of chemotherapy she never wavered. Presently, Mrs. Vincent was discharged, Against Medical Advice.

She died 2 weeks later in another hospital, dejected, with her divorce not yet final.

This clinical vignette raises many critical questions. Why did the health care system not at least attempt to respect her stated wishes and support the desires she cherished? Why was she not sent home, not with the hand-washing formula "Against Medical Advice" but with essential medical advice, buoying support, and compassionate follow-up care by home visiting nurses and physicians? In a real sense Mrs. Vincent was mistreated not because she had given up on life but because she had refused standard treatment, a treatment that ironically offered not a trace of chance for cure. She had stepped out of the established "system" and now, it seemed, had to be punished for it. Joe attempted to recognize her all too human yearnings. Unfortunately, as commonly happens, the medical team found a multitude of reasons to ignore him.

Why did this happen? Perhaps the medical staff was so caught up in their own definition of curing disease that they lost sight of Mrs. Vincent herself, of her real desires at the close of her life, her own goals and needs. But simply to condemn the doctors who cared for her is too easy and it does not help. Rather, we must try to empathize. This may provide some clues as to why this tragedy happened. Often when there is no cure, doctors feel impotent and helpless—as if they have personally failed. This is irrational, of course, but terribly common. Far too often doctors pressure themselves to achieve the impossible. They demand of themselves cures that simply do not exist and, in the process, forget that even when cure is not possible there still remain many opportunities to facilitate a healing process. Acceptance. Listening. Support. Keeping hope alive. Truly knowing what it means to walk in the patient's shoes and being able to communicate that knowledge. These are human acts, always available to the physician, interventions he can and sometimes must choose to make, especially when the hope for cure is long since past, when, as was true for Mrs. Vincent, the patient seeks not biomedical recovery but compassionate, human support, spiritual transformation, and final peace—the healing a person seeks when he knows that death is at hand.

Mr. Moore

First our pleasures die—and then
Our hopes, and then our fears—and when
These are dead, the debt is due,
Dust claims dust—and we die, too.
Shelley

Picture an abandoned farm house. It is rotting somewhere out on a prairie where roads no longer go. Slowly the skeleton of a place that once held life is baking to death. Perhaps this is transpiring on some parched, waterless, indifferent Texas plain. The windows are shattered and long since devoid of any remaining glass. The rooms of the farmhouse are completely gutted and have been for years. A door still hangs by one rusty hinge. Now and again it flaps idly against its frame, bestirred by some ghostly, invisible breeze.

Now, try to imagine the incredible physical deterioration that has taken place over the last 6 months in Mr. Alan Moore. He is 6 feet 3 inches but weighs only 107 pounds. Daily he scorches with a body temperature of 101°F or more. Antipyretics and antibiotics repeatedly fail to bring it down. Malignant melanoma has gutted and ravaged him. He is very close to the end. Everywhere, throughout his body, tumor cells proliferate in uncontrolled anaplasty, choking out normal cells the way weeds crowd out healthy vegetation around an abandoned farmhouse. His liver, bowel, and lungs are all terminally infested with histopathological chaos. Mr. Moore is 33 but he looks 50. Dissipation funnels through him like some hot Texas wind, and death peeks out surreptitiously from the shadows of his eyes, like a tramp hiding in the barn, waiting only for nightfall to make his final move. Mr. Moore never complains or makes demands, but from the hallway outside his room one hears wretching and choking, muted moans. Against the stark hospital wall one sees his emaciated shadow, like some ghostly Giaccometti sculpture, hunched over an emesis basin, throwing up incessantly. The end is proving to be horrible—there is just no way to soften or romanticize it.

We met Mr. Moore because his suffering affected one of our junior medical students very deeply.

Paul had gone as always on daily rounds with his medical team. The junior resident was presenting the latest laboratory data, all of which confirmed Mr. Moore's relentless decline.

The group spoke well outside the patient's earshot. Finally, one of the residents, after crisply reciting the latest numbers, had put Mr. Moore's chart back in the rack with a sigh. He had then shrugged his shoulders, turned his palms upward toward the ceiling, and exclaimed, "Why isn't this patient dead!"

He had not meant this with any malice; but, the next thing that happened was dramatic indeed.

Slowly, an intern on the case began to giggle. The attending put his fingers to his lips and tried but failed to suppress his own laughter. Soon, the whole thing broke wide open. Six doctors of varying age, rank, sex, and experience were all laughing, repeating over and over, "Why isn't this man dead?"

Each time the question was repeated, the group would once again shake with laughter.

Doubtless, some would say that such behavior was scandalous, but we believe it was understandable, human. The medical team, in our opinion, was releasing torrents of almost unbearable pain. The tears that we saw streaming down their cheeks were not just tears of laughter. Practicing medicine can be very difficult.

Still, the question disturbed Paul. He presented Mr. Moore's case to us. Quite somber now, Paul again asked, "Why isn't this man dead?"

It was a good question. An important one.

Why indeed?

The first thing we asked Paul was if the medical team had shared its amazement with Mr. Moore. Had anyone asked *him* where he got the courage and strength to endure? Such a question from our perspective was not simply an admiring compliment. We *did* admire Mr. Moore, but as physicians we knew it was more important to understand him. Consider the parallel: Almost any doctor would feel comfortable asking his arthritis patient how, despite advanced debility, she still managed to sew and do the dishes. Was asking Mr. Moore how he endured his disfigurement and pain any different? Yet because of the inhibitions and taboos that people feel about death, no one had asked. Thus Paul's reply was not unexpected.

"No," he said, "We routinely discuss his case in the hallway, outside of his room. We only spend brief moments . . . actually with him."

Paul continued, "When we are with him, it's mostly to monitor his drugs, like his pain medications. You know, whether he needs more or less. That kind of thing. We always tell him to let us know if he needs more. Nobody wants the poor guy to suffer. But, you know, we don't get into what's really going on with the guy."

"Let's go in and see him."

Paul nodded solemnly and loosened the knot in his tie.

When we entered the patient's darkened room, we entered a cathedral of silence, a silence broken only by the rustle of bedsheets and a low continuous murmur of pain. Mr. Moore was extremely cachectic. He resembled a survivor of Nazi atrocities. But as hideous as his physical condition was, his expression was lively and alert. We had hardly expected this! To our considerable surprise, his eyes were bright, engaging, and (dare we say?) full of hope. He was in obvious pain. Shortly after we entered the room, he suddenly clutched his abdomen, gasped, and began to wretch and heave. He groped feebly for his emesis basin, apologizing meekly, and slumped over it, commencing to vomit.

One of us put our hand on his shoulder. Another held the emesis basin under his chin. We tried our best to comfort him. Finally, Mr. Moore again grew quiet. The paroxysm appeared to pass. We introduced ourselves. Was he comfortable enough to be interviewed?

"Oh yes! Sure!"

In a raspy voice he said that he had been looking forward to the interview and was feeling "all right."

It was obviously a painful, faltering start. However, once the interview had gotten under way, everyone became quite engrossed, including Mr. Moore.

One of us finally popped the question, "How do you keep going? . . . It's so *severe*. Your illness . . . The way you keep going . . . It's remarkable."

Mr. Moore smiled.

"Maybe I'm stubborn. All I know is, I'm not ready to die. Uh Uh! Not yet!"

During the course of the interview, Mr. Moore became increasingly energetic. Especially, his eyes sparkled as he talked lovingly of his wife. He told us also about his parents. It gave him great pleasure that in recent years he had once again grown close to them. "It's amazing how much they've matured in the last few years!" he laughed. He and his wife were planning to spend the summer with them. They had a cottage on Lake Huron. It would be the perfect place to recuperate,. draw and paint.

Drawing and painting—these were things he had done much earlier in his life but had somehow grown to neglect in recent years. He had always seemed too busy, too caught up in one thing or another to find the time. Now, just here recently, he had reembraced his old love. Once again he found himself seized by an insatiable passion to create.

"Art is one of the things I have to live for," he said. "Does that make any sense?"

Several of us nodded.

Especially, he had been drawing and painting nonstop since his most recent admission to the hospital. Some of his drawings were "visualizations." These he had done in conjunction with his irradiation and chemotherapy. Although his physicians had been skeptical, saying only, "Do whatever you want," Mr. Moore believed these exercises might be helpful. He worked with a psychologist interested in such matters. Collaborating, they mapped out a strategy whereby he would draw pictures to aid his own immune system. Many of his drawings depicted his image of his own white blood cells fighting the cancer. He portrayed them as powerful, ravenous warriors, unstoppable in their appetites, gnawing away relentlessly and finally overpowering the ugly, ill-formed cancer cells.

Suddenly his face lit up.

"Would you like to see some of my work?"

A rustle in the room. Shifting of feet. Then, nods and smiles.

Characteristic of his independence and strong will, Mr. Moore in sisted on getting out of bed unassisted. Very painfully and very slowly he hobbled over to his dresser and opened the top drawer where he kept his drawing tablet. Cradling it in his arms, he inched his way back to the hospital bed. But now, back in bed with his artist's notebook open, animation and vigor seemed to return. Enthusiastically he began showing us his drawings, describing them, relishing them. The first was a portrait of a woman he had done before.entering the hospital. It was executed in charcoal—large gashing strokes, jagged intersecting black lines, bold and incomplete. Starkly, in black and white, the portrait conveyed to us the artist's angst—rage, despair, fury, and loneliness, all of these feelings at once.

He showed us this piece hastily and without comment.

"Here's another one," he said, flipping the page, "I think you'll like this one."

Now he showed us a colorful pastel. This drawing had been completed more recently, shortly after he was admitted to the hospital. It depicted how the radiation treatment (drawn as multicolored "rainbow energy") maimed and killed the cancer cells, while his white blood cells victoriously gobbled up the injured and dead cancer cells.

"Now," he said with unmistakable pride, "Here's my favorite!"

He showed us a drawing done the day before. It was another portrait, again of a woman—but unlike the first one, this piece was full of softness and tender beautiful detail. He had executed it with very fine, delicate strokes. He had filled the page completely with shading and color. The portrait was so realistic it seemed almost like a photograph.

Paul, the medical student, exclaimed with delight, "That's your wife, isn't it? Golly! It looks just like her!"

Mr. Moore turned to Paul and grinned. "Yes, it is. It is my wife. Do you like it? I drew this one with a whole lot of love in my heart! It shows, huh?"

"Wow!" Paul said, drawing closer, "I mean *that's* really something!" Without thinking about it, Paul now reached out his hand and touched Mr. Moore. With the index finger of his left hand, he very delicately traced the drawing. With his right hand, he now clasped his patient's shoulder.

"You like it?" Mr. Moore asked, looking up at Paul, visibly beaming.

"Yeah!" Paul replied. "Oh, yeah, Oh, yeah . . . Really!"

Several years have passed now since that day when we all talked with Mr. Moore. We still muse from time to time and wonder, "Might he still be alive?" It is unlikely. Of course if we really wanted to find out, we could. Perhaps we prefer to remember him just as we last saw him, with Paul's hand on his shoulder, his eyes full of excitement, joy, and pride.

Who can assess the true worth of a human being's effort to communicate the meaning of life, even as he is leaving it? Our meeting with Mr. Moore had been remarkably meaningful for us all. As human beings, we were touched. As physicians, a number of things struck us as quite remarkable. During the interview, Mr. Moore never once grimaced with pain. He showed no sign of feeling nauseated. He did not once vomit or wretch. During the period when he showed us his art work he especially appeared to be utterly pain-free. . . . Why?

Equally noteworthy was the lack of awareness among Mr. Moore's physicians that he drew and painted at all. . . . Why? The residents knew vaguely about his "visualizations." Because he had insisted on being allowed to try, they had even given their begrudging permission, but they acted as though such endeavors were trivial and slightly far out. . . . Why? It is true that scientific evidence supporting the effectiveness of visualizations so far remains scanty—but so what? To Mr. Moore this therapy clearly meant a great deal. Why was this trivialized and ignored? In one phase of the interview, Mr. Moore talked about his spiritual life. He was a member of an Eastern religious sect. Part of his worship included daily prayer and meditation. Yet none of this was deemed at all important by the medical staff. . . . Why?

Still other questions: Does the will to live help one to go on in the face of death? This notion has long been entertained anecdotally. Is it true? If so, how does it work? Why have we not studied it?

Do creative pursuits, such as Mr. Moore's drawing and painting, conceivably decrease the experience of pain? How does this happen? Does being creative somehow promote healing? If so, how does this function at the level of brain chemistry? Do the intangibles of hope, love, faith, and belief reinforce a person's will to live? What is the effect of loving? Of being loved? How did Mr. Moore's deep love for his wife affect him? His rapprochement with his parents?

What of prayer, meditation, faith, and belief in God? Over and over our patients tell us that these things are very important. Yet they are mentioned with extraordinary infrequency in the medical literature. Is this because they are actually unimportant? Why have such phenomena not been considered more carefully? How has such a fertile field of investigation gone uncultivated and allowed to lie fallow under our scientific noses for so long?

Touching

The observant reader will note that a significant part of Mr. Moore's interaction with us involved touching. At the start of the interview, there was little physical contact. Indeed, the first thing that greeted the students had been a sepulchral somberness, a room filled with so much that was sad, ominous, and dark, a room that resonated with the sound of human pain. By the end of the interview, however, everyone had drawn closer. Paul and Mr. Moore were touching each other. The other students kept reaching out. This was no social contrivance or cookbook recipe regarding "physical contact in the medical interview." Far from it. What happened between Mr. Moore and the students was both natural and extremely powerful—a consequence of their growing rapport, deepening empathy, and budding awareness of a mutually shared humanness. This closeness was all the more powerful because it grew like a bright flower in the shadow of life's ultimate darkness, death. Perhaps the most important message of all that Mr. Moore and the students conveyed to each other came not in words at all but in physical contact, in the touch of a hand. Listen to Lewis Thomas (in *The Youngest Science*) on the matter:

> Medicine was once the most respected of all the professions. Today, when it possesses an array of technologies for treating (or curing) diseases which were simply beyond comprehension a few years ago, medicine is under attack for all sorts of reasons. Doctors, the critics say, are applied scientists, concerned only with the disease at hand, but never with the patient as an individual, whole person. They do not really listen. They are unwilling or incapable of explaining things to sick people or their families. They make mistakes in their risky technologies; hence the rapidly escalating cost of malpractice insurance. They are accessible only in their offices in huge, alarming clinics or within the walls of terrifying hospitals. The word "dehumanizing" is used as an

epithet for the way they are trained and for the way they practice.
The old art of medicine has been lost, forgotten . . .

What is it that people have always expected from the doctor? How,
indeed, has the profession of medicine survived for so much of human
history? Doctors as a class have always been criticized for their
deficiencies. Montaigne in his time, Molière in his, and Shaw had less
regard for doctors and their medicine than today's critics. What on
earth were the patients of physicians in the nineteenth century and the
centuries before, all the way back to my professional ancestors, the
shamans of prehistory, hoping for when they called for the doctor? In
the years of the great plagues, when carts came through the town
streets each night to pick up the dead and carry them off for burial,
what was the function of the doctor? Bubonic plague, typhus,
tuberculosis, and syphilis were representative examples of a great
number of rapidly progressive and usually lethal infections, killing off
most of the victims no matter what was done by the doctor. What did
the man do, when called out at night to visit the sick for whom he had
nothing to offer for palliation, much less cure?

Well, one thing he did, early on in history, was plainly magic. The
shaman learned his profession the hardest way: He was compelled to go
through something like a version of death itself, personally, and when
he emerged, he was considered qualified to deal with patients. He had
epileptic fits, saw visions, and heard voices, lost himself in the
wilderness for weeks on end, fell into long stretches of coma, and when
he came back to life he was licensed to practice, dancing around the
bedside, making smoke, chanting incomprehensibilities, and *touching* the
patient everywhere. The touching was the real professional secret,
never acknowledged as the central, essential skill, always obscured by
the dancing and the chanting, but always busily there, the laying on of
hands.

There, I think, is the oldest and most effective act of doctors, the
touching. Some people don't like being handled by others, but not, or
almost never, sick people. They *need* being touched, and part of the
dismay in being very sick is the lack of close human contact. Ordinary
people, even close friends, even family members, tend to stay away
from the very sick, touching them as infrequently as possible for fear of
interfering, or catching the illness, or just for fear of bad luck. The
doctor's oldest skill in trade was to place his hands on the patient. . . .

Pause and consider for a moment the real significance of touch, the
craving that human beings have to be embraced when they are suffering
and in pain. When we cease to romanticize the phenomenon and consider it objectively, our amazement hardly diminishes. In fact, it is bound
to grow. As documented by James Lynch (see reference in Suggested
Reading), there is astounding power in a human's touch. Yet touch
appears to be on the decline in medicine, too often denigrated, ignored,
and unappreciated. Some, in the name of some ill-conceived notion of
therapeutic purity, have actually advocated that it be abandoned.

The sheer complexity of modern medicine—its growing anonymity—discourages expressions of connectedness, closeness, and warmth. As Thomas observes, in our modern medical complexes, the most protracted personal interaction a patient often has occurs not with a doctor or a nurse but with a clerk at the admissions desk. The most intimate aspects of a patient's life elude the doctor but are fed instead into an accountant's computer terminal, to be spit out onto an insurance form.

"Name?"

"Address?"

"Mother's maiden name?"

"Previous hospitalizations?"

"Relative to contact?"

Each question is dutifully answered, as though by rote. In the process, the interrogator seldom nods or even makes eye contact.

"Annual income?"

"Place of employment?"

The patient obediently replies. The computer's keyboard clatters. Hieroglyphics of a life appear on the TV screen.

What a travesty it all seems to have become at times!

Touch, intimacy, closeness, a sense of belonging—many fear that their disappearance from medicine deeply hurts patients. Sadly, this is true, but we worry about something beyond this. Such alienation is also taking its toll on the doctor.

One of the great joys of medicine comes from the fact that the work we do is often highly meaningful. We should never forget how truly blessed we are to have a profession so full of purpose, importance, and meaning. Six-figure incomes pale in comparison with this kind of wealth. Often, however, our work is also emotionally and spiritually draining. Sometimes we must endure a kind of pain and responsibility that is truly excruciating and harrowing. The essence of what we do is connected with what is most elemental and mysterious in life. Above all, we confront life's deepest riddle, death. We cannot and should not flee this. The evasion just will not succeed. Physicians must come to grips with their philosophical burdens and opportunities. It goes with the territory, as they say; there really is no choice. To flee from these things only leads to numbness, loss of purpose, confusion, and professional misery. The task of educators is not to find shortcuts to escape hatches—it is to help students master what they face, increase in wisdom, and grow from the challenges they confront. This is true whether the challenge is a new procedure to be learned or the human dimension of a physician-patient encounter. Much of what we fear, and long for, is embodied in the doctor-patient relationship and that most elemental part of it, the human touch.

Reaching out. Healing. It can be beautiful, but it can also be terrifying, exposing us to some of the most painful and trying of human situations. We should not make light of it or blame any lapses simplistically on "technology." The pain of dying is hard, very hard. This was true long before CAT scans, SMA 34 panels, and protein electrophoresis. The loneliness of illness, the sheer awfulness of dying are profound, these things frighten us to the core and always have. How naive to blame all our dread on a fickle and faddish infatuation with high technology. Let us be honest—it is frightening to be a doctor. It always has been. Yet if the doctor can reach out, can touch, can reach across that dreadful existential chasm, so much that is profound, inspiring, beautiful, and uplifting really can be achieved. The doctor-patient relationship *is* astounding and incredibly beautiful—but we should stop pretending that it is easy. Sometimes touching *can* help, amazingly so. Take Mr. Moore: suddenly he is no longer an apparition—he is again a human being, a person with hopes *even now*. He is someone alive and sentient with very simple yet vital human needs. Above all, he is a person who needs others, someone longing for human contact. Like his ancestors through the centuries, he is afraid and longs for human touch. Responding to this need is one of the doctor's most ancient and critical responsibilities. When we touch Mr. Moore, we are not simply being supportive of our patient. We are engaged in healing, responding to his anguish. It is all part of our calling, one of the demands we must be prepared to make of ourselves.

One final point about touching: It is closely connected with what we refer to in Chapter 1 as Acceptance, a basic principle of medicine as a human experience. Think about it: We begin life as physical organisms. Long before language and abstraction develop, we know the world through our sensations, through what we feel. It is through touch that we begin to identify love, safety, and indeed survival.

Mother holds baby. Baby touches mother. It *is* a lovely picture. We could say the sight is *touching*. This is also the biology of survival. Human touch is one of the first and most highly critical events in the process of mother-infant bonding.

Currently our scientific model tends to regard such matters as trivial. Generally, we have failed to recognize the rich vein of important knowledge that awaits a curious investigator—it is more than a vein, it is a mother lode. As Lynch has shown a scientific inquiry into the impact on patients of touching tells us so much of critical importance. However, such matters are apt to be ignored until medicine begins to grasp their significance within the systems perspective. Until then, all of these matters will remain enshrouded in folklore and sentiment—or worse still, be belittled as "unscientific." For the most part, they await the inquiry of perspicacious and curious minds.

Healing and the Biopsychosocial Model

Currently medicine is a house divided. We are painfully cleaved on many issues: Private practice versus publicly financed medicine; specialists versus generalists; physicians providing health care versus nonphysicians providing health care. The list goes on and on. At times the only thing that does seem to unite us is our shared belief that something is wrong with medicine, perhaps desperately wrong. We live in the wealthiest nation in the world and find ourselves devoting ever greater proportions of our total budget to health care. With each passing year, people seem more unhappy, more alienated, and more angry at American medicine. On the other side, exasperated physicians respond defensively and ask bitterly, "What do people want anyway?" Anger, disappointment, and pain: these emotions, more than any sense of common resolve, seem to be what unite us. As a consequence, many of us find ourselves longing for the "good old days." Then, we like to fantasize, everything was harmonious, happy, and whole.

Of course the good old days never really existed. People were no more trusting of physicians in Montaigne's time than they are today. Leaving aside our current deficiencies and excesses as a profession, ambivalence about doctors is probably inevitable. In truth, it is inconceivable that a calling so closely linked to life and death, to human fate, would ever be regarded without profound conflict. Despite the currently politicized climate and a nimble rhetoric of "holism," the problems that beset us are not new, and the solutions certainly no simpler. If only they were simple! Charlatans may prey on this longing, but physicians must not. For anyone who does not succumb to easy answers, the current climate is disquieting.

Increasingly the schisms that divide us seem to grow: "holistic" versus "technological," "primary care" versus "specialty care," the "art" of medicine versus the "science" of medicine. Whatever dichotomy one selects, there is clearly a *perceived* schism between "scientific" medicine and "humanistic" medicine. Yet what nonsense! It is the sort of nonsense that would not be so serious if it did not threaten patients. Permit us to concretize this. Consider once again the medical management of Mr. Moore. Recall that with begrudging "permission" from his medical team Mr. Moore undertook some visualization exercises. Here indeed is a case in point. The time will come when, through science, the efficacy of visualizations has been proved or disproved. Let us presume for a moment that the outcome is positive. Hopefully, though by no means automatically, such proof can lead to acceptance and application of such techniques by "traditional" medicine. Until then, most reasonable people would agree that there is little apparent *harm* in visualizations. This is especially true if the patient believes in them and embraces them as part of his treatment, in concert with established forms of therapy. Clearly Mr. Moore was no fanatic; along with his visualizations he accepted and had faith in the chemotherapy and radiation treatments his physicians provided. Mr. Moore's care thus seems to have been logical, noncontroversial. Yet considerable controversy actually coalesces around even so seemingly simple and rational a care plan as this. Especially, feelings and rhetoric run high on both sides over the issue of "scientific" versus "naturalistic" medicine.

Let us elaborate on this controversy and begin by articulating, as best we can, the views of both camps in this noxious but important controversy. On one side, we have the views of what we shall call, for simplicity's sake, the "holistic" movement in medicine. Proponents on this side of the schism argue that biotechnical medicine must pay attention to visualizations. Visualizations are a product of naturalistic, homeopathic trends within medicine. Such trends emphasize the importance of self-healing, which the modern medical establishment perhaps ignores. So far, so good. Who could disagree? However, from here the rhetoric may expand, becoming more strident and extreme. Some say: Not only should Mr. Moore engage in visualizations, he should eschew the harmful drugs and chemicals that establishment doctors are forcing on him. All such substances are part of a medical conspiracy, worse than poison! He should turn to nature for healing! No more drugs, no more synthetic vitamins! Only *natural* will do. Honey, please. No sugar! From here, Mr. Moore may be exhorted to meditate, to think about the unity of nature and all of life. He may be exhorted to adopt a macrobiotic diet and renounce the evils of Western scientific thought. . . . Saved, in the nick of time!

What about the other side of the schism, the traditional Western medical establishment? Is this camp really any more reasonable? Here too the reasoning probably starts out sensibly. *Of course,* some doctors assert, patients *should* be allowed to have a say in their own treatment. "Obviously" the patient's wishes and religious beliefs should be considered. Still, as the passions behind the argument swell, you hear the prejudices churning underneath that rational surface. For instance, many physicians are convinced that, by definition, nonphysicians (e.g., clinical psychologists) who attempt to treat patients with nonmedical interventions (e.g., visualizations) are ineffectual. Such a prejudice is never directly acknowledged, yet every nonphysician and many physicians who are honest with themselves know this bias exists. As for people who believe in meditation, diet, and prayer—well, these people are at best well-intentioned fad followers and at worst quacks. Many physicians try to adopt a stance of reasonableness in the face of these trends, but underneath they are quite incensed and if prodded explode, telling you that the whole holistic health movement is really a lot of nonsense. Furthermore, they say, doctors are tired of hearing patients question physicians about practices that are being attacked in shallow, trendy newspapers and magazines. Rubbish, handholding, and snake oil is all it really comes down to. When will people wise up?!

Obviously taken to extremes, neither camp is "right." There is truth on both sides of the chasm. How, then, has it happened that each side regards the other as so incorrigible, willful, and incompetent? At the core, what is wrong actually has nothing to do with intentions or intelligence. There are bright and sincere people polemicizing on both sides of the schism. What we are actually witnessing is confusion, a confusion that inevitably results from an inadequate underlying scientific model. Despite obvious differences in the scientific model that each side invokes, in critical respects they are surprisingly similar. Especially, both camps use models that rely heavily on cause-and-effect and reductionism. This is a provocative assertion. Therefore allow us to expand: The antimedical, "holistic" camp invokes a model of nature that is essentially identical to that found in all prescientific cultures (of which it is an example). Such cultures attempt to explain natural events by "displacing upward" on the systems hierarchy. For example, these cultures explain illness by invoking causes that are larger, greater, and more removed than the person himself. Thus the ancients blamed illness on "the gods" or malalignment of the stars.

Though the direction of displacement in this model is upward, its effect is no less reductionistic. Nor is this "displacement upward" restricted to primitive cultures and historical antiquity. Some forms of contemporary psychological reductionism, for example, are similar and just as unhelpful. Thus some people naively assert that a person got an ulcer "because he is unconsciously mad," or a woman developed asthma because she "could not tolerate separation from her mother." Here the displacement is upward from the ailing body to the mysterious unconscious with its unseen gods and demons. Likewise, displacement upward is the favored etiological explanation for the current "naturalistic" movements within medicine. For instance, so-called "iridologists" claim that they can discern all diseases by looking into the eye—a sort of window to the body and soul. The counterpart in primitive cultures would be the witch doctor who discerns patterns in the rocks and bones he has scattered on the ground. The problem in many diseases is purported by these "naturalistic" practitioners to be some imbalance, a disruption in the harmony of Yin and Yang, which in turn reflects a discordance contrary to some higher universal balance. Such thinking, of course, is no different from the ancients who cited horoscopes and pointed to the confluence or divergence of certain stars.

Western "scientific" medicine, with its emphasis on objective evidence and Cartesian dualism as well as reductionistic explanations of cause-and-effect, is far more empirically rational but equally hobbled ultimately by its insistence on a *linear quid pro quo* to explain all natural phenomena. It seeks etiological explanations by *displacing downward*. To explain illness at the person level, biomedicine attempts to *analyze* the problem (which literally means to break things into smaller component parts) and hopes in this way to find the "ultimate truth" at a cellular, molecular, atomic, or subatomic level. The biomedical model inherently encourages physicians to confuse "smaller" with "closer to the truth."

Throughout this book we have advocated the biopsychosocial model, based on systems theory, as a sensible and practical path toward reconciling many apparent polarities and schisms. We believe that proponents of the so-called "holistic" movement in health care cannot be entirely ignorant and without substance. They are resonating with some legitimate perception on the part of many people, not all of whom are ignorant. At the same time, many scientifically committed physicians, including the authors, are dismayed by the complete noblesse oblige and uncomprehending caprice with which such movements commingle common sense, conjecture, and outright quackery. We acknowledge that physicians are not always effective at protecting patients from the dangers of their own biomedical excesses and too often ignore natural, intrinsic modes of healing. Thus it comes as no surprise that many "naturalistically" inclined people view physicians with fear. Physicians are also accused by this movement, correctly, of failing often to see the suffering person who exists behind the x-rays and enzyme profiles. We physicians seem so eager to isolate (at considerable cost) and analyze smaller and smaller parts of the human whole. This can be wrong, but a rejection of the scientific method would be equally destructive and absurd. As we stated at the outset, solutions are not simple. However, at the very least, the biopsychosocial model shows how many apparently disparate "truths" are actually equally valid phenomena observed *at different levels* of the systems hierarchy. It points a way toward a view of people as not *either* heart-and-soul *or* cells-and-mitochondria but *both*—all of this and much, much more—functioning as a fantastic whole of incredible intricacy, coherency, purpose, and design.

Medicine's Existential Quest

In Andre Malraux's famous novel, *Man's Fate,* there is a depiction of altruism in the face of death. The novel concerns the struggle of Communist freedom fighters in China during the revolution. The scene takes place in 1927. The protagonist is Katow, a hardened Russian revolutionary now fighting with the Chinese Communists. Katow is no stranger to death; he fought in the Russian Revolution, has been shot at by a firing squad, and has been a prisoner at hard labor. Now he is again a prisoner, among many, all of whom are condemned to die. The less prominent and influential will be put to death by shooting before a firing squad. Important and influential people, such as Katow and his friend Keo, are to be cremated alive in the boiler of a locomotive. From outside the prison the condemned hear the piercing wail of the locomotive's whistle. Each peal signals that another prisoner is being burned to death. Both Katow and Keo possess a cyanide tablet. Now, groping in the dark, Katow discerns that Keo is dead. He has already swallowed his poison. In the darkness Katow hears two young boys, revolutionaries but barely out of their teens, sobbing in terror. He makes one of the most difficult decisions of his life, and breaking the tablet in half, gives each of them one-half tablet of his cyanide.

• • •

It is the winter of 1981, Washington, D.C. In a horrifying airline disaster, a commercial jetliner, its wings heavily iced, has skidded off the end of the runway and plunged into the Potomac. Hundreds die. Commuter traffic stops as horrified onlookers behold the catastrophe in stunned silence from an overhead bridge. Suddenly a Washington office worker who had been commuting home emerges from his car, proceeds to the river bank, and leaps head first into the water. Nearly losing his own life in the process, he is able to pluck a drowning passenger from certain death.

• • •

In Canada, an athletic young man develops an osteosarcoma. In rapid succession he experiences amputation, chemotherapy, and radiation treatment. Equally important, he now must adjust to a severely altered self-image. He is suddenly "an invalid," a "cancer sufferer," and "disabled." His name is Terry Fox. In a stupendous feat that combines obstinacy with courage and ecstasy with suffering, Terry Fox attempts to run across the continent raising money for cancer research. As most people know, he did not make it. He died 2000 miles into his odyssey after metastases developed in his lungs. By the time of his death, however, he had galvanized the pride of an entire nation, inspired countless young people with cancer, and generated a huge outpouring of financial support for cancer research and treatment. His was truly an inspired act of creative madness—it made no sense and yet it made so *much* sense. It was the sort of divine folly which only human beings seem driven to and capable of.

The above vignettes are especially dramatic, inspiring instances of human transcendence. Through heroes such as these we all hold a mirror up to ourselves and feel heartened. They remind us of the beauty, courage, and grace of which people are capable. (We already have far too many reminders of our baseness, destructiveness, pursuit of power, and arsenals of death.) Ultimately heroes would be less important than they are, however, if they did not also help us to hold up smaller mirrors to our quieter, more personal moments of courage, love, creativity, and hope: A volunteer who will never make the newspapers reads passages of great literature every Thursday to a woman who is blind. A young man with Ivy League credentials and a promising job in a law firm joins the Peace Corps. A busy resident physician in Pediatrics is about to rush by the room of a frightened 10-year-old. She has much to do—IVs to start, physicals to be performed, medication orders to be written—but something makes her stop. She enters and for a few minutes plays with the child, tucks him into bed, and kisses him goodnight. Her kindness will never be reported. In fact, she herself regards it as far too trivial to mention the next day on morning rounds. Yet indelibly, undeniably, in the mind of the child it has occurred. It may be, in fact, that the most profound evidence of our humanness is not to be found in instances of great heroism but in small, everyday acts—the touch of a hand, a look of understanding, a willingness to really listen. Reflect on the medical students' actions with the three patients in this chapter and throughout the entire book. It is heartening to remember that our profession has the real possibility of remaining a healing profession, and it is encouraging beyond measure that our students are so often at the vanguard expressing their ideals.

Altruism. Courage. Dignity. Creativity. Love. Humor. Gentleness. Pride. Compassion. Joy. Hope. Sensitivity. Honesty. Selflessness. Charity. Where do we put these intangibles in the systems hierarchy? Is the courage of a man who jumps into the Potomac a function of processes at the organ system level? Is bravery a matter of epinephrine, norepinephrine, and catecholamines? Is it mediated by axons, synaptic clefts, and storage granules? Certainly this must be part of the answer—but not all of it. Courage seems to be a matter of this and so much more. Is it experiences at the two-person system that are key? Something in the way this man was raised? Something taught to him of altruism by a mother or father or loving grandparent? No doubt. We are certain of it. But what more? Does he belong to a subculture which, despite our colossally narcissistic society, still condones sacrifice and selflessness? What are his religious convictions? For that matter, where *do* we put spiritual beliefs and longings in the systems hierarchy?

The truth is, we do not know where to place such intangibles. They do not fit neatly anywhere, yet they seem relevant everywhere. They are embedded in the essence of medicine, and we encounter them everywhere in our practice of it. Walk down the corridor of any hospital, and you will witness dramas unfolding that all pivot on intangibles. To the participants in those dramas, the intangibles are everything. Our patients are not statistics but people, struggling with the most profound and important events of their lives . . . events measured not by sodium concentrations and hematocrits but by intangibles. Imagine 100 patients, 100 identical men with identical cancers of an identical organ (as though such were possible!). Imagine that the pertinent enzymes are all elevated to identical levels. The x-rays cast identical worrisome lucencies on identical films of lung and brain. You would still be witnessing 100 vastly different human events. Each one of these "identical" men has had a different life, different values, different memories, hopes, dreams, wives, children, grandchildren, and friends. Each feels differently about pain, discouragement, fear, fighting on, or giving up. Histopathologically, perhaps, they are all nearly the same, but the essence of their struggles, defeats, triumphs, and setbacks is not found here. It is found in the intangibles. For each, the experience of life is unique. For each, it is comprised not of enzymes and cardiac glycosides but of memories and ideals—our quest for meaning, our capacity for faith and love, our ability to trust and to accept solace, and ultimately of the existential and spiritual underpinnings of our souls.

Clearly, modern medicine has tended to ignore these matters, though they are what is usually *most* on our patients' minds. Still, some argue that the importance and significance of such concerns lie outside the purview of medicine proper. Some say these are issues for philosophers, perhaps for clergy. Some even assent that such matters are personal, private—that a doctor should not intrude (how reminiscent of the sexual prudery of a few decades past!). We believe, however, that here is a place where a doctor can, indeed must, learn to feel comfortable and belong.

What to call these things? Where to put them? Throughout this book we have urged the reader to view patients from the perspective of the systems theory and the biopsychosocial model. Such a view broadens and deepens our understanding of human beings suffering from illness; it renders us more capable and better informed. In summary, it enables us to be more effective doctors. Beyond this we believe that a full understanding of our patients requires attention to the universalities, to the intangibles, to the existential nature of so much that we do. Here it becomes as difficult as it is critical to find the right words. For some, religion explains what we are attempting to describe. Such people are comfortable with terms such as "God" and with such concepts as the "spirit" and "soul." Yet others feel put off by such a vocabulary—people who still feel the power of these universalities and instinctively appreciate their immense importance. Many such people recoil from terms that have religious overtones. How do we find the words to express such matters to them? Finally, there are some who feel that all such considerations are antiscientific, inherently in opposition to the rational, analytical, empirical thrust of our Western scientific tradition. Such individuals are sincere, but we believe they fail to understand much of what medicine, and life, consist of.

In the end we find ourselves stymied. We cannot find the right words, but our experience in medicine has taught us not to reject what we still have failed to capture. We believe that someday someone will. The same yearning to capture the essence of the intangibles in life may have been on the mind of Walt Whitman when he wrote the following poem. It was first published in 1863 but was still being revised in 1881. Evidently he had trouble finding the right words too.

> A noiseless patient spider,
> I mark'd where on a little promontory it stood isolated,
> Mark'd how to explore the vacant vast surrounding,
> It launch'd forth filament, filament, filament, out of itself,
> Ever unreeling them, ever tirelessly speeding them.
>
> And you O my soul where you stand,
> Surrounded, detached, in measureless oceans of space,
> Ceaselessly musing, venturing, throwing, seeking the spheres to connect
>   them.
> Till the bridge you will need be form'd, till the ductile anchor hold,
> Till the gossamer thread you fling catch somewhere, O my soul.

Healing

There is a vast difference between curing and healing.* A patient can be cured but not healed. There are also many times when a physician can help a patient to heal, even though he cannot cure him. Sometimes the latter opportunities provide the highest joys and privileges a physician can hope to know. We close this chapter with such an example . . . the story of David, a little boy, and his family who were helped to heal by a deeply caring physician. The story of David is not ours. He was the patient of a very gifted and special doctor, Dr. Frances Sharkey. Her account of David is one of several in her superb book, *A Parting Gift*, a book that should be read by every medical student and every doctor who still has a longing to grow and learn.

David was a pale, taciturn 2½-year-old when pediatrician Dr. Sharkey first encountered him in her waiting room. He came accompanied by a brief referring note from his general practitioner. The note was only two words long. It read, "Hemoglobin 6." From the outset Dr. Sharkey suspected leukemia; yet she was reluctant, as many physicians would be, to accept a diagnosis that seemed to extinguish hope:

> I patted the bruised little leg. How about a diagnosis of aplastic anemia? That wasn't a nice disease, but it could be treated and not prove fatal.

> One part of the baby remained to be examined before I could make even a provisional diagnosis in my mind of cancer or leukemia—a diagnosis that meant almost a death sentence for this beautiful child. I must feel his abdomen to see if his spleen is enlarged.

> I unbuttoned his shirt and look at his abdomen. It was fat like all 2-year-olds. Or was it fatter? I put my fingers on his chest. He bent his head and watched my hand. Soft skin, firm little ribs moving up and down with each breath. The pulsating of his heart was strong and normal. I ran my fingers downward. Then, light as was my touch, with no wince from the baby, I felt an enlarged spleen. . . .

From the outset Dr. Sharkey related not only to David but his parents. They did not warm up instantly to her; rather, the relationship grew, and over time a powerful bond between them replaced shyness and distrust. Dr. Sharkey's relationship with Mr. and Mrs. Carver was marred early on not by any lack of warmth but by her initial misinterpretation of the medical facts. When David's leukemia was being diagnosed, the fields of hematology and oncology were changing so rapidly that most general pediatricians could not hope to keep up. Within several years, during the decade of the 1970s, acute lymphocytic leukemia (the

---

* To *cure* comes from the Latin word *curare* and means to take care of, to take charge of, and denotes successful medical treatment. To *heal* comes from the ancient English word *haelen* and means to make or become whole; it is closely related to the word *holy*, also derived from the same root.

form David had) ceased to be a uniformly fatal illness—truly a death
sentence—and became a potentially curable disease. This astonishing
biomedical progress has continued to the present. Now children suffering from the disease are more likely to live than to die—but initially Dr.
Sharkey knew none of this. She broke the painful "truth" to them, comforted them when they wept, and only later discovered that she had been
quite wrong. Her courage in admitting this mistake in the book, her
willingness to share with her readers that she was fallible and human is
one of the traits that make Dr. Sharkey and the book so remarkable.

> Tears ran down Mrs. Carver's cheeks and she wiped them away with
> the back of her hand. I sat back and took my hand from hers. "There
> are good, effective drugs with which leukemia can be treated, at least
> for a while," I said.

> For the first time since I had sat down with them, she looked directly at
> me. Shock marred her young face. Her husband shifted uncomfortably
> in his chair. "How long—how long . . . ," he began. His voice faltered.

> "How long will he live?" I filled in for him. He nodded. . . .

As physicians, we cannot witness illness and suffering in our patients so intensely without, on occasion, glimpsing intimations of our
own mortality and that of the people we most dearly love.

> That night as I tucked my children into their beds, I put my hand on
> their abdomens and surreptitiously felt to see if any one of them had an
> enlarged spleen. It would be months before I lost the need to reassure
> myself they didn't.

David responded well to the drugs administered to reverse his
acute crisis. Color returned to his face, liveliness and vitality to his play.
Dr. Sharkey was soon able to send him home. There is a passage in the
book at this point that captures for us the essence of medicine as a
human experience. Dr. Sharkey is talking with David's parents before
his discharge. What she has to say makes it clear that it is never a matter
of "either" humanism "or" science. It is inevitably an amalgam of both.

> "There's another way therapy has been improved just recently.
> Although it's new, I want David to have it—radiation to his brain . . .

> "I already did a spinal tap on David and injected methotrexate into his
> spinal fluid. That also decreases the chance of malignant cells growing
> around his brain. The spinal tap wasn't painful, but he had to be held
> tightly, which scares most children. Not David! He cried for a minute
> and then quieted down and just lay trustingly in the arms of the nurse.
> He's a wonderfully calm baby."

> Mrs. Carver nodded her head and kissed David's cheek lightly.

"Here," I said, reaching into my bag and bringing out a sheaf of journal articles, "these are for you to read. The past few days I've reviewed the literature on leukemia. It's marvelously encouraging and speaks of 50 percent cure rates with current therapy."

I handed Mr. Carver copies of the articles I had read. "A week ago I said that David's disease was fatal. I hadn't read up on leukemia then. My statement may already be out of date. I certainly hope it is."

"You can take David home. . . ."

In the ensuing months Dr. Sharkey assumed responsibility for all parts of David's treatment. Instead of sending him to a specialist for his anticancer drugs, she consulted the specialists but administered the treatments herself. With each office visit David seemed to grow stronger—and with his physical rebirth, hope too began to thrive:

Safe in his mother's arms David regarded me with wide eyes. He's 2½ years old, I thought. In 5 years, if he lives, he'll be in the second grade. Could that be possible? Would I be saying to these parents someday in the future, "David is cured. . . ."

So too did the relationship between Dr. Sharkey and the Carvers deepen and thrive:

Mr. Carver shook hands with me. The contact of our hands was firm and reassuring. Mrs. Carver smiled as if I were an old friend. She held David in her arms.

"He doesn't say many words yet but I've taught him your name. Come on, David," she coaxed, "You know it."

David looked shy and then, knowing how much it would please her, he flung his chubby arms up and said, "Docta Shark."

Months blended into years. David's response to the radiation treatment was good, and there were no further signs of leukemia. He and his family began to feel that perhaps, just maybe, they were not treasuring life under the shadow of death. Mrs. Carver soon became pregnant.

David lived to enter kindergarten, then first grade. Both passed without incident. The little boy Dr. Sharkey once thought doomed to die was now an active, rambunctious 6-year-old asserting to his father that the training wheel just had to come off his bicycle, that instant! When David came to Dr. Sharkey's office now it was was with pride, and just a hint of a boyish flirt, that he pulled off his shirt and flexed his biceps for her.

Finally, after 5 years of chemotherapy, the time had come to stop David's medication. Taking him off the drugs was a huge step. Everyone wondered what might happen after they relinquished David's now familiar and reassuring chemical safety net. However, as a consultant had correctly remarked, "We can't keep him on the drugs forever." Dr. Sharkey and David's parents realized that they must find the courage to let go.

The drugs were stopped. David remained well. Dr. Sharkey began to cut back from the schedule of weekly office visits. He seemed cured, and it was time to let him leave the medical nest.

When David turned eight, however, tragedy struck. Dr. Sharkey discovered it during a routine physical:

> . . . I ran my hands over David's familiar body. He was, despite the radiation therapy and drugs, a big child. Recently his body shape had matured and his muscles were chunkier. As usual, at the end of the exam I felt his testes. David no longer giggled the way he had when he was younger but tolerated this patiently. All at once I was alarmed. Was I imagining it or did his testes feel larger? There were no hard lumps and there was nothing irregular about them, but they definitely had increased in size.

Because leukemia of this type was most apt to recur in the testes or brain, the finding was frightening. It also posed very difficult decisions regarding what should properly be done at that point. No discrete mass in the testes had been found, but by the time a mass was found it might be too late. The question she struggled with was should they irradiate his testes immediately? It might be effective but it would sterilize David for life. He was eight; the growth of his testes *could* be early enlargement prior to puberty. Should anyone risk sterilizing David just on the *chance* that his leukemia might recur? Either way, they had to play a fearsome game of Russian roulette with David's life and future at stake. They decided not to irradiate.

Several months later the time bomb exploded. Dr. Sharkey had just returned from a trip to India. She had gone in to the hospital to make rounds on a hospitalized child. She was sitting at the nurses' station:

> As I sat there, an intern and a resident came by making their evening rounds. They were discussing each patient briefly.
>
> "Welcome back," one said. "You've got Theresa's chart. She did really well while you were gone. She even gets up and walks to physical therapy now."
>
> Leaving me, they went on to talk about the next patient. Although I was reading Theresa's chart I could hear their words.
>
> "In this room is a child with leukemia in relapse."
>
> Suddenly Theresa's chart felt as if it weighed a hundred pounds. Unconsciously I held my breath, waiting for their next words.
>
> "Whose patient is it?" the resident asked the intern.
>
> It was David.

The prospect now was very depressing. When leukemia had recurred only in the testes, the literature indicated a fighting chance. When it had recurred only in the bone marrow, there was also still hope for a cure; but if malignancy was discovered in both sites, the odds of a child's living more than a year were virtually nonexistent. This is what had happened to David.

Heroic efforts nevertheless continued. New drug protocols were coming out all the time, and with courage and fierce hope Dr. Sharkey fought on, struggling to find the magic combination of drugs and irradiation that might still offer David a chance.

In the end it was a fight she lost. Now, not only did she anguish with the pain of her own grief, she also struggled to find the right words with which to say all those things to David and his family.

> David now came to my office once a week. He'd gone to school a few times, but it tired him badly. He looked so ill his classmates were frightened. We arranged for a home teacher to come to his house every day. She asked me how much work she should give him. Did I ever expect him to rejoin his class?

> "No," I said sadly, "but he must continue with his schoolwork. Taking it away from him would be like telling him he was going to die."

> Now when he came into the office, he needed my help to climb onto the examining-room table. He was embarrassed by his weakness. In his thin face his smile had lost none of its sweetness.

> He knew his disease was back, and he knew it was leukemia. I wondered if he had ever seen a television program about anyone dying from leukemia. I wondered if he thought this was happening to him. I hadn't said anything to him about dying. For that matter, I hadn't said anything to his parents, either.

With the reality of David's death now a certainty, Dr. Sharkey also had to relive the misery she had experienced when other children had died. Many of these deaths had been painful and terrifying. Worse still, they had come in a hospital, with the anguished child separated from his parents when he needed them most. Hospitals, Dr. Sharkey was beginning to think were *not* where children should have to die. In the hospital children tended to die alone—and their parents suffered alone. Dr. Sharkey began to wonder: was this really in the name of optimal patient care? Or had the elaborate system of rules, regulations, protocol, and hospital routine actually been erected to protect the staff from the pain *they* might feel if the struggles of these children and their families suddenly became too real?

> Late one afternoon I asked Betty and Stan to come to my office. Finally, I had to tell them there was no hope; there was nothing further I could do for David. Until that was said, there was no way we could

plan for his death. I was terribly depressed. By admitting that there was nothing more I could do for David, I felt I was no longer needed. Yet on a deeper level I realized I was needed more than ever.

We sat in front of the window in my office for a few minutes and watched the shadows lengthen on the hills. I finally broke the silence. "David gets closer to death each day. I've said nothing to him about dying. I must soon. I've always been uncomfortable watching the children who die in the hospital. It seems to me that children hate being in the hospital and would be much more at peace in their own homes. Before I tell David he's dying, I want to know what your feelings are about where he should die."

Betty reached out for her husband's hand. Tears filled her eyes. "We want David where it is best for him . . . We'll keep him at home. . . ."

Dr. Sharkey now had to endure a tremendous outpouring of defensiveness and disapproval from her colleagues. Her natural tenderness, open expressions of love and affection—all these had already led some uneasy colleagues to accuse her of being "overly involved," of "losing professional detachment." Her decision to send David home was more than most of them could bear. They accused her of losing all sense of professional responsibility. She was upbraided for not giving *every* new regimen on the horizon a try. More than one physician came close to accusing her of depriving David of a chance for cure. When Dr. Sharkey held her ground, colleagues finally shrugged their shoulders and said, "Well, it's your case," thus isolating her and ensuring that she would feel alone and unsupported.

We can only imagine the loneliness and pain that she had to endure at the hands of "colleagues." Already she suffered deeply at David's impending death. She was trying to help his family. Surely she too now needed all the support and empathy that her colleagues could offer. Instead, she was ostracized . . . "It's your patient." The message was clear: "If you want to confront what we're afraid of, we'll push you away. You'll do it on your own."

What a lonely path she was forced to take for doing what she believed was right:

Time was running out.

I took his frail body in my arms and cradled his head against me.

"David, most of the time when we're sick, we take medicine and it makes us better. But sometimes the medicine doesn't work and we don't get well. We die." I felt his body tense. I held him closely and rocked him as if he were a baby. "I'm going to die someday, and your mommy is going to die someday, too. Usually mommies die before their children, but sometimes . . . sometimes. . . ." My voice failed me. I kissed the top of his head and saw my tears fall on his hair. His arms were around me. He tightened them as he nestled closer.

"Am I going to die?" he asked, his voice muffled against me.

"Yes, David."

"Does my mommy know?"

"Yes, and John and your daddy know, even Mary. They want you at home with them."

"Will it hurt?" asked this child who had never let us know he was frightened.

"No, I don't think so. It'll just be like going to sleep. And your mommy will be with you."

We held each other in a profound silence. I realized with wonder that what I had said had not shocked him at all. Why had I waited so long, making excuses to myself that I needed the perfect moment? There is no such thing as the perfect moment. We make all our moments, and by the truth and love we bring to them, we make them perfect. David had probably thought he was dying for at least a month, maybe longer. His innate sensitivity had made him keep that from us.

My arms were cramped. "Is there anything you want?" I asked, shifting his weight.

"Would you rub my back?" he said. "It hurts."

I couldn't save him, and I couldn't tell him what death was like. But I could rub his back.

Finally, the day came for his discharge from the hospital.

The next morning when I entered David's room, the intravenous line had been disconnected. The heparin lock was neatly taped in place on his hand.

"Are you actually discharging him?" asked the resident doctor.

"Yes."

"And his mother is going to treat his bloodstream infection? Isn't that asking a bit much of her?"

I didn't answer him.

"Why don't you keep him here a few weeks and treat him properly for the infection?" he persisted.

"Because he doesn't have a few weeks," I snapped. "He'll be treated just as properly at home as in the hospital. Does it matter whether a nurse or his mother injects the antibiotics? But even if we could clear up the bloodstream infection, it wouldn't save his life. If he doesn't go home today, I'm afraid he'll never go home again."

"He's your patient," the resident said sarcastically and walked away.

I wrote the discharge order. David, wrapped in a blanket, was carried out of the hospital in his father's arms.

Every day Dr. Sharkey visited David. One of her own children, aware of how absorbed her mother had become with this mysterious dying boy, also groped to understand. Finally she went and fetched a book of poems, tattered from use, and gave it to her mother to read to David. It was her favorite book.

That afternoon Dr. Sharkey read David the poems from her daughter's book while David smiled and lay curled in her arms.

As time went on, David grew very weak and ill.

I leaned over him. His breathing was rapid. His face was warm with fever. I sat beside him and listened to his chest with my stethoscope. My touch awakened him. He looked at me with recognition and smiled weakly. I stroked his hair. "Do you want a poem?" I asked softly. He nodded and closed his eyes.

I sat with my arm around him and read him a very short one. He didn't seem to be listening. "Do you want another poem?" I asked. He shook his head and closed his eyes. I put my cheek against his and then kissed him.

Here is the closing passage from the book:

On Saturday morning when Stan was home from work David awakened, once again inexplicably interested in his surroundings. He got out of the big bed and went to the bathroom and then walked back to his own bed in the dining room. He lay down but didn't fall asleep. Betty was surprised by this and heartened by the fact that he was up again. She'd scarcely left his side for 3 days. She thought, "He's so alert, he can't possibly die right now." She kissed him on his forehead and asked, "Is it all right if I go shopping for a little while?" He touched her hand and nodded his head. She noticed that his dark eyes seemed more beautiful than ever. She left, anxious to get the shopping over with and be back with him.

David lay on his bed and looked out of the window. He could see his sister playing on the front lawn. The kitten was on the window sill, trying to catch a fly.

After a little while David asked his father for some morphine. He swallowed a spoonful and made a face. He asked for some juice. Stan went to the kitchen to get some from the refrigerator. He could see David all the time. David was lying on his back on the bed. He held his hands in front of his face, looking at them. He stretched out his arms and then brought his hands in close to his eyes. He seemed to be examining each finger the way a baby does when it first discovers its hands.

Stan turned his attention to pouring the juice. When he brought it to the bed, David was dead.

David hadn't made a sound. His father couldn't believe it. He sat by David, almost expecting him to breathe again. David's eyes were closed. He looked as if he had just fallen asleep.

Stan sat by David awhile and then went outside and called Mary and John. The two children went to the bed where the body of their dead brother lay. Mary ran her finger along David's arm and put her head down next to his on the pillow. John stood looking at David and then went to the window and picked up the kitten. He brought the kitten to the bed and curled it up next to David, placing his dead brothers's arms around the kitten in the position it had rested so often.

When Betty came home that was how she found her family.

Is this painful? Yes! Excruciatingly so. Yet it is also excruciatingly beautiful. It is healing just to read it.

Every student should read Dr. Sharkey's book. It is a masterpiece. Suffice it to say here, the book is about far more than death, though it is certainly about this, too. It is about love, courage, altruism, mystery, and awe—the human essence of our work. Though it is painful to touch on these things, in the end it is only by fleeing from them that we ourselves will fail to heal.

Medicine *is* a human experience, propelled forward by science but guided by love.

Suggested Reading

Boyd, W. 1966. The Spontaneous Regression of Cancer. Charles C Thomas, Springfield, Illinois.

Cassell, E. J. 1982. The nature of suffering and the goals of medicine. N. Engl. J. Med. 306:639–645.

Cousins, N. 1979. Anatomy of an Illness as Perceived by the Patient: Reflections on Healing and Regeneration. Norton, New York.

Cousins, N. 1983. The Healing Heart: Antidotes to Panic and Helplessness. Norton, New York.

Lynch, J. J. 1977. The Broken Heart: The Medical Consequences of Loneliness. Basic Books, New York.

Rosen, D. H., and Blackwell, B. 1982. Teaching psychiatry in medicine: The development of a unique clinical course. Arch. Intern. Med. 142:113–115.

Sharkey, F. 1982. A Parting Gift. St. Martin's Press, New York.

Thomas, L. 1983. The Youngest Science: Notes of a Medicine-Watcher, pp. 55–60. Viking Press, New York.

Tumulty, P. A. 1978. The art of healing. Johns Hopkins Med. J. 143:140–143.

Weiss, P. A. 1978. Causality: Linear or systemic. In: Psychology and Biology of Language and Thought, pp. 13–26. Academic Press, New York.

Epilogue

Desiderata

During the sixteenth century in England an anonymous individual carved a series of desiderata in a wooden church door. They were apparently offered as guides to young novitiates on how to lead effective, harmonious lives. During the 1960s and 1970s these desiderata were rediscovered and widely circulated on posters which found their way onto many walls. Centuries later, the world is still in colossal turmoil, and the desiderata still make sense. The lyricism and wisdom of the desiderata are, in fact, remarkable. There is so much beauty in them that even repeated reading discloses something fresh and new.

What we offer here is far more modest. Our desiderata are short and to the point. However, we felt it appropriate somehow to close this book with some "words of wisdom" to the young men and women whom we are attempting to teach, who have embraced the impossibilities of this fascinating and excruciating calling.

Remember that being a doctor is a privilege. When you face the trauma and savagery that man can inflict on his fellow man, that life sometimes inflicts on us all, when you see human beings reduced to an ugliness that you once thought unimaginable; when you see doctors, nurses, and even yourself treating people with a callousness you once never dreamed would be possible—remember, you are privileged. It is true that doctors are no longer held in blind esteem by the general public. This is for the better. But you remain part of a powerful, respected, and protected profession. Certainly there are financial rewards, but the privilege is really a much deeper one. By your choice of calling, you have been invited to be a trusted and intimate participant in the most elemental and basic moments of human life: birth, death, regeneration, decline; madness, pain, and instances of unbelievable clarity. Very few will ever be so permitted or so graced. You have been granted communion with life's most important mysteries. Artists and priests go where you go; but they lack your knowledge and skills to help scientifically. On the other hand, do not ignore their capacity to see beauty where others see only the mundane or ugly. Learn the poet's appreciation for man's nobility and transcendent spirit. It is within your reach. When your privilege begins to feel like a burden—and at times it will—remember how fortunate you are to live life so fully.

Remember that you are free. There are few professions in which one is as free to choose as medicine. You can go to NIH and study mitochondria. You can go to Appalachia and treat coal miners. It is all up to you. Your education confers a staggering number of options. Yet medical school education is so often hierarchical, constrictive, and authoritarian that students lose sight of this. Sadly, by graduation time many new doctors have forgotten what it means to be free, even after the chains and shackles have been removed. This is the saddest tyranny of all.

If enough young physicians remember that they are free, there will come a true renaissance in medicine—many different styles and kinds of practice will flourish and coexist. We will no longer be so distrusted and envied as a profession. True, many attack us from the understandable wish to have what we alone possess. It must be said, that at times our wealth, power, and privilege do seem to be excessive and unreasonable, especially in a world so full of suffering, deprivation, hunger, and want. In the end, however, only our own failure to remember that we are free will cause us to go the way of the dinosaur. This seems very unlikely to happen. Mostly it rests with you, the next generation of physicians.

Empathize with the plight of your fellow professionals. When your resident dumps on you, when the nurses are cold, when the attending humiliates you, when you see people treating patients like castoffs instead of human beings—remember they are really only people too, like yourself. They are struggling with the same questions, torments, and responsibilities that you are. Have compassion, especially for the house staff. Their pressures await you. The demands are awesome, and the help these young doctors get is almost nonexistent.

Remember why you decided to be a doctor. If you are like most of us, you did not choose medicine solely to do pure research, and it certainly was not to own a huge home on the first tee of the golf course. Remember, too, as you are being trained in an academic setting, that you did not necessarily choose medicine to be famous and important. You chose medicine because you are interested in healing the mind, body, and spirit and because—sentimental as it sounds—you care about people. Remember this when someone humiliates you for not knowing everything about everything. Keep it in mind when you are tempted to recoil from patients who seem ravaged beyond hope, almost beyond human recognition. You chose medicine because you care.

Medical school does not last forever. This is difficult to remember sometimes, but it is true. If you are a junior, your formal education will average another 6 years. This is a long time but not forever. Remember the human, gentle qualities that you cherish in yourself and that seem to go underground during these years. You may fear at times that these traits are hopelessly lost forever. However, be assured, they can and do come back. Do not be overly discouraged, either, by the sometimes callous behavior of house officers; their struggles are huge ones. Do not be overly impressed or dismayed by your academic teachers. Teachers are important, and we need them. Medicine needs researchers and scholars as well. Sometimes, too often perhaps, the academicians who teach you are people who have failed to grow up in some ways. They remain "in training" forever—always climbing the ladder of success, always competing, always conscious of the hierarchy. Do not let their mockery of the practicing physician dissuade you. Certainly private medicine has its share of incompetents. So does academic medicine. There are many wise, happy, and mature doctors in both settings as well. Seek out the role models you respect for both their knowledge and the care they provide. Hold on to the realistic conviction that you can get there eventually.

Forgive yourself. Just as you should forgive those around you, learn early to forgive yourself. You will make mistakes. You will do terrible things—not as often as you fear, but now and again. You will fail to be perfect. You will blunder technically, and on occasion your sadism toward patients may shock and depress you. However, this is a line of work filled with impossibilities. Show yourself generosity. It will make you a better doctor for your patients as well.

Accept ambiguity and personal limitations. Despite our wish for certainty, medicine is and will always remain an ambiguous field. Those who think that science will ultimately eliminate this ambiguity are dreamers. The more our science advances, the more fundamental and deeply vexing the ambiguities we face will become. If you cannot learn to

tolerate ambiguity in medicine—and it is very difficult for most of us—
your life as a doctor will be filled with torment. If you can learn to accept
ambiguity, you will see beauty and splendor where others see only disor-
der and frustration. Accept your own limitations. You cannot know
everything. You cannot do everything. You cannot be everything. Some
people will be better at some things than you. You will never gain full
mastery—ever. Accept this, and peace will replace frustration and fear.
Refuse to accept it, and you will drive yourself into a life of pettiness,
envy, and despair. Do not be afraid to draw boxes. We all do. We must.
It is fun to have a little corner where things are less ambiguous and
where our mastery, relatively speaking, is greater. However, beware of
people who draw boxes, pretend that everything inside those boxes is
certain, and denigrate what lies beyond the perimeters of their own
narrow conceits. Keep your eyes peeled. Watch out especially for any
doctor who puts another doctor down just because he is different.

Physician, heal thyself. In recent years there has been growing
concern over the dehumanizing and fragmented nature of medical practice. Most of the attention has focused on the destructive effects this has
on the patient. The emergence of such concern is appropriate and
heartening. The title of this book reflects our conviction that our experience in medicine must be human and humane. This includes our
patients and ourselves but as a group, we—doctors—have been
curiously, and often tragically, neglected. There is just now a beginning awareness of the severity and prevalence of physician impairment. Suicide. Alcoholism. Drug addiction. You have all heard the statistics—and do not say it could never happen to you, because it could. A
number of these eight desiderata were constructed with just this concern
in mind. No book can replace a humane and informed system of education. On the other hand, we seriously doubt if any physician truly could
follow the spirit of these eight desiderata and become impaired. Full of
hurt, in need of help—yes; but hopelessly isolated, alone, devastatingly
impaired? We doubt it. Beyond this, we are just as concerned about the
"unimpaired physician," the driven, workaholic perfectionist who cannot unwind or have fun, who never sees his family and seems a likely
candidate for a heart attack. A pillar of the community, he is hardly
impaired. Yet we fear he may be lost—so much of the joy and wonder of
medicine seems to elude him. The alcoholic or addicted physician is a
tragedy, but he is only the tip of an awesome iceberg. It is an equally sad
fact that too few physicians are actually very happy. You would be surprised to learn how widespread this unhappiness really is. This is terrible, for our calling offers so much potential for growth, creativity,
beauty, and meaning. Something clearly is wrong with the way we are
educating doctors. It is a complicated problem, with origins in realms as
diverse as the knowledge explosion, economics, and politics. We have no
wish to oversimplify the problem, but we are convinced that a major
source of physician unhappiness lies in the lack of compassion and em-

pathy with which we treat ourselves. We are not talking here about anything as simple as overly demanding call schedules (though we are talking about that too). We are talking about a more silent yet malignant view of physicianhood which ignores, indeed attacks, the rights and needs of physicians themselves to be sensitive, to feel pain, to be human beings. Doctors are taught and then reinforced in countless ways that they should hold feelings in, go it alone, never let their vulnerability show. Never, it seems, should one reach out, express vulnerability, experience and permit human needs. No wonder doctors are so poor at permitting these same vital needs to emerge in their patients! When this kind of socialization becomes coupled with other traits so common to physicians—a driving perfectionism, unforgivingly high self-standards, a tremendous need for mastery and control—then we have a situation which is very dangerous. For every addicted physician, there are a hundred unhappy workaholics. For every suicide, there are a thousand quietly lonely, vaguely depressed doctors who do a wonderful job with their patients but somehow never get to see their children grow up, never experience deep love and peace. These are doctors who wonder too late, "Where did my life go and what did it all mean?"

Although the issue is admittedly complex, we believe that ultimate revolution in medical education will come from within. We must begin to nurture the needs, hopes, and sensitivities of the promising young men and women who have elected to adopt this unique, stressful, beautiful, and perilous career. We must encourage introspection, healthy relationships, play, openness, and joyous, creative expression. We must spawn a generation of doctors who are not afraid to love.

Index